Enjoying Power

Dame Eugenia Charles

Enjoying
Power

Eugenia Charles and Political
Leadership in the
Commonwealth Caribbean

EDITED BY

Eudine Barriteau and **Alan Cobley**

University of the West Indies Press
Jamaica • Barbados • Trinidad and Tobago

University of the West Indies Press
7A Gibraltar Hall Road   Mona
Kingston 7   Jamaica
www.uwipress.com

10 09 08 07 06   5 4 3 2 1

CATALOGUING IN PUBLICATION DATA

Enjoying power: Eugenia Charles and political leadership in the
Commonwealth Caribbean / edited by Eudine Barriteau and Alan Cobley.

p. cm.

Includes bibliographical references.

ISBN-10: 976-640-191-8
ISBN-13: 978-976-640-191-7

1. Charles, Mary Eugenia, Dame, 1919–2005. 2. Political leadership –
Caribbean, English-speaking. 3. Women in politics – Dominica.
4. Women prime ministers – Dominica. 5. Dominica – Politics and
government. I. Barriteau, Eudine. II. Cobley, Alan Gregor.

F2051.C5 E64 2006   972.9841

Cover illustration: Shadrach Burton, *Rainy Day at Trafalgar Falls* (2002).
Courtesy of the artist. Photographed by Charles James.

Book and cover design by Robert Harris.
Set in Bembo 11/14.5 x 24
Printed in the United States of America.

In memory of

MARY EUGENIA CHARLES

15 May 1919–6 September 2005

Contents

Preface

This book is the second in a planned series of publications associated with the project Caribbean Women: Catalysts for Change, sponsored by the Centre for Gender and Development Studies at the Cave Hill campus of the University of the West Indies. The first in the series was edited by Eudine Barriteau and Alan Cobley, *Stronger, Surer, Bolder: Ruth Nita Barrow, Social Change and International Development* (Cave Hill, Barbados, and Kingston, Jamaica: Centre for Gender and Development Studies and the University of the West Indies Press, 2001). One output of the project includes the Caribbean Women: Catalysts for Change lecture series in which Eugenia Charles delivered the inaugural lecture in 1995. Another major aspect is the acquisition and cataloguing of the Dame Nita Barrow Papers and the acquisition of the Dame Eugenia Charles Papers. These two important collections are housed in the Main Library at Cave Hill and are available to researchers in the Dame Nita Barrow Women in Caribbean Development Specialist Collection, which has been set aside especially for them. These acquisitions also include many hours of taped interviews, which were used by researchers in the preparation of the two edited collections published to date.

Connie Sutton, professor of anthropology at New York University, planted the seeds for this project when she first asked why it was that a cohort of Caribbean women had emerged in the second half of the twentieth century who had made seemingly disproportionately large contributions on the international scene to debates on gender and development issues. From the early 1990s, when this idea was picked up by members of the Women and Development Studies Group at Cave Hill, to the present, many have contributed to its development as a major research project at the University of the West Indies. It would be impossible to name them all individually; however, special mention must be made of the staff of the Centre for Gender and Development Studies at Cave Hill who have carried the administrative burden of the project since its inception. They include Veronica Jones, Jacqueline Morris, Deborah Deane, Carmen Hutchinson Miller and Olivia Birch. The project has also counted on the professionalism and cooperation of our colleagues in the Main Library, Jo-Ann Granger, but especially Jeniphier Carnegie, who was responsible for cataloguing the Dame Nita Barrow Papers. Sharon Alexander-Gooding, campus archivist, joined phase two of the project and was responsible for the sorting, shipping, initial storage and classification of the Dame Eugenia Papers. Without their unfailing commitment, energy and professionalism, much less would have been achieved.

This book would not have been possible without the gracious and unstinting support of Dame Eugenia Charles. During the course of the research on which this book is based, Dame Eugenia hosted every member of the research team in her private office in Roseau, and gave each the opportunity to tape an interview with her. Despite ill health, she responded to hours of probing questions about her public and private life with the same honesty and forthrightness that had been the hallmarks of her political career, often concluding interviews only when fatigue overtook her. She also gave the research team completely unrestricted access to her papers, which were stored in neatly labelled boxes lining the shelves of her office, and readily honoured a commitment made in 1997 to donate them to the University of the West Indies, so that they would be available for future academic research. Individually and collectively, we owe her a great debt of gratitude.

Apart from Dame Eugenia herself, more than thirty friends and associates from her more than three decades in public life gave interviews to members of the research team. Some individuals were interviewed several times. A full list is contained in the references at the end of the book. We thank them all for giving so freely of their time and for sharing their memories of "Miss Charles" with us. A special word of thanks is owed to Mrs Marilyn Zamore, Dame Eugenia's private secretary, who dealt with our numerous requests efficiently and in other ways smoothed the path for the research team in Dominica with many kindnesses and unfailing courtesy. Ms Edith Bellot of the University Centre in Dominica and Dr Lennox Honychurch graciously fielded our questions and provided valuable insights into Dame Eugenia's tenure.

Dame Eugenia Charles died on 6 September 2005. Her passing is emblematic of the end of an era of charismatic Caribbean leaders whose personalities rather than policies created a more lasting impact on their publics. There is a tendency to speak of Dame Eugenia more as a charismatic, commanding character than as a policy maker. Therefore part of the responsibilities of the Centre for Gender and Development Studies was to "capture critical elements of the life, times and motivations of one of the Caribbean's most imposing political leaders".

It is a daunting task to try to capture the essence of a life lived in the heat of political controversy, or to weigh in the balance the contributions made by any individual to the community, the society and the world of which they were part. Such success as has been achieved in this collection is owed to the help we have received from so many in the course of its preparation. The responsibility for any failings or shortcomings that may remain is, of course, ours alone.

Eudine Barriteau

Alan Cobley

Abbreviations

CARICOM	Caribbean Community and Common Market [now a fifteen-member grouping of independent Commonwealth Caribbean countries and British-dependent territories, including the republics of Suriname and Haiti]
CEDAW	Convention for the Elimination of All Forms of Discrimination Against Women
CNS	Committee for National Salvation [Dominica]
CPA	Country Poverty Assessment
CSA	Civil Service Association
DFP	Dominica Freedom Party
DHA	Dominican Huskers Association
DLP	Dominica Labour Party
DNCW	Dominica National Council of Women
DUPP	Dominica United People's Party
NDFD	National Development Foundation in Dominica
NGO	non-governmental organization
OECS	Organisation of Eastern Caribbean States
UNICEF	United Nations Children's Fund
UWI	University of the West Indies
WAWU	Waterfront and Allied Workers Union

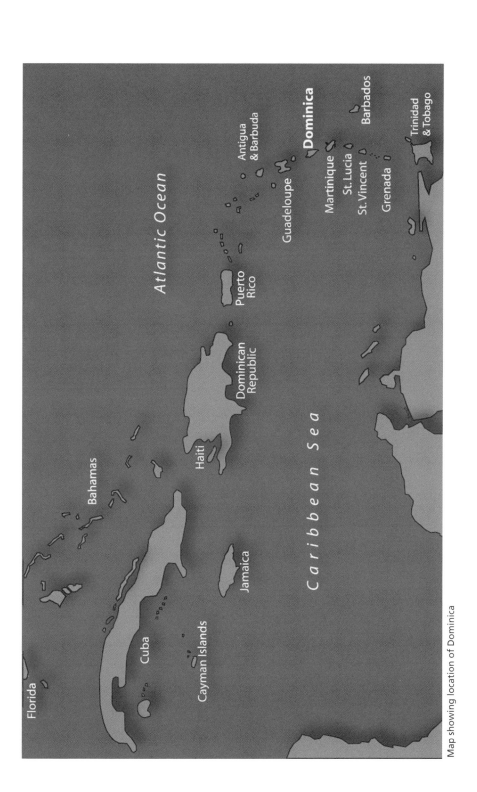

Map showing location of Dominica

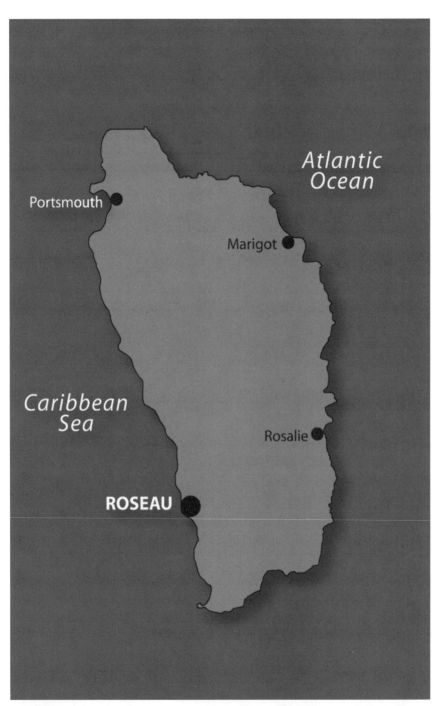

Map of Dominica

PART 1

Eugenia Charles

and Political

Power

1

Enjoying Power, Challenging Gender

EUDINE BARRITEAU

Because women who hold power are generally resented, and women and power have an ambiguous, uneasy relationship, women's leadership occupies a contradictory political space. Women who are leaders exist and operate in the borderlands of power. They are within the paradigms of leadership because of the positions they hold; simultaneously they are on the borders because ideologies of gender encode their sex to be the objects of power and not the initiators of decisions. (Barriteau 2003a, 26)

Introduction

Eudine Barriteau: How would you like to be remembered?

Eugenia Charles: As a person who said what she meant even though it annoyed people.

EB: What is the greatest untruth about you?

EC: That I don't care about people. I am not going to sit here and say I love everybody, because I don't, but I care very much about people making the best of themselves.

EB: People here [Dominica] say you are troublesome.

EC: [laughing] They say I am troublesome? I think I was. I didn't take no for an answer. I didn't give up

3

because they said no. You kept looking for ways to make them change their minds and give in. I was always troublesome, from a little girl, I would keep asking my parents for things and they said, "No, no", and I kept asking, and they eventually said "yes". (Charles 2002d)

This analysis of the political leadership of Mary Eugenia Charles is an ambitious effort of the second phase of the research project Caribbean Women Catalysts for Change, by the Centre for Gender and Development Studies at the Cave Hill campus of the University of the West Indies. The project examines "the experiences of Caribbean women who have influenced change in our societies". In phase one of the project we stated, "Our goal is to examine and locate the activities of outstanding Caribbean women in six overlapping arenas of the contemporary public domain", and we listed these as follows: regional and international development, politics and political participation, women organizing and the women's movement, trade unionism, education, and agriculture and food production (Barriteau 2001a, 7).

The Centre chose Eugenia Charles as our subject in order to investigate the public life of a woman who broke new ground in politics and who achieved a number of firsts in political leadership in the Commonwealth Caribbean. Yet her style of leadership and activities as prime minister disturbed many national and regional constituencies. As the researchers demonstrate, in the words of the Bajan vernacular, Eugenia Charles was no "sweet bread" (Allsopp 1996, 541). Here was a woman who relished castigating publicly the domestic decisions and foreign policy of male Caribbean leaders who were held in high regard for their approaches to Caribbean sovereignty, even if they were often criticized for their domestic policies. At various times Eugenia Charles was critical of, and in turn was highly criticized by, Forbes Burnham of Guyana, Errol Barrow of Barbados, Maurice Bishop of Grenada and Fidel Castro of Cuba, among others (Charles 2002d). Her views and her actions aroused strong emotions and often polarized public opinion.

Yet persons opposed to Eugenia Charles's conservative politics and policies have not grasped the significance of subjecting her political tenure to scholarly scrutiny.[1] Interrogating Eugenia Charles's peculiar style of leadership is a necessary project. Undertaking this analysis enables the Centre to give proper attention to one of the Caribbean's most prominent leaders of recent years. Simultaneously, dissecting the policies and practices of such a controversial woman leader demonstrates the maturity of feminist scholarship by destabilizing the notion that the intent of a feminist focus is somehow to romanticize the female subject and excuse all excesses.

My colleagues and I did not find Eugenia Charles an easy subject. However, the ethos of the Centre for Gender and Development Studies has never been to produce a halcyon manifesto of virtuous feminist fables. Nita Barrow, the subject of phase one of the Project, was considerably less controversial than Eugenia Charles (Barriteau and Cobley 2001). But Nita Barrow was not chosen merely because she was an acceptable public figure whose international activities tended to draw commendation rather than hostile criticism (Nettleford 1988). In both cases the subjects were chosen because their public lives exemplified the themes of a project designed to document, dissect and disseminate the contributions of Caribbean women in the six major areas listed above. Eugenia Charles personifies the Caribbean woman who, as politician and political leader, has had the greatest impact on politics at the national and regional levels. This made her an obvious choice for research and analysis.

There is a pervasive misunderstanding in the region that a key goal of Caribbean feminism is to "sanitize" the image of women, and to have them appear always as the more virtuous sex (*Trinidad Guardian* 2000; *Barbados Advocate* 1996; Wint 1989). However, a primary thrust of feminist scholarship is to claim women's subjectivity – whether women appear as saints or sorcerers. It is not necessary for Eugenia Charles to be Dominica's Joan of Arc[2] for her to merit scholarly investigation. What is relevant is that she occupied a position of power and leadership for a period of time significant enough to effect change. It is the business of the researchers to document and assess the scope of this change. The contributors here have done just that.

As the various analyses unfold one can sense the tension and difficulties some of us felt in grappling with the contradictions and contrariness of Eugenia Charles. Part of the tension arose from an anxiety to be fair, balanced and responsible in documenting the career of a woman who at the time of our interviews with her was eighty-three years old and in ill health.[3] The tradition of respect for elders in Caribbean societies has not disappeared, even for elders whose actions may sometimes have infuriated, disappointed or embarrassed us in the past. In addition, researchers have a peculiar responsibility not to misrepresent the views and actions of their subject, especially when they feel out of sympathy with those views or actions. We have tried to ensure that this responsibility to objectivity is met in the pages that follow.

Women and Political Power

Another source of tension in research on women as political leaders is the difficulty in dealing with simultaneity. Researchers are challenged to reject Cartesian binaries that require a dichotomous, hierarchical assessment and ranking of women's personal and political motivations. There is a temptation to succumb to fossilized stereotypes of women leaders. They can be hard, mechanical, crusading leaders like Indira Gandhi, Margaret Thatcher or Benazir Bhutto, or alternatively they can be benign maternal figures, struggling to mother unruly nations in the mode of Corazon Aquino or Violetta Chamorro (Saint-Germain 1993; Genovese 1993a, 1993b; Col 1993; Anderson 1993; Everett 1993). Very few studies incorporate a sense of the range of complex influences and interests confronting women leaders (Sykes 1993).

Powerful, political women like Eugenia Charles defy conventional interpretations of their motivations and ambitions, and the researchers have avoided pursuing a linear interpretation of her life. We have sought to reveal her subjectivity with all its complexities. In addition to the Western philosophical tradition of defining politics to exclude the participation of women in public life (Jones 1988, 12), when women are involved in politics, the convention is still to evaluate their public performance and relevance against the values and virtues of women in the private sphere: "Because women were associated with the private realm, public life became in the classical tradition, not only without women, but against women and the devalued virtues of the 'oikos' [the household]" (Jones 1988, 13).

The popular tendency to analyse women's public performances against some unstated but implicit scripting of their private, domestic lives remains in the foreground of several of these analyses. Many Caribbean female politicians or women leaders experience inordinate pressure to try to convince the public that they do care and desire a traditional domestic life bounded by children or, at the very least, a husband. In the 2003 general elections in Barbados a newspaper ran a feature on the fact that the female politicians in one political party were all mothers and had eleven children, compared to the childless status of their counterparts in the other political party. There was no similar information on the reproductive patterns, fatherhood status or number of children of male politicians in the two respective parties (Hoyte 2003, 9). More recently, the minister of housing and lands in Barbados, Elizabeth Thompson-McDowald, was congratulated by government senator Sandra Husbands for bravely mixing marriage and politics. "I think Minister Thompson[-McDowald] is now blazing a new trail by being married and we want to wish her extremely well in her marriage endeavours", she said, noting that it will give hope to other women who look at politics and may want to make that contribution. She further queried, "How does the male deal with the fact that you are up front, up top, visible and how does he deal with that in terms of the marriage relationship?" (*Barbados Advocate* 2005, 5).[4]

The key point missed by Senator Husbands was how socially sanctioned responsibilities for the reproductive work of the household can impede women interested in a political career. Eugenia Charles was entirely uninterested in pandering to such conventional notions of a private, domestic role, challenging the customary expectations of women's gender identities. Yet the ideological constraints of relations of gender make it expedient that political women appear comfortable and desirous of traditional roles, while the material limitations of having to sacrifice time and personal resources to carry out these responsibilities are generally ignored in assessing the scope and success of women's political participation. Eight years earlier, Minister Thompson-McDowald, speaking at a public meeting about her experiences as a female politician, cabinet minister and member of parliament, said, "One has to work much harder to achieve success" (*Sunday Sun* 1997, 10A).

A very significant feature of women and politics in the Caribbean is that the majority of women who contested elections in the Eastern Caribbean between 1951 and 1971, twenty, or 66 per cent, were married (Barriteau 1998a, 15). Bledsoe and Herring, speaking particularly of the United States, comment, "The low incidence of women in elected public office is at least partly a response to very practical restrictions on political mobility imposed by child care responsibilities, a duty that is still disproportionately placed on women" (Bledsoe and Herring 1990, 214; Barriteau 1998a, 15).

Eugenia Charles was never married, had no children, and seemed disinterested in any version of traditional domestic roles. Her unwedded, childless status was the subject of frequent and base political bantering during her electoral years as was her utter contempt for the attempts by political opponents to turn this into some kind of liability.

Traditionally women in the anglophone Caribbean have been locked out of the corridors of parliamentary political power by the gatekeepers of political parties.[5] In Jamaica between 1962 and 1983 the proportion of female candidates contesting general elections never exceeded 13 per cent, but in the six general elections held in that period, female candidates averaged only 6.2 per cent of all candidates (Henry-Wilson 1989, 242). When political parties run women as candidates, with few exceptions, the majority are sacrificed in seats the parties have privately surrendered. Frequently political parties place women as the opposing candidates to the strongest candidates of rival political parties (Barriteau 1998a).

Historically, regional governments have been more comfortable with women as ceremonial heads of state. Regionally and internationally such appointments make a country appear progressive, and the practice can even boost a country's ranking on the Gender Empowerment Measure of the United Nations Development Fund. Since 1974 five women have served as governors general in the anglophone Caribbean: Dame Hilda Bynoe (Grenada), Dame Nita Barrow (Barbados), Dame Ivy Dumont (Bahamas), Dame Pearlette Louisy (St Lucia) and Dame Minita Gordon (Belize). Linette Vassell (2003) observes that women have gained visibility in some regional parliaments because of their positions as president or vice president of the Senate, or as Speaker of the House of Representatives.[6] She concludes that even though these appointments show an area of responsiveness by political parties to issues of gender balance, they do not bring women into the sensitive areas of decision making, and unless these women use these positions creatively they will remain hostage to partisan interests (Vassell 2003, 8–9).

In 1997 the Inter-Parliamentary Union found that, in the Caribbean, the filling of senior positions by women in parliamentary assemblies followed the proportion of women in the bodies concerned (Inter-Parliamentary Union 1997, 128; Barriteau 1998a, 22). They conclude that instead of acting as enlightened elites, parliaments merely follow the electorate in maintaining nominal involvement of women (Barriteau 1998a, 22), while benefiting from the publicity garnered by these nominal appointments. In a ranking of women in parliaments worldwide, Cuba ranked the highest in the region, in seventh position with 219 women elected out of 609 seats, representing 36 per cent. This was followed by Guyana in fourteenth position, with 20 women elected out of a total of 65 seats, representing 30.8 per cent, while Grenada was ranked at nineteenth with 4 elected women out of a total of 15 seats representing 26.7 per cent of all seats held (Inter-Parliamentary Union 2005).

Among independent Commonwealth Caribbean countries, Billie Miller was deputy prime minister of Barbados from 1994 until Mia Mottley succeeded her in that position in May 2003. In the Bahamas, in May 2002, Cynthia Pratt was appointed deputy prime minister and minister of national security. In Jamaica, Portia Simpson Miller, previously a senior cabinet minister, was elected leader of the People's National Party in February 2006 and succeeded P.J. Patterson as prime minister on his retirement a few weeks later in March 2006. In St Lucia, Morella Joseph led the United Workers Party unsuccessfully into the 2001 general elections, but had to relinquish the position since the party's constitution does not allow an unelected member to be its leader. It was the first time in the country's political history that a woman had led a major political party. In Trinidad and Tobago (independent since 1962), and Barbados and Guyana (both independent since 1966), a woman has served neither as political leader of any major political party nor as the country's prime minister.[7] In all other countries of the Caribbean Community (CARICOM) including Suriname no woman has served in any of these capacities.[8]

Although the situation remains variable, the evidence from the contemporary Caribbean political environment reveals that women have begun to penetrate the senior leadership positions of political parties and governments. Though still in the minority as cabinet ministers, women are no longer political neophytes. This was not the case in 1980 when Eugenia Charles crafted her political leadership of the Dominica Freedom Party (DFP) to emerge as her country's, and the Caribbean's, first female prime minister.

The thematic issues emerging from this study of Charles's political career and public life straddle foreign policy, the use of law as an instrument of state control, women and political leadership, trade unionism and co-optation, the experiences of the Rastafari community with state power, party politics and power, the gender issues confronting women leaders including gender stereotyping in the print media and economic development issues. The researchers investigated Charles's involvement in simultaneously criticizing and contributing to the regional integration movement, mapped a psychology of her leadership, outlined the path she carved to achieve political power and dissected her discourse of rights and freedoms in relation to her choices about legislative and legal processes. She is analysed as emblematic of the end of an era of charismatic Caribbean leaders who, according to Keturah Cecilia Babb, were elected at a time when governance had been severely fractured. Charles's economic philosophy is assessed and the impact of that neoliberal philosophy on enterprise development and poverty alleviation in Dominica is discussed.

The combination of Eugenia Charles and Dominica was that of a rugged leader confronting and trying to tame a physically rugged, politically rebellious and economically regressive country. From the vantage point of transformational leadership the scenario was dismal even though Charles remained undaunted. In the words of the *Economist* (2005), "the Dominican economy Charles tried to manage, remained vulnerable to everything".

Eugenia Charles was a woman who dominated decision making in her party and parliament. She commanded the corridors of political power and intimidated many of the men and women who crossed her path. Many feminists seeking an alternative approach for women to achieve elected office and exercise political power perceive her model and practice of leadership as problematic. It has been argued that key features of Eugenia Charles's practice of political power were traditional – and masculinist. She was decisive and domineering, consistent and controversial, powerful and partisan, well organized with an oligarchical hold on power within her party and country.⟩

Paradigms of Leadership

Keturah Cecilia Babb offers an incisive and personal account of the experiences of the Rastafari community with the Eugenia Charles administration in chapter 6. "Mary, Mary, Quite Contrary" highlights Charles's controversial politics and practices from the vantage point of a Dominican, Rastafari woman and development planner. Babb grapples with doing justice to Charles's significant national achievements even as she castigates her for the harsh decisions and politics she saw as insensitive to the poor and marginalized groups within Dominican society. She highlights the demise of trade unionism, which she argues resulted from the trade union movement's tacit compliance with Charles early in her administration and then the weakening of their power by heavy-handed legislation. What is unique about Babb's analysis is that she uses the medium of the calypso to chronicle, dissect and highlight the high-handedness and flaws in Charles's tenure. Babb's analysis substantiates Patricia Mohammed's point that calypso can be an important tool in nation building. Mohammed states the calypso functions as a tool,

> not just for creating conformity or shared ideas among a people, but equally for its capacity to decolonize thought and diffuse the ideas which one nation invents to rule another, which rulers invent to rule over other nations or which individuals invent to define each other. . . . [C]alypso . . . has the capacity to speak with seeming irreverence of sentiments which could not be stated otherwise without creating violence of different kinds, including a violence that can suppress everyday interactions and exchanges between people who have to love and survive in the same small space. (Mohammed 2005)

Babb demonstrates effectively how calypsonians deployed calypso to record their concerns with the direction in which Eugenia Charles was taking the country.

Eugenia Charles represents an enigma to relations of gender, power and politics in Caribbean societies. She was the first Caribbean woman to lead a Caribbean political party successfully. From 1980 to 1995 she led the DFP to victory in three consecutive elections. She served simultaneously as prime minister, minister of finance and economic affairs, and minister of foreign affairs and defence.[9] In 1993 Eugenia Charles resigned as political leader of the DFP, but she remained as prime minister until the 1995 general elections when she retired from active politics.[10]

Her political leadership in the Caribbean is unprecedented. Her detractors find this difficult to acknowledge, concede or recognize. She was an ideologically conservative, right-of-centre politician who was unafraid to publicize or (benefit from) her conservative views in an era when it was more fashionable, even if unprofitable, to articulate a progressive political philosophy. What informed her leadership style? In chapter 5, Joan Cuffie develops a psychological profile of Eugenia Charles's leadership. She isolates key components of leadership as developed in the theorizing of leadership. Most leaders are motivated by the need for power. Cuffie develops this idea as the desire to acquire prestige, status and power over others. Alternatively, some leaders are motivated by the need for achievement. This is presented as the desire to do something exceptionally well for its own sake. Cuffie completes these two features with the observation that all leaders tend to be highly ambitious, highly energetic and willing and able to work under pressure. Cuffie suggests that Eugenia Charles possessed both types of motivations for leadership but weights Charles's personal characteristics, skills and capabilities as very significant in her development as a political leader.

In chapter 3, Cynthia Barrow-Giles investigates the political durability of Charles, particularly in the context of a lack of critical mass of women in politics in the region. She examines the factors that defined Charles's political ambitions, seeking to unearth early political activity before her official involvement in party politics. In the context of the constraints, challenges and opportunities represented by the Westminster model of political arrangements, Barrow-Giles assesses the factors that propelled Eugenia Charles into the political leadership of the DFP and Dominica. While noting that the Westminster model should be more accurately termed the Whitehall model, Barrow-Giles provides an incisive summary of the principal features of this form of democratic governance. She notes that its essence is majority rule and the fusion of the legislative and executive authority, accompanied by constitutional flexibility. Even though the Westminster model gives tremendous power to the prime minister, Barrow-Giles calls attention to the sobering principle of the no-confidence motion, which provides a mechanism for the opposition to unseat the government.

Barrow-Giles traces the origins of Charles's political career to her pivotal role in the formation of the Freedom Fighters, a coalition of citizens opposed to the Seditious and Undesirable Publications Act. She concludes that it was Charles's leadership of this pressure group, which evolved into a new political party, and her election to its presidency that prepared her for national leadership. She identifies the factors that made Charles, in spite of her lack of political experience, the ideal person to lead this new political party.

The Shadow of "the Father" . . .

An intriguing feature of this study of Eugenia Charles, and the lingering question it poses for feminists and social anthropologists to explore, is the dominant role played by her father in her life. Both in her stated recognition of his influence and in the many ways his figure permeates this work and her life, a study of Eugenia Charles seems in some ways to be an exploration of the long political shadow of her father. The exploration of the influence of the father figure in the lives of Caribbean girls and women is an overdue project. When fathers are absent from Caribbean homes, public commentators wring their hands in despair over the negative effect on boys (*Sunday Sun* 1998, 14A). These assessments never turn to the effect on girls. Yet in a study of four outstanding Caribbean women leaders, including Eugenia Charles, all identified their fathers as instrumental in building their confidence and negotiating their entry into public life: "They all commented on strong, supportive relationships with their fathers. They stated their mothers were supportive too but they each singled out the relationships with their fathers and the high values their fathers conveyed as decisive in growing into leadership roles" (Barriteau 2003a, 9).

Mary Hartman underscores that this situation is not unique to the

Caribbean. In a study of thirteen powerful women leaders from around the world she notes that they cite supportive families, especially fathers, but mothers as well, as critical to their success (Hartman 1999, 14; Barriteau 2003a, 9). Given the prominent attention paid to the negative influence of fathers and other male figures in the lives of girls and women, these findings suggest that Caribbean feminist analysis must engage with the dynamics and implications of women's positive relations with their fathers. Alicia Mondesire's analysis emphasizes the strength and influence of Charles's relationship with her father by noting that his political activism and prominence in Dominican politics and business were a crucial source of inspiration for her. Mondesire is careful to mention that Charles's mother, Josephine, was a resourceful, decisive woman who was equally an authority figure in the home and "in charge of" the family's small dry-goods store. Yet it was Charles's father who was the planter politician.

Nowhere is the lingering political shadow of Charles's father more discernible than in the opening of Alan Cobley's investigation of her approach to Caribbean integration. In chapter 4, Cobley uses the United States invasion of Grenada in 1983 as a counterpoint to interrogating and revealing the contradictions in Charles's philosophy of Caribbean regionalism. Before addressing the substantive concern of his analysis, Cobley alludes to the political future of Eugenia Charles by locating her as the thirteen-year-old daughter of planter politician J.B. Charles, a colonial patrician character. The teenaged Charles attends a regional meeting held in Dominica to discuss a closer union of Britain's Eastern Caribbean colonies. It is a meeting that her father attends as a prominent member of the local planter elite. Cobley makes it clear that in spite of Charles's protestations, her views and attitudes towards regional integration were derived from a conservative ideological orientation similar to that of her father. However, he also establishes that her philosophy on regionalism transcended her father's views in key areas. Similarly the influence of Charles's father intrudes in several other chapters. I trace her economic philosophy to the ideas of a colonial, landed peasantry of which her father was a main proponent. Cynthia Barrow-Giles also comments that Charles credits her father with being a major political influence in her life.

. . . But Mother of the Nation

Eugenia Charles's political leadership of Dominica enabled the conflation of two powerful images. Powerful women are not perceived as "normal" women; sometimes they are not even seen as women. The public struggles to deal with images of powerful women as "normal" because normal in this context refers to the traditional images of women who in political theory and the national psyche are wards of the state or of their spouses (Pateman and Shanley 1991). Alicia Mondesire quotes John Compton, former prime minister of St Lucia, as saying of Eugenia Charles:

> You can be in a room . . . there is a lot of cross talk. Eugenia takes the floor and there is silence. She has accumulated the respect. *It was not a woman that was there, it was a person with a strong personality. She transcended womanhood. She was an intellect, in woman's clothes . . . . She was more than being just a woman. Here is a woman, just behaving in this very extraordinary manner. So it was not only her intellectual capacity, which you would normally expect in a man. Coming from a woman, you would not expect that kind of thing.* (Compton 2002; emphasis added)

John Compton struggled unsuccessfully to accept Charles's intellect as normal because he respected her very much, but given the strength of her personality and the significance of her intellectual capital, he seemed forced to conclude that she was not a woman, she transcended womanhood. Where do confident women fit in the popular imagination? For Compton and many others Charles became something else. Powerful and domineering, she personified the archetype of the strong matriarch. Detractors and supporters invoked the mother figure to comprehend and contain Charles, "the Powerful Woman Leader". Charles "mothers" Dominica through economic crises and natural disasters. Babb, Hutchinson Miller, Mondesire and Robinson allude to her image as "Mama" and "Mamo", the female charismatic leader. Fitted into the niche of "not quite woman", but, nevertheless, "mother of the nation", the personality of Eugenia Charles became more palatable.

The construction and iconography of the nation as female and feminine reoccurs throughout the theorizing of political philosophy. The nation is female, to be ruled and controlled by men, to be domesticated and developed into a civic society. In Dominica we have the ultimate irony:

Dominica, the mother country, controlled by Eugenia Charles – the matriarch as politician.

At Ease with Power

Eugenia Charles came to power precisely at the time when the US administration of Ronald Reagan became increasingly concerned to ensure no additional Caribbean countries would join Grenada in experimenting with the policies and politics of socialism or in pursuing close ties with Cuba. In the early 1980s the US administration hastily crafted a foreign policy approach toward the Caribbean that introduced an effective departure from the acceptance of ideological pluralism by President Jimmy Carter (Sally Shelton, quoted in Barriteau 1982, 13).

Carter's Caribbean policy had been defined by a significant support for economic development; a firm commitment to democratic practices and human rights; unequivocal respect for national sovereignty; and strong encouragement of regional cooperation and an active role in Caribbean affairs (Sally Shelton, quoted in Barriteau 1982, 13).

On the other hand, the Reagan administration promoted a policy that recognized the Caribbean as the third border of the United States; principally provided military and economic support to those nations which pursue political policies compatible with US interests; assisted like-minded governing parties in introducing economic policies that would strengthen their position; specifically encouraged friendly nations to adopt a higher regional profile (described as an attempt at fostering less stable nations); offered bilateral aid in a manner concurrent with the above points, and lessened economic support wherever possible to multinational agencies (*Caribbean and West Indies Chronicle* 1981, 1; Barriteau 1982, 13).

These policies coincided with Eugenia Charles's views. Dominica and Jamaica, led by Prime Minister Edward Seaga, benefited from friendly relations with the United States and a higher profile within the region. In many ways the Reagan era defined the foreign policy thrust of Eugenia Charles.

Alan Cobley explores the apparent paradox between Eugenia Charles's criticism of the CARICOM and her specific contributions to the

Caribbean integration movement. Cobley argues that Charles's idea of regionalism was motivated more by the desire for functional cooperation in the pursuit of common goals than by a commitment to regional integration involving shared political structures and practices of governance. The historical relationship between Dominica and the francophone countries of Martinique and Guadeloupe, and also a preoccupation with the security of small island states, were additional factors influencing her approach to regionalism. Cobley's analysis substantiates the infiltration of a new strain of US influence in the region through the formation of "a powerful neoconservative, pro-capitalist, authoritarian bloc against socialist and communist influences in the region in the early 1980s" by Edward Seaga, Tom Adams and Eugenia Charles. He argues that Eugenia Charles shared with these two other leaders a view of integration as a vehicle for mutual security, a platform for capitalist development and a bulwark against socialism and communism. Cobley identifies the singular issue that exemplified her foreign policy and her approach to regional integration as the set of events surrounding the intervention in Grenada by US forces in 1983. Cobley considers that this was the defining moment of her career as a Caribbean leader and dedicates a third of his analysis to assessing the impact of this involvement on her legacy. He concludes that the articulation of a widely shared notion of inter–West Indian bonds of kith and kin caused her to emerge, albeit briefly, as a popular regional leader in this moment of crisis. He maintains that her actions reflected a deep emotional engagement with events in Grenada that was shared by a cross-section of the anglophone Caribbean community.

"I Am Perhaps Not a Feminist": Ambivalence about Feminism and Gender

Charles used every opportunity afforded her to disavow any significance to being a woman who exercised power at the pinnacle of political leadership. This seeming contradiction should not be construed as a desire on the part of Eugenia Charles to be self-effacing or to become entangled in the ambivalence researchers have noted that some women leaders harbour about holding and exercising power (Moglen 1983; Statham 1987;

Kitzinger 1991, 113–14; Pohlmann 1995). Like Nita Barrow, Eugenia Charles was an extremely confident woman and was very sure about her abilities to lead. Whatever her limitations and political shortcomings, a reluctance to embrace power, authority and the responsibilities of political leadership was not among them.

By her own admission Eugenia Charles enjoyed exercising power: "I enjoyed my years of government" (Charles 2002c). She relished being in a position where her actions could engineer different, even unanticipated outcomes. It may not have been the developments that many of her critics would have preferred but Eugenia Charles embraced her unique location in Dominican and Caribbean politics even as she stated she did not see herself as a *woman* creating change. She insisted she did not see herself as crusading on behalf of women or creating affirmative action programmes for women. Still, she admitted, "we had a strong women's bureau. There were good women in government and I had to be able to put them to use" (Charles 2002c).

While Charles was very comfortable exercising political power, she displayed a public ambivalence about issues of feminism and the significance of the social relations of gender in Dominican and Caribbean society. In a 1985 address at the opening of a national symposium on women and gender in Jamaica she remarked:

> When I became Prime Minister one of the first things I did was to appoint a woman speaker to the House of Parliament. I did so, not because she was a woman, but because she was the most knowledgeable person on the Parliamentary rolls. On congratulating her some of the men Parliamentarians said that they were getting a little concerned about things in Dominica, and they felt they should ask me to create a Men's desk to look after the affairs of men because women were already so well looked after in Dominica. I have not conceded to their request. I think they can look after themselves individually. (Charles 1985, 6)

To an audience overwhelmingly of women, dealing with issues of women and development, she chose to emphasize her appointment of a woman, Marie Davis Pierre, to a senior parliamentary position as Speaker of the House of Parliament (a position she held from 1980 to 1989). To avoid her statement being interpreted as feminist or pro-woman, Charles immediately retreated into describing this appointment as due to this person being the most knowledgeable. Yet she continued to suggest she understood the need for a focus on women by stating that, although the male parliamentarians asked for a men's desk to look after men's interests, she ignored their request. In that same speech to women in Jamaica she stated, "I am perhaps not a feminist, but I believe that women are more capable of doing detailed work than men. They seem to have more patience than men. And running a government, where there is no money to run it requires a lot of patience" (Charles 1985, 8–9). She also stated, "When persons ask me 'how do you feel about being the first woman Prime Minister of the Caribbean?' I say, 'I just wonder why it took so long to be the first, because in fact our women have always stood out strong' " (Charles 1985, 7).

Seventeen years later Charles reinforced her claim that she chose individuals for positions on the basis of their skills and not their sex in an interview:

> I did not choose women to do things, I chose people to do things. The people who could do it were men. I did not look at men as different. I worked with Charles Maynard, Brian Alleyne, Charles Savarin. We didn't always agree but they knew they could put their point of view forward and be heard. (Charles 2002c)[11]

A pertinent question is, why are women leaders continually asked to justify the appointment of women to senior office in ways men in leadership roles are never asked? When men appoint women to senior positions, the former appear progressive for choosing women who may be seen as deserving and who perhaps would not have been recognized without the affirmative action of the male leader. When the leader is female, her appointment of other women raises suspicions that she may be promoting undeserving women. This explains Eugenia Charles's public eagerness to underscore the qualifications of the women she promoted.

Two of Eugenia Charles's lasting contributions to public life in Dominica are creating greater opportunities for women to work at senior levels of government and serving as a role model for women who aspired to exercise public leadership. Former attorney general David Bruney believes, "Women have managed to surpass men in all the professions in Dominica. Dame Eugenia changed women's view of themselves. She showed them where they can reach. She changed attitudes" (Bruney 2002, 20)

Whether she acknowledged it or not, Eugenia Charles used her understanding of the pivotal role Caribbean women play in maintaining communities to create an effective political strategy based on harnessing this role to advance her political goals. Lennox Honychurch describes how she combined her skill for political organizing with a recognition and appreciation of the networking activities of Dominican women and how these could be deployed in servicing constituencies on the ground:

> Every Thursday evening she held constituency meetings for her constituency. These were packed with women. Women were controlling the yards. Parts of Roseau have little territorial names, women knew everything happening there and brought it all back. She had the loyalty of these women and the rural peasants. She was concerned with women who were single headed households, she always assisted and helped. (Honychurch 2002)

Chapter 10, by Alicia Mondesire, is probably the one a feminist audience may find the most fascinating. In this chapter, Mondesire scrutinizes Eugenia Charles's feminist politics or lack thereof to attempt to reveal any feminist inclinations in Charles's personal philosophy. In the process Mondesire addresses Charles's ambivalence to issues of feminism and gender. Mondesire provides a unique vantage point for us to comprehend the character of Charles. She interviews a wide cross-section of personal and political associates including Charles's secretary of fourteen years, Marilyn Zamore, cabinet colleagues and Sir John Compton, a former prime minister of St Lucia. Mondesire skilfully weaves in and out of their accounts to construct a feminist reading of Charles. Still, by the conclusion of her analysis the conundrum Charles constitutes in comprehending women's political leadership remains.

Mondesire states Charles helped women in her personal capacity but introduced no state policy on behalf of women. However, Mondesire acknowledges Charles established a day-care centre, appointed women to senior parliamentary and public sector offices and during her fifteen-year tenure laid the groundwork for policy, legislation and institutional measures to strengthen women's advancement. Mondesire's analysis calls attention to the ambivalence of Caribbean women, especially older women, working on behalf of women, to identify with feminism. Nita Barrow was adamant she was not a feminist and did not pursue a feminist agenda (Barriteau 2001a). Charles also resisted naming herself as feminist.

In practising law, Eugenia Charles emphasized what she saw as her neutrality on the question of gender and representing women and men. She said, "A lot of women came to see me on affiliation orders, I did a lot of these and I am very proud of that" (Charles 2002c). However, she stated she was equally pleased to represent men. "When a man came to me, I was proud they chose a woman to do a case against another woman" (Charles 2002c). Implicit in these comments is the recognition that many men and women do not believe women who are professionals are as competent as men. To be pleased to be chosen by men for cases against women exposes her satisfaction that men think she is a good lawyer and trust her to represent their legal interests.

Charles may have perceived her legal actions as a practising lawyer as gender neutral, as questionable a concept as that is. However, in chapter 2, Tracy Robinson raises several provocative, if not troubling, theoretical and practical questions about Charles's approach to law as a citizen, parliamentarian and legislator. Law and freedom seemed to matter very much to Eugenia Charles. One can say the desire to protect the right of association and expression propelled Charles into civilian and then electoral politics. However, in Robinson's incisive analysis of Charles's practice of political citizenship through the use of law, a different scenario emerges. Robinson tracks Charles's repeated claims that the Dominican state was violating constitutionally protected rights and freedoms but shows that rarely were these claims converted into judicial proceedings. Why did Charles make these claims and why did she not seize existing opportunities to press these claims over alleged violation of civil liberties?

Between 1968 and 1980 Charles chose platforms outside of parliament to make some of her most important arguments about law and human rights. Robinson maintains that while Charles frequently criticized Labour Party governments for abridging the basic civil liberties enjoyed by citizens, both in opposition and in government Charles eschewed using legal processes at her disposal to address the primacy of fundamental rights and freedoms. Robinson argues Charles practised a civic republican conception of citizenship, subscribing to the political philosophy that "pushes the notion of citizenship beyond rights to duties and responsibilities and emphasizes the collective good in contrast to individual autonomy".

Eugenia Charles prided herself on having a hands-on approach to

engaging with development issues and was very confident in her understanding of the cultural nuances of Dominican society and what part that
understanding should play in economic development:

> I remember once there was a World Bank team helping us to build roads. One
> morning I saw them going to work and they were all dressed in tweed pants. I
> called to them and said, "You have to wear dungarees." I listened to them on tech-
> nical things but they had to listen to me on facts on the island. I lived here all my
> life. (Charles 2002c)

While Charles cannot be faulted for her confidence and hands-on
engagement, her folksy, populist strategies for economic development were
archaic and more suited to the Dominica of the 1930s, of her childhood.
Dominica as an independent country needed an economic development
strategy that would carve out an economic niche to cushion the coming
crisis of the collapse of the banana industry. As it turned out, the disappear-
ance of agriculture as the mainstay of the economy was the first indicator
of the coming ravages of globalization.

In chapter 7, I assess Eugenia Charles's economic philosophy as origi-
nating in the benevolent ideologies of a colonial landed peasantry. I view
the economic strategies Charles pursued as pedestrian and inadequate even
though they were well intentioned. Eugenia Charles did not have the economic skills and political vision required to create a long-term economic
development policy for Dominica. She faced tremendous political and
economic obstacles, both indigenous and exogenous, on assuming the
prime ministership, but after fifteen years the cumulative strategies followed still seemed *ad hoc*, piecemeal and reactionary to unfolding
economic and political events. Charles seemed unable to think beyond
the immediacy of securing donor financing and a rudimentary appreciation of an "industrialisation by invitation" strategy. In the *Daily Nation* on
4 December 1981, she queried, "How do I ask investors to come to
Dominica when there are no roads to move their products?" (quoted in
Barriteau 1982). There is never a doubt that Eugenia Charles wanted to do
the best for the economy and was still perhaps the best qualified to hold
the finance portfolio. That was not enough. I conclude that her educational
background and her economic philosophy did not predispose her to be
innovative. She constantly used the past, especially her childhood, as her

point of reference for economic planning, and her articulation of what was required betrayed nostalgia for an earlier time and a simpler society. Yet Dominica, more than any other Eastern Caribbean economy, needed to be catapulted into the twenty-first century. Eugenia Charles attempted to keep corruption at bay but she was unable to produce a viable or any economic blueprint as part of her political legacy.

The inherent weaknesses of her economic strategies are borne out in Jonathan Lashley's assessment of her approach to enterprise development in chapter 8. Lashley examines Eugenia Charles's approach to enterprise development and poverty alleviation in the context of the neoliberal development paradigm that dominated international political economy throughout Charles's fifteen-year tenure. The Bretton Woods institutions of the World Bank and the International Monetary Fund, which actively promoted this paradigm, were the two institutions Dominica depended upon most heavily for macroeconomic financing throughout the 1980s. Lashley demonstrates that one effect of the neoliberal development paradigm is the separation of strategies formulated to achieve economic growth from the strategies used to address the problem of poverty. He reveals that the approaches pursued by Charles in relation to enterprise development and poverty alleviation were twofold and created a paradox for her administration. She believed the strategy of creating an enabling environment would stimulate investment and create economic growth. It is not surprising this approach assumed benefits would trickle down from the enabling environment into enterprise development to create jobs and thus combat poverty.

The trickle-down theory of economic growth was a major plank of the economic philosophy of Ronald Reagan that became known as Reaganomics. Eugenia Charles subscribed heavily to both the political and economic ethos of the Reagan administration and these views were in keeping with her own pragmatic and limited strategies for economic growth. According to Lashley, on poverty alleviation Eugenia Charles expected the benefits to emerge from the creation of a social infrastructure through investments in health, education and roads. He states the paradox existed because Charles the prime minister clung very closely to the neoliberal, trickle-down, Reaganomics model of development while Charles the citizen-politician utilized welfare-type approaches to supporting her constituency and the wider community, including giving monetary handouts and paying school fees for students.

In chapter 9, Carmen Hutchinson Miller dissects the portrayal of Eugenia Charles in the region's print media. She underscores the significant role media play in perpetuating inequalities experienced by women in societies and goes on to demonstrate how the print and broadcast media chose to convey stereotypical images of Eugenia Charles as an ageing, childless, unmarried, outspoken woman and politician. Again we observe the continuity in popular commentary and media strategies of using women's maternal or spousal status to draw inferences about their political relevance. Hutchinson Miller is careful to emphasize that Eugenia Charles never accepted these caricatured images but was not averse to exploiting certain statements made about her to gain political advantage. In reacting to the media's portrayal of her, Eugenia Charles again proved herself to be a confident politician unafraid of confronting statements and negative coverage. Hutchinson Miller concludes that Charles was a leader who not only understood the dynamics of political power but immensely enjoyed the exercise of it.

As Eugenia Charles was a political leader and the first woman to lead a political party and serve as prime minister for three consecutive terms, the assessment of her contribution to Dominica's public life must turn on political categories. Her contribution to the concepts of citizenship, equality, freedom, justice, the spheres of the public and private, matter to a project that assesses outstanding Caribbean women as catalysts for change (Pateman and Shanley 1991, 1). Did Eugenia Charles's political leadership alter the practice of politics for women in anglophone Caribbean society? There is credible evidence that her occupation of the pinnacle of political leadership had a tremendous demonstration effect for Dominican women. Whether admired or resented, Eugenia Charles stood out as a woman who held her own among an elite circle of Caribbean male leaders. Whether they admired the woman or not, Dominican women and men could single out a woman who was not intimidated by regional or international political developments. They could also take comfort in a political leader who possessed a heightened sense of nationalism and attempted to root out the excesses of governmental corruption even though there were lingering or new areas for concern.

Yet there is no definitive concluding statement to be made about Eugenia Charles. She entered and exited the Caribbean political stage as a conundrum. Publicly disavowing feminism, she facilitated an enabling environment for Dominican women to flourish in the public sphere. Championing Dominicans' right to freedom of expression, she callously avoided dismantling the seditious and undesirable publications legislation that catapulted her into public life. Widely regarded as introducing accountability and measures of restraint in public finance, her administration continued the economic citizenship programme that, whatever its justification, allowed individuals to buy a Dominican passport and access to the rights and privileges of a member of the Caribbean Community and the British Commonwealth for US$30,000.

At the end of this study, I do not think we have unpacked the paradox that was Eugenia Charles. However, I believe the research team has made a significant contribution to documenting, analysing and disseminating knowledge about a Caribbean woman who enjoyed political power and defied traditional categories of gender. Her refusal to fit into pre-existing definitions forces a rethinking of the existing classifications of women's political behaviour and leadership along conventional, linear readings of gender. Eugenia Charles gave much to the people of Dominica. Her gift to Caribbean scholarship is a public life that challenges feminist theoretical claims and insists upon new generalizations about political leadership. Eugenia Charles led against the grain.

Notes

1. I have been subjected to several incredulous inquiries, some even verbally hostile, as to why the Centre for Gender and Development Studies was doing a book on Eugenia Charles, the woman who, in the words of one person, "stood as Aunt Jemima on television with Ronald Reagan".
2. Her diehard supporters, however, certainly see her as Dominica's saviour.
3. Dame Eugenia Charles died on 6 September 2005, after undergoing surgery in Martinique for a broken hip.
4. These remarks were made at a meeting of the Inter-Parliamentary Forum of the Americas' first regional Forum for the Caribbean and North America. The focus of the meeting, ironically, was Enhancing Women's Leadership to Strengthen Democracy. Evidently, the senator was unaware of the research by Patrick Emmanuel that shows that the majority of female candidates in political contests in Barbados and the Eastern Caribbean were married women (Emmanuel 1992; Barriteau 1998a, 13).
5. For an earlier study of women and politics in Barbados, see Duncan and O'Brien 1983.
6. For example, in Grenada, Leslie Ann Seon serves as president of the Senate, while in Dominica, Marie Davis Pierre was appointed to serve as Speaker of the House during Eugenia Charles's first two terms.
7. On the death of her husband, President Cheddi Jagan, in 1997, Janet Jagan became president of the Cooperative Republic of Guyana. While she had a long-standing political career spanning decades, it was her husband's death that catapulted her into the leadership of the country. Citing health reasons, she relinquished the position to Bharrat Jagdeo in 1999. In Bermuda, Jennifer Smith was premier from 1998 to 2003. Kamla Persad-Bissessar was appointed as leader of the opposition in Trinidad and Tobago in April 2006, the first woman to hold that position. However, at the time of going to press the question of the leadership of her party, the United National Congress, outside parliament had not been resolved.
8. In Haiti, on 13 March 1990 Ertha Pascal-Trouillot was sworn in as interim president and became the first and only woman to hold that office, albeit briefly. She was appointed in her capacity as Supreme Court justice to hold power until elections could be held. The presidency passed to Jean-Bertrand Aristide in February 1991 after he won the presidential elections convincingly in December 1990 (Heinl, Heinl and Heinl 1996, 731–34). Also in Haiti, Claudette Werleigh served as prime minister from 1995 to 1996 (Neft and Levine 1997, 20).
9. No other Caribbean female politician has held these combinations of portfolios

or, until 1994 when Billie Miller was appointed minister of foreign affairs in Barbados, any of them. In 2002 Allyson Maynard-Gibson was appointed minister of financial services and investment in the Bahamas, but the prime minister, L. Christie, remained the minister of finance.

10. Eric Williams, prime minister of Trinidad and Tobago, won every election at the helm of the People's National Movement, the party which he founded and which won its first general elections in 1956. A Caribbean historian and intellectual, he died in office in 1981.

11. Charles Maynard, Brian Alleyne and Charles Savarin were all ministers holding various portfolios in the three administrations Charles led. They were also senior cabinet colleagues and would become engaged in differing leadership contestations with Charles during her last term of office.

PART 2

Situating Power,

Politicizing Law

and Regionalism

2

Law, Freedom and Politics
The Praxis of Political Citizenship

TRACY ROBINSON

Introduction

Eugenia Charles is fashioned into a politician in 1968 in a very particular historical moment – Britain had conferred associated status on Dominica a year earlier; and Charles emerges into formal political life in a distinct way – by identifying law as a key site of state repression and innovatively employing the language of justice, freedom and rights to create critical spaces for political intervention. In 1967, Dominica had gained associated status, in effect a "partial grant of independence" (Alexis 1983, 54), which meant the country had full power over its internal affairs and the power to move unilaterally to independence (Alexis 1983, 15n8). Associated status was a far more dramatic devolution of power in the decolonization process than independence some ten years later, and it consolidated the hegemony of the then-ruling Dominica Labour Party (Paravisini-Gebert 1996, 229). That government was now virtually autonomous from Britain, had no meaningful political opposition within Dominica and had become increasingly intolerant of dissent.

Associated status had other implications. It constructed a new order of constitutional governance signalled by a constitution whose very first section read: "Whereas every person in Dominica is entitled to the fundamental rights and freedoms . . ." (Constitution of Dominica 1967, s. 1). Written constitutions were the chief instruments of decolonization in the Caribbean and became the supreme law of the land; all other laws to the extent of their inconsistency with the constitution were void. The 1967 Dominica Constitution, like its successor, the 1978 Independence Constitution, did more than define the contours and distribution of governmental power; it placed crucial limits on what the state could do. The chapter designed to protect fundamental rights and freedoms that began at section 1 became the "moral core of the constitution" (McIntosh 2002, 227). Very importantly, it gave the *citizen* constitutional prominence in ensuring a system of limited government. Now any person whose fundamental rights were infringed by state action or legislation had a constitutional right to bring proceedings in the High Court for judicial review of those Acts of Parliament or acts of the executive (Constitution of Dominica 1967). By the same token, courts gained new eminence as guardians of the constitution.

It is in this new milieu that Eugenia Charles entered the political stage. Both the formation of her Dominica Freedom Party in 1968 and its rise to government in 1980 were set in motion by challenges to legislation that limited freedom of speech, assembly and association (Seditious and Undesirable Publications Act 1968; Industrial Relations Act 1979; Libel and Slander Act 1979). I am intrigued (admittedly thinking most like a lawyer) that Charles, already by the 1960s a skilful and very successful barrister, so conspicuously focused on political, not legal, processes to challenge the actions of the state. Charles described the foundation of the state that had been established by the constitution as "a society of free men, human dignity and human rights" (Charles 1987, 3) and encouraged graduating lawyers to offer advice, take action and follow through with concrete solutions on the interpretation of the constitution (Charles 1983b, 6). But rarely did she transform her claims that the state was violating constitutionally protected rights and freedoms into challenges in the form of judicial review proceedings.

As a prominent lawyer she had all the means to exploit judicial review and, at least in theory, many reasons to do so. She was acutely aware that she was opposing a Labour Party government which had enormous popularity and strong grassroots appeal, and that she was doing this as an identified member of the urban elite, one who would struggle for years to build popular political support. Judicial review has an appeal to minority interests and political oppositions because of its counter-majoritarian nature. Looking at judicial review from this angle, it is a power given to undemocratically selected judges to apply and construe the constitution against the wishes of a legislative majority or primarily elected executive where these organs of government fail to pay proper regard to the provisions of the constitution (Bickel 1962, 20). But instead of taking the state to court about civil liberties, between 1968 and 1980 Eugenia Charles chose platforms outside the House of Assembly and the floor of the House of Assembly to make some of her most important arguments about law and human rights.

My point is not that Charles's work as a lawyer had no bearing on her political life. Far from it; while in opposition, Charles consistently acted as a barrister on behalf of clients who were challenging the state on different fronts. And, despite her protests otherwise, this work was not divorced from her political agenda. My argument is quite specific to Charles's claims during her opposition years that the government was abridging the basic civil liberties enjoyed by the citizen, and the infrequency with which she pursued that very argument in the High Court of Dominica through judicial review proceedings. In other words, while one could in very general terms say that Eugenia Charles took the state to task both as a lawyer and a politician between 1968 and 1980, the crux for me is that, on the narrower question of fundamental rights and freedoms, her advocacy was almost exclusively as a politician and rarely as a lawyer.

In this chapter I offer a way of thinking about Charles's discourse of rights and freedoms and its relation to her choices about legislative and legal processes. The key is what I see as her version of a civic republican conception of citizenship. Republicanism pushes the notion of citizenship beyond rights to duties and responsibilities and emphasizes the collective good in contrast to individual autonomy. James Pope highlights the distinction between republicanism and liberalism:

> In contrast to liberalism's negative freedom, a "freedom to be left alone . . . that implies being alone", republicanism offers the hope that "freedom might encompass an ability to share a vision of a good life or a good society with others." . . .

> Where liberalism embraces or at least accepts the politics of self-interest, republicanism expects citizens to place the general good ahead of personal gratification. (Pope 1990, 296)

Though Charles utilized rights talk, she was neither liberal nor is she correctly styled as a libertarian. Eugenia Charles was a conservative, remarkably unmoved by the radicalism of the 1970s. She saw rights as tied to responsibilities of participation and viewed freedom not as something you simply enjoyed but as vigorously practised. And always, the rights that mattered most were those that facilitated involvement in political life, frequently her own. Her goals were political, and, pragmatically, so also were her means. Her interest in rights almost always revolved around politics.

In Caribbean constitutional democracies, we have tended to glorify the role of the courts in constructing constitutional vision (P. Craig 1990, 7) and often view politics as base, dangerous and lacking any virtue. Invariably we treat politics as an undesirable mechanism for working through matters of civil rights and freedoms (Waldron 1999). This fixation with courts in constitutional theorizing has left us with an inadequate explanation of the recent past in the Caribbean. We continue to narrate how rights issues are resolved almost entirely through accounts of what judges say, paying little attention to what happens in and outside Houses of Parliament. "Politics" and "rights" are constructed as static antagonists, missing the complex and dynamic relationship between the two in which rights are continuously renegotiated in political time and politics is transformed through rights debates. Charles's political orientation and strategizing are quite central to my analysis in this chapter. Parallel to that study of Eugenia Charles is my fascination with the broader import of her method and political life. In my view both, even if somewhat obliquely, invite us to reflect on and rethink the preoccupation of traditional legal thought with the courts and judges as the guardians of the fundamental rights and freedoms protected by our constitutions.

Even as we remain invested in narratives of our political stability, crisis, the kind that registers in political and constitutional terms, has been emblematic rather than atypical of modern Caribbean life. Nowhere is this truer than Dominica during the period from the beginning of Charles's political career at the end of the 1960s to her ascendance to the position of prime minister. There were the Civil Service Association's strikes between 1973 and 1979, the Dreads crisis, Hurricane David in 1980, and two coup attempts and high-profile kidnappings in the early 1980s, to name a few. With crises come crucial contestations about civil liberties, most of which never make it to court. To be sure, that may be a deep disappointment; we may have wished that the High Court, for example, had ruled on the constitutionality of the infamous Dread Act passed in 1974 in Dominica. The danger of this kind of dissatisfaction is how it can easily proceed into an erasure of the roles played by legislatures and the citizenry in shaping the fate of such legislation. The mobilization Eugenia Charles helped to lead in the gallery of the House of Assembly and outside it in 1968 around the sedition legislation, the transformation of the House she helped to engineer in 1979 in response to restrictive industrial relations and libel and slander laws, even the feeble criticisms she provided of the Dread Act within the House in 1974, were all decisive moments in the evolution of civil liberties in Dominica. The judicial decisions found in law reports will yield little of these stories.

This chapter looks at the first half of Eugenia Charles's political career – from her years in opposition to the beginning of her first term as prime minister. This early postcolonial period of 1968 to 1981 in the Caribbean was one of formative nation building as well as discontent and crisis of a character that would no longer be possible after the 1983 United States invasion of Grenada. Charles oddly existed in this time as a political leader who was conservative ideologically and yet intent on being a disruptive and destabilizing political force. She found her political feet through crises and she proudly helped instigate some of them. I see her during this time as performing from a sense of citizenship that was focused on the value of political life, deeply respectful of majority sentiments, grounded in notions of the common good, and articulating an understanding of freedom and rights that was shaped by the pre-eminence of those concerns.

Political Citizenship: The Democratic Gadfly and Wasp

Eugenia Charles's idea of citizenship always, to borrow from Anne Phillips, "returns us emphatically to the political sphere" (A. Phillips 1993, 85). A good citizen for her was an active citizen, one who knew how to speak vigorously against her government. Consistent with the civic republican tradition, freedom and autonomy are located in the public activities of citizenship (Young 1995, 178), and political community is a good in itself (Beiner 1995a, 14). Speaking out was the centrepiece of valuable citizenship for Charles. At the end of her political career Eugenia Charles could still be heard maintaining, "I am a Dominican and I have the right to speak" (*Daily Nation* 1998, 21), just as she had thirty years before. In describing the key human rights issues that the new graduates of the Norman Manley Law School would face in their legal careers in 1983, Charles not surprisingly spoke first of freedom of speech, then freedom of the press and last the right to vote in a free and fair elections – all rights to facilitate involvement in political life (Charles 1983b, 6). Charles's insistence on the pre-eminence of freedom of speech on occasion defied logic. In describing the violence of apartheid in South Africa, Charles noted the oppression of black South Africans, and she said that "above all they have been refused the right of freedom of speech and the right of freedom to travel to go further to be educated" (Hansard, 8 July 1971, 16).

This ethic of speech Charles learned at home. Hers was an argumentative family in which everyone in the household regardless of age had the right to express their opinion at the dinner table (Charles 1995a, 2, 11; Higbie 1993, 77). Of her own home Charles would say that it "has always been, and still is open to anybody who wants to talk, anytime" (Dowe and Honychurch 1989, 5). Forthrightness and formidability were distinctive features of her personality that were inextricably tied to her political method and secured within familial foundations. Charles could be fearless and defiant in her opinions. In 1964, the bishop of Roseau wrote to her saying he had planned to send a petition to the Holy See asking to have her admitted as a permanent lay observer at the council, as a "worthy representative of the devout feminine sex" (Boghoert 1964). The Bishop indignantly complained: "And now comes your impious letter. . . . On many points you seem to agree with the arch-conservative Cardinal Ottaviani, but then there is your stubborn stand on Free Love. . . . You will admit that this would be another 'pill' difficult for him to swallow" (Boghoert 1964).

Charles's first abstract thought as a child was based on the slogan, "No taxation without representation" (Charles 1995a, 2). This became a central plank of her political philosophy – her right *and* responsibility as a taxpayer to speak out on any matter relating to the affairs of the country and to challenge even the most senior government officials and politicians. Charles could be trenchant in her criticisms of those who failed to face up to their responsibilities as public citizens. She castigated women later in her career for sitting back and letting the sacrificial few bear the brunt of the jobs that in the long run were beneficial to all. She was adamant it was up to women "to mobilise the resources at their disposal for a better future for themselves and the national good" (Charles n.d.). This notion of the responsibilities of citizens also had its wellspring in her family life because her parents had clearly laid before their children their responsibilities, and each child was expected to fulfil their expectations (Dowe and Honychurch 1989, 11).

Eschewing membership in a political party did not mean that you ignored the wrongs being perpetrated on citizens, Charles explained (Charles 1995a). In 1967, she quoted the following in a letter titled "Freedom from Criticism": "People who do not know how to talk against their government do not deserve a democracy. And the best government in the world when it is deprived of the goading democratic 'gadflies' soon gets bored with its own virtue and dies of inanity" (Higbie 1993, 85).

The "Shut-Your-Mouth Bill": The Right to Dissent

A goading democratic gadfly is what Charles had proudly become by 1968. She once boasted of herself: "I know I am much more annoying than a wasp" (Charles 1974). Dr Nicholas Liverpool, former dean of the Faculty of Law at the University of the West Indies, described her as "contentious, a warrior, and someone who liked to fight" (Liverpool 2002). She began her professional career as a barrister in 1949 in Dominica, having completed her studies abroad. In the 1950s and 1960s, she developed a reputation for tenaciously representing civil servants and other clients in disputes with the colonial government. From the late 1950s through the 1960s she had been writing regularly to the newspapers on various local issues, often using pseudonyms (Higbie 1993, 80). Of her newspaper writings, it was said that "her satire was barbed, her pen was dipped in acid" (Dowe and

Honychurch 1989, 13). By the late 1960s Charles had become a harsh newspaper critic of the Dominica Labour Party and its leader, Premier Edward LeBlanc, who was a very popular politician with strong rural ties as a former agricultural extension officer (Honychurch 1984, 180). Her letter in the *Chronicle* in May 1967 asked of the LeBlanc administration:

> Why are they so sensitive to criticism? Surely they must know that the freedom which they are so proud to obtaining for us cannot be maintained if the liberty to speak and write on any matter concerning the affairs of this island, including that of government, is not permitted to all, even to those whom they describe as enemies of the government. (Higbie 1993, 85)

The Labour Party, which Phyllis Allfrey had co-founded and was later thrown out of after her criticism of the government, she now described as "a petty little group of nationalist islanders calling themselves Labour" (Paravisini-Gebert 1996, 230). With no effective opposition inside parliament, the major newspapers played the role of providing political commentary and criticism (Honychurch 1984, 181). Phyllis Allfrey at the *Star,* Stanley Boyd at the *Chronicle* and Edward Scobie from the *Herald,* "a trio of liberal, light-skinned, Roseau-based newspaper editors" (Higbie 1993, 86) were all rankling the government and LeBlanc.

Eugenia Charles's formal political career was set in motion in 1968 when she, these newspaper editors and other critics of the government learned that the government planned on introducing the Seditious and Undesirable Publications Bill in parliament. In 1968, sedition legislation limiting political speech and what one could say against the government existed all over the Caribbean, including Dominica,[1] and reforms to sedition legislation were key political tools to contain the disaffection of the late 1960s and early 1970s in the Caribbean.[2] The Dominica Labour Party government insisted that the bill was intended to provide guidelines for higher and better standards of journalism, not to stifle the press (Attorney General L. Austin, in Dominica 1968, 11), but not surprisingly, the law was viewed as targeting the newspapers and their writers, like Charles, who had intensified their criticisms of the Labour Party government in the preceding years. Once they heard of the impending introduction of what became famously dubbed by Charles as the "Shut-Your-Mouth Bill", the group of critics, who later formed the core of what became known as the "Freedom

Fighters", mobilized. The night before the bill was introduced in parliament a public meeting was held in Roseau where Charles joined a platform of speakers condemning the introduction of the legislation. Charles represented the Employers' Federation and she analysed the draft provisions of the proposed legislation in "devastating detail" (Higbie 1993, 88). Charles also drafted a critique of the legislation that was signed by a number of persons and sent to the attorney general that day.

On the encouragement of Charles and others, protesters filled the gallery of the House of Assembly on 5 July 1968, the day the bill was introduced. The loud, large crowd in the gallery, which included Charles, plainly produced discomfiture in the House. In opening the debate, the attorney general almost immediately referred to the letter he had received the day before "signed by responsible citizens of the community pointing out certain things they would have liked removed from the Law" (Dominica 1968, 8). Ronald Armour, minister of communications and works, described the letter as written by the "eminent professional virgin" (Dominica 1968, 15). The attorney general responded to some of the points raised by the letter and indicated places where amendments had been made in light of the letter. Though modest, Charles's efforts had an impact on the legislation even before the debates meaningfully began. The hostility of the members of the House towards Charles and her coalition that day was patent. The minister of trade and industry, N. Ducreay, said,

> I am very happy to see at this moment that certain people have found it necessary to come here today and this is what I enjoy. [Members] who for many years have never found it necessary to come here to listen to meetings of the House of Assembly have now in their wisdom come here at this time to attend this meeting. This is a very great thing. (Dominica 1968, 11)

Armour was more caustic. He said,

> I am very glad today that there are so many people here. If the crowd would see that all this juvenile disturbance is coming from big business men . . . [and] professionals like Eugenia Charles. . . [W]hat we are seeing here is a concerted effort of a few rich people . . . who want to confuse Dominicans living outside of Dominica. (Dominica 1968, 16)

The House of Assembly passed the law, repealing the earlier ordinance and expanding the definition of sedition. Now included was exciting dislike of, or discontent with, the government by means of any false representation or wilful misrepresentation of facts or of the motives or intentions of the government or any officer of the government. Also included as an offence in the new law was advocating, teaching or defending the use of force, violence, terrorism or physical injury to person or property as a means of accomplishing any governmental change. The new act introduced a more severe maximum fine of $2,000 for persons who did acts or published materials with a seditious intent, but a lower maximum sentence of imprisonment was introduced. The most significant additions were concerned with seditious publications and were directed at the newspapers. If a newspaper habitually contained matter with a seditious intention or had the object of inciting any person or class or persons to use unlawful violence or of promoting feelings of hostility between different classes of the community, the court could prohibit publication for a year. The court could also prohibit the editor or publisher of that paper from publishing or editing or writing for another newspaper for a year. Additionally, the printing press of the paper could be seized for a year.

The group of critics, by then known as the Freedom Fighters, launched an island-wide petition to repeal the legislation and gathered 3,317 signatures. A demonstration of up to three thousand persons took place outside the House of Assembly at the next sitting on 23 September to present their petitions, and LeBlanc famously announced, "We are here to rule and rule we will" (Honychurch 1984, 182). In that moment Charles made a speech which turned out to be "a vibrant barrage on democracy and constitutional law" and "flung herself unflinchingly into the political arena" (Honychurch 1984, 182). Nominated member Eustace Henry moved a motion for the repeal of the act on 25 September 1968 unsuccessfully. But from that moment, the Dominica Freedom Party under Charles's leadership was born. Charles and her colleagues did not thwart the passage of the legislation nor did she initiate judicial review proceedings to challenge the constitutionality of the newly enacted law. Her victory was that the 1968 law, once enacted, was never enforced – a matter of pride for the Freedomites. Charles and the Freedom Party would later lose some credibility because they did not attempt to repeal the law during Charles's fifteen-year tenure as prime minister between 1980 and 1995.

Eugenia Charles has in later reflections admitted to a measure of unsophistication in this early period. Her instinctive political sensibilities told her "it was terrible that you would not be able to say what you wanted to say" and that "everybody had a right to talk easily about the things that mattered", but she did not always frame her arguments using the words "freedom of speech" or ground them explicitly in the new constitution of 1967 (Stern 1995, 16). The Freedom Party's first policy statement after its founding in 1968 used Franklin Roosevelt's four freedoms – freedom from fear, freedom from want, freedom to worship and freedom of speech and expression. This liberal, social democratic document was not a strong indication of Charles's orientation; rather, it bore Phyllis Allfrey's imprint and was not dissimilar to the objectives of the Labour Party written by Allfrey in 1955 (Paravisini-Gebert 1996, 233).

As Charles matured politically so, to a fair degree, did her discourse on speech rights. By the mid-1970s, Charles began speaking forcefully about the *right to dissent*, very influenced by a 1973 article by Lord Denning (Denning 1973). During the independence celebrations in 1978, she tried to embarrass the Labour government and then premier Patrick John in her welcome address to the UK delegation by castigating John's administration for failing to recognize that the right to dissent must exist in a democratic society, and for treating criticisms of it almost as if they were acts of treason (Dominica 1978b, 2). Charles became known for this skilful rhetorical appeal to freedom of speech, and freedom of assembly and association for political effect and for her insistence on these three freedoms for her political development.

The Little Revolution: The Right to Protest

In 1970, Charles joined the House as a nominated member, having unsuccessfully contested the election for the Roseau North seat. The next year the Freedom Party took control of the Roseau Town Council. There was a breakdown in relations between the council and the government, and demonstrations took place outside the House of Assembly on 16 December 1971, the same year the Freedom Party took control of the town council. Charles and other Freedomites were arrested for participating in a public demonstration without the necessary permission; she was acquitted and helped raise money for the fines of those convicted. Thereafter, for Charles demonstrations and strikes emerged as pivotal forms of dissent against the government. Many in the opposition saw demonstrations as the only way their views would be heard by a government that had grown indifferent to criticism with continued success at the polls (Liverpool n.d., 2).

By 1975 Charles was sitting in the House as an elected member and as the leader of the opposition. The Dominica Labour Party was still firmly in place but its new leader was Patrick John, who took the country into independence in 1978. Her advocacy on behalf of civil servants crystallized into a strong political and professional alliance with the Civil Servants Association (CSA) that began in 1969. Charles had attended a course on trade unionism in 1968 and spoke often in the 1970s about workers' rights. Charles was politically adept and maintained her growing political base through the CSA alongside her representation of the Employers' Federation. Missing no opportunity to link rights and freedoms to a verbal lashing of those whose politics she detested, she once said, "Had [Maurice] Bishop honoured his promise to entrench the rights of the workers, the trade unions and the people of Grenada, no doubt he would today not only be alive but he might well have been a hero of the region" (Charles 1984c, 2). Against a backdrop of deteriorating relations between the CSA and the government, proposed general strikes and wide criticism of deals being made by John to set up a free port, on 29 May 1979, the House of Assembly read and passed the Industrial Relations (Amendment) Act 1979-6 and the Libel and Slander (Amendment) Act 1979-4. The opposition campaigned intensely for about two weeks prior to this, and approximately ten thousand demonstrators protested outside the House of Assembly on 29 May, just as they had in 1968 (Honychurch 1984, 205). Charles took her seat in the House, understanding this to be her rightful place and fearing that she would be arrested if she gave a speech outside to the demonstrators (Charles n.d.). Then the Defence Force opened fire on the crowd, killing a youth. On hearing of the events outside, Eugenia Charles as opposition leader protested the continuation of proceedings and led a walkout of opposition members. A majority of the remaining members passed the legislation.

The amendments to the Libel and Slander Act allowed the plaintiff in a libel suit to seek the court's permission to require the editor to produce information and particulars as to the name of the writer of any article published in the newspaper alleged to be libellous. Failure to do this where ordered by the court was made an offence. The Amendment Act further provided that the directors on the board of a newspaper were jointly and severally liable for the payment of damages ordered by the court in a libel suit. Editors were prohibited from publishing any article that criticized any person in his or her professional or official capacity or which ascribed to any person conduct which may have the effect of lowering that person in the estimation of others, unless the article carried an indication at the top of it as to whether the article was political or purported to be factual, together with the name of the writer of the article. The attorney general assured the House that nothing in the Libel and Slander Bill was unconstitutional, pointing out that there were many lawyers supporting the law (Hansard, 29 May 1978, 37). The law "aims at giving every citizen his right . . . each and everyone of us has constitutional rights and it is only when everybody regards these constitutional rights, that harmony and peace prevail" (Hansard, 29 May 1978, 38).

The amendments to the Industrial Relations Act were more extensive and gave the relevant minister greater powers to respond to strikes. It was "an emergency valve or device", according to L. Austin (Hansard, 29 May 1978, 13), to stop the "industrial warfare" (Hansard, 29 May 1978, 12). Workers engaged in essential services were prohibited from strike action. Any trade union or other organization that called for industrial action in these services was guilty of an offence. Providing financial support to an organization that called for industrial action in an essential service was also an offence. Members of the public, prison, fire, teaching and nursing services were all prohibited from taking industrial action. The Amendment Act established a National Arbitration Tribunal to determine disputes in the Public Service. Courts were given jurisdiction to issue a stop order for industrial action in the national interest on the application of the minister.

The events that ended John's leadership and paved the way for the rise of the Freedom Party to government in the 1980 elections began on 29 May 1979. This became known as the "little revolution", a not-coincidental comparison to the Grenada Revolution that toppled the Gairy government two months earlier. The country was locked down in a national strike after the laws were passed and soon various ministers of the government began to resign. Charles acted constructively in the crisis as a member of the Committee for National Salvation that assumed *de facto* leadership of the country. Her leadership in the House of Assembly was both restrained and vital. On 21 June 1979, Eugenia Charles asked members present in the House of Assembly to indicate whether they had withdrawn their support for the prime minister, Patrick John, and would support an interim government made up of a coalition of political partners. She then successfully led a motion in the House for the establishment of an interim coalition government, but she took no office in the interim government. Charles said of these events: "So the PM was wrong to boast that the people must learn that the Government cannot be prevented from passing laws by use of violence. Instead he must learn the lesson that he cannot pass laws under the protection of violence against the wishes of the citizens of Dominica" (Charles n.d., 3).

On 19 July 1979, the offending sections of both statutes were repealed by parliament (Libel and Slander (Amendment) Act (No. 2) 1979-11; Industrial Relations (Amendment) Act (No. 2) 1979-13). A year later, on 20 July 1980, the Freedom Party won its first elections, and Charles became prime minister of the Commonwealth of Dominica. Charles would recount and reconstruct the events around and after 5 July 1968 and 29 May 1979 often in interviews and speeches. These were defining moments of her political life and the life of the nation in which the political landscape was radically altered as citizens mobilized quite literally inside and outside the House of Assembly around matters of civil liberty and freedom. Parliament, as the site of formal political power, became the primary arena of citizenship. Still, many of the critical engagements of this period, such as those the Committee for National Salvation was involved in, took place in the balconies and on the steps of the House, and further afield, by men and women who were choosing a deeper involvement in public life (Michelman 1988, 1,531).

Majoritarian Justice and the Common Good

Charles was presented by her party in 1980 as the single most important figure to have "bravely defended the rights of Dominicans and fought to maintain the rule of law" (DFP 1980). Yet so variable and moderate was her advocacy of human rights that this frequently was not a plausible claim. She could be an exacting "law and order" proponent; Charles was pro-capital punishment, saying that she had "always been convinced that it [was] less merciful to imprison a person for life than to carry out capital punishment" (Charles 1993). She argued that the cat-o'-nine-tails was inhuman but supported whipping as a lawful punishment (Dominica 1974a). Where she did attempt to explain the contradictions, Eugenia Charles did so by nuancing her conception of human rights with the idea of common good. For her this meant that the interests and rights of the majority or larger community superseded the rights of the individual or a few individuals. For instance, she urged stern censorship of films in the Dread Act debates, blaming films for providing the vocabulary for "dread language". The rationale she offered for limiting freedom of expression was the larger interest of presenting a few good films from which people could learn something (Dominica 1974, 34).

The common good was typically a discourse of defence – a justification either for her support while in opposition or her introduction as prime minister of measures that limited civil liberties. Charles turned traditional notions of human rights as imposing obligations on the state towards the citizen upside-down and argued that each citizen must have a civic responsibility towards other citizens and the state, in the interests of the common good. In her independence address in 1981 she said,

> But it is not only Government which must act fairly. The people of Dominica must act fairly also. They must be fair to themselves, to their neighbours, to their leaders and to Dominicans as a whole. We must not permit our own selfish desires for our own personal aggrandizement to block our view of what is fair for others. The national cake is small but it must be shared among all parts of the island and among all people of the island. (Dominica 1981a, 4)

Charles's appeal to the common good further locates her within this civil republican tradition I mentioned earlier. Civic republicanism claims that citizens rise above their self-regarding lives and the pursuit of self-interest by engaging in public life, and in that process take up a general position from which they agree on the common good (Young 1995, 178). Her sense of the common good proceeded from a notion of community and common identity that was grounded in the experiences of her child-hood. Her parents, she said, taught her and her siblings that they could not have everything and made them feel, despite their wealth, that they were no different from others who were less well off (Dowe and Honychurch 1989, 2). She said she began to understand the meaning of community life at the Convent High School because they were all taught to do things together (Dowe and Honychurch 1989, 1).

Charles turned to the common good in her early political career as a way of minimizing class divides that compromised her political viability. She insisted that there were no class distinctions in Dominica and charged that it was the government that had spread class hatred (Dominica 1973b, 36). Class distinctions were artificial, she said, because

> we all come from the same sort of background – some of us are ambitious and make a better thing of life than others; but no-one is born with a silver spoons in one's mouth. . . . [I]f we wish to build a nation we must put aside those pettinesses and judge a man by his achievements and his behaviour and not by who his parents were, what his profession is; and how much money he is thought to have. (Charles 1974, 17)

In a similar way, Charles used the word "taxpaying" rhetorically to legit-imize her participation in public life as someone who was not (yet) a politician and, more important, to counter the criticisms that she was part of a small Roseau-based wealthy elite and unfit to represent the interests of the majority.

Taxpaying served to secure her within a common identity as citizen and also to distinguish her within it. It was not simply that she paid taxes, but that, as a very successful lawyer and businesswoman, she paid *a lot* of taxes, to which she turned to strengthen her legitimacy as a critic of the state. Though promoting the idea of a common identity and the common good that lay outside of class distinctions premised on the commonality of tax-paying, Charles was inscribing a notion of citizenship that excluded those who failed to contribute meaningfully to the political and economic com-munity by paying taxes and making something of themselves in a "class-less" society. Persons who opted out of contributing in this way in her view did not deserve the rights of citizens. This conception of citizenship lay at the heart of Charles's response to the Dread Act.

The Dread Act: The Common Good, Non-Citizens and Limited Rights

The Dreads were a disparate community of young people who had been very influenced by the Rastafari religion and way of life and the Black Power movement. Like Rastafarians, they were distinguishable by their dreadlocked hair. Within the community there were different ideologies and practices and no clear leadership, but, on the whole, they shared common ideas of "returning to nature", and made strong demands for land; also, many expressed a belief in Jah as the Supreme Being (Dominica 1975, 10). They understood their way of life as a disavowal of the established political, economic and social life of the country. Many Dreads lived off the land in the hills, some on family land and others squatting on private and state land. Many smoked and grew marijuana, though this was not unique to the Dreads (Dominica 1975, 13).

By the early 1970s, the Dreads had gained a reputation for criminal activity and violence. The rising and well-publicized incidence of crime in the country, including attacks on tourists, murders, armed robberies and larceny of crops, was being attributed to the Dreads. By 1974 the Dreads were viewed as Dominica's greatest problem (Dominica 1975, 3). The premier, Patrick John, bombastically described the Dreads as a minority terrorist organization working on a communist takeover (Dominica 1974a, 22, 24). The extent of their criminal activity and their degree of organizational structure were greatly exaggerated, but public anxiety and fear were intense and the demands for strong government action were overwhelming.

On 19 November 1974, Patrick John introduced in the House of Assembly the Prohibited and Unlawful Societies and Associations Bill which defined an unlawful association, designated the Dreads an unlawful association and criminalized their existence. It was intended to "preserve law and order and to dispel the climate of fear and apprehension visible because of the behaviour of the Dreads" (Dominica 1974a, 22). The law, which became known as the "Dread Act", was unanimously passed by the House of Assembly and had wide public support. In what would best define the tenor of the legislation, the premier promised:

> we will fight fire with fire, and who don't hear will feel. We will use Moses' law and the Communist terrorists are bound to yield – it's tooth for tooth, an eye for

an eye, gun for gun and bomb for bomb, hand grenade for hand grenade, raid for raid, blade for blade, knife for knife and Mr Speaker, life for life. (Dominica 1974a, 25)

Eugenia Charles had no sympathy for the defiance (or what she saw as the deviance) of the Dreads and expressed support for fighting "fire with fire" (Dominica 1974a, 35). She showed little understanding of their origins and simplistically claimed that the Dread crisis had been created by rampant drug use (Dominica 1977c, 105) and lost no opportunity to criticize the Labour Party for contributing to the development of the Dread crisis through its own party rhetoric of "gros bourg" and "petit bourg" (Dominica 1974a, 31). Having abandoned the traditional political and economic community, the Dreads represented the paradigm of the "noncitizen" for Eugenia Charles. This is, of course, the danger of a classical republicanism that ends up excluding those whose voices would "threaten disruption of a community's normative unity" (Michelman 1988, 1,495). A good citizen in conflict with the state was expected to follow her example during the ten years the government attempted to "crush" them as the opposition: "we continued paying our taxes, we did not refrain from paying the taxes, which we knew were being misused and wrongly pocketed . . . we continued as citizens of this country and stayed and did our part as citizens" (Dominica 1981b, 18).

The Dreads fell far short of this and were deemed subversive, and Charles would turn to the interests of the common good to explain her support as an opposition member of the repressive and draconian act of 1974.

Opening the session of the House of Assembly after lunch on 19 November 1974, she began:

I rise in support of this Bill. I do so reluctantly. It is regrettable that the day should have arrived when we ourselves must take away one of our human rights enshrined in our Constitution. But this is almost beyond our control. Because in this bill, there is no doubt, an erosion of the fundamental freedom of association . . . However, it becomes necessary, Mr Speaker, because a greater majority of people's freedom is being eroded and that is the freedom from fear. There is no doubt that in the past few months the community has lived under a reign of fear. (Dominica 1974a, 30)

Charles's overarching claim was that the measures were necessary to protect the freedom of the majority of people – the common good. She presented the human rights concerns in the narrowest of terms, for the act's impact went well beyond freedom of association. This right was of great importance to Charles generally, but for the Dreads, who were never properly an organization, it was the least significant of the infringements they would suffer. The act restricted virtually every enumerated right in the Constitution of Dominica – protection of the right to personal liberty, protection from deprivation of property, protection from arbitrary search and entry, provisions to secure the protection of law, protection of freedom of conscience, expression, movement, and protection from discrimination and above all the right to life.

Ostensibly the legislation was concerned with prohibited and unlawful societies and associations, but it was designed to address the Dread crisis. The act established what was an unlawful association and made any person who was or became a member of an unlawful association guilty of an offence under the act. Section 3 of the act outlined a number of indicators of an unlawful association or society. These included an association or society whose members conspired to affect public safety and public order adversely, or practised acts of terrorism or enticed young people under the age of eighteen to join their membership, thereby preventing them from attending school. Some of the indicators were explicitly linked to protection of the rights and freedoms of others. Thus, any association or society whose members prevented the peaceful enjoyment of rights over property by the destruction of crops, animals or buildings or by acts of violence was an unlawful association or society. Similarly, an association whose members assaulted, beat, wounded, hindered or prevented other persons from enjoying freedom of movement or association on the grounds of their economic status, class, social background, race, place of origin, colour or religious persuasion was unlawful.

Eugenia Charles was anxious that the law would be unwittingly extended beyond the Dreads to political organizations like her own. She had a concern that the definition of association was so broad it would cover organizations like the Dominica Freedom Party. As a result, to remove doubt, it was made clear that the association or group must share a common *unlawful* objective (Dominica 1974a, 58). The section outlining the activities of an unlawful association was reconstructed in the Committee of the House largely due to Charles's suggestions, with strong concurrence from the premier, to include additional grounds such as an association whose members, among other things, attempt to adversely affect public safety (Dominica 1974a, 58).

Charles objected strenuously to the manner in which the Dreads were designated an unlawful association. There were two methods of designating an unlawful association under the act. First, the minister had the power after the passage of the act to designate a society or association engaging in any of the named practices as unlawful. Second, an association could be so designated by the schedule to the act itself. The Dreads were designated an unlawful association or society in the latter manner. The other method, a later designation by the relevant minister, carried with it a right of appeal to the High Court. Charles suggested they remove the schedule, pass the legislation and the next day the minister could bring an order to designate the Dreads an unlawful society, thus giving them the right of appeal. She wanted everybody, including the Dreads, to have a right to challenge the designation (Dominica 1974a, 66). On this point, she failed to convince her fellow parliamentarians.

Charles was also concerned that the act gave a minister rather than parliament the power to designate an association unlawful. She preferred to have this done by the House of Assembly because the bill was so far-reaching (Dominica 1974a, 65). On this point she urged more strongly than others:

> I don't want the Minister to make regulations. . . . As I said, this is an infringement almost of our Constitution; it is a necessary step and I am all for it. But I want it to be curtailed . . . I want to prevent any further infringement. . . . [L]et us meet and let the House itself decide these things. Let us not leave it to a Minister to pass orders which nobody knows about until they are laid on the Table two or three months later on. (Dominica 1974a, 36)

She unsuccessfully moved to have this provision deleted. She was successful in urging that a clause giving the minister power to make changes to the legislation be removed. She argued that the legislation took away people's rights, or at least circumscribed them, and that it was important that the House of Assembly be involved in any changes to the law (Dominica 1974a, 66–67).

Charles did not question the designation of the Dreads as an unlawful society, just the method of designation and the author of designation. She confirmed in response to a question from the chairman of the Committee of the House that she was sure that the Dreads should be declared an unlawful society (Dominica 1974a, 66). Charles stated this in spite of her acknowledgement that there were different categories of Dreads: she described these as created by unemployment, by frustration with society, and by family neglect, association with bad company, criminals, drug use and brainwashing (Dominica 1974a, 31). Not all Dreads were involved in criminal activities, on her account, but she raised no concerns about all being subject to the severe penalties of the act. The Dreads could not properly be described as an organization or association because there was variation in beliefs, ideologies and practices and an absence of any hierarchy or leadership (Dominica 1975, 9). The committee appointed by the government to report on Dreadism in 1975 confirmed that some Dreads were involved in criminal activity, but said that the numbers of Dreads involved in criminal activity had been exaggerated (Dominica 1975, 12, 21).

In consequence of the designation of the Dreads as an unlawful association, any person wearing any distinguishing mark or manner of wearing their hair that was associated with the Dreads was guilty of an offence and was to be arrested without warrant by any member of the police force. Charles raised no objections to this provision. It was later strongly criticized by the Dreadism Committee, which urged that those searching for identity be tolerated in society "once such action is peaceful and does not infringe the rights of others", and further urged that the growing of hair in dreadlocks should remain a personal matter and that the focus be on character and behaviour, not appearance (Dominica 1975, 5). Persons deemed to be Dreads and arrested were not entitled to bail but were to be taken before a magistrate within forty-eight hours of arrest. Charles agreed that no bail should be available; her only concern was which gaol could hold the "two hundred, these four hundred, these six hundred when we pick them up" (Dominica 1974a, 34). She was unhappy about all members of the police having the power to arrest without a warrant a member of an unlawful association in public. She thought it should be restricted to police officers from the rank of sergeant upwards; however, she did not move an amendment to this effect (Dominica 1974a, 60). She argued that persons arrested without a warrant should be brought before a magistrate within twenty-four hours, urging that the person be brought "strictly and quickly to justice", and the House agreed on forty-eight hours (Dominica 1974a, 61).

On the first conviction for being a member of the Dreads, one was subject to a mandatory sentence of nine months' imprisonment, and for a subsequent conviction, to two years. The bill started off with mandatory sentences of eighteen months and two years respectively. Member Ronald Armour pointed out this was unprecedented and advocated discretion for first offenders. Charles said she, too, was unhappy with the provision, stating she would like the law to come up for review every six months and hopefully to be repealed after the first six months (Dominica 1974a, 67). Charles never moved for the introduction of a provision to this effect and it was Armour who suggested a reduction from eighteen months to nine months, which was accepted.

These overly broad provisions of the Dread Act criminalized many non-violent Dreads, such as

> a young man of 17 [who] decides he is going dread, he has not as yet beaten up anybody, he has not as yet stolen, he has not as yet cursed anybody, he is still hesitant but in fact one day he is anxious to grow his hair long and comes in public and you hold him. (R. Armour in Dominica 1974a, 39)

Charles raised no concerns about this in the debates. The Committee appointed by the government in 1975 and chaired by Reverend A. Didier to report on the problem of Dreadism concluded that many of the Dreads ultimately detained and imprisoned pursuant to the powers provided by the Dread Act were non-violent, peaceful and law-abiding (Dominica 1975, 13). Prison warders commented on the peaceful nature and tolerant attitude of some of the youths imprisoned under the Dread Act (Dominica 1975, 5). The incarceration of innocent Dreads among hardened criminals just because of their appearance "resulted in suspicions and a lack of confidence among youth, widening and hardening the gaps and prejudices in the society" (Dominica 1975, 13).

The act authorized the police with a warrant issued by a magistrate or justice of the peace to enter any home by force, by breaking doors if necessary, to search if the police had reasonable cause to suspect a member of an unlawful society to be hiding therein. Charles noted that justices of the peace had never issued warrants in Dominica but said that the provision was acceptable if they were given a "little seminar" (Dominica 1974a, 64). She also said she was unhappy about the inclusion of "breaking of doors" but again she did not move to have it deleted from the section. She raised no questions about the section granting the police full indemnity against criminal or civil proceedings for action taken in performance of duties under the act. Most extraordinarily, the Dread Act provided that no proceedings, either criminal or civil, could be brought or maintained against any person who killed or injured a Dread found at any time inside a dwelling house. The bill was broader, originally referring to persons found in "private premises", not a "dwelling house". Charles was firmly in support of the section, but proposed it be restricted to dwelling houses: "[Imagine] [y]ou get up during the night and you see a person with his tam and slits for his eyes", she said (Dominica 1974a, 63). And then she turned to the law in Jamaica which, she claimed, allowed you to kill anyone found in a dwelling house at the wrong time of night: "Jamaica has had this provision in the early nineteen hundreds and for a person of an unlawful society. If at night you see a hand over your windowsill – that's inside your house – you shoot him. Jamaica's law has always been that way" (Dominica 1974a, 64). No one, including Charles, was troubled by the scenario presented by member Ronald Armour: "Suppose the man says 'Oh! I thought this was somebody's house, or, I came to collect my change' " (Dominica 1974a, 63). The section was approved with "dwelling house" substituted for private premises.

There have been few laws enacted in the Commonwealth Caribbean in the last century as brutal or offensive as what became known as the Dread Act. There was a legitimate state interest in containing the growing violence in Dominica in the early 1970s, but the measures introduced were astonishingly disproportionate and inexact in addressing that problem. Ultimately, Eugenia Charles did little to oppose the most reckless excesses of the measures introduced in the Dread Act, but she made a contribution to the marginal moderation of the law through her participation in the parliamentary debates. Armour, by comparison, was far more strident in his interventions. Charles's professional and political colleague Brian Alleyne was even bolder in his critique of the Dread Act. In an article published in the *New Chronicle* on 7 December 1974, Alleyne offered the view that

> this [act] is the inevitable result when people (and more so with a body of people rather than an individual) allow themselves, in fits of emotion, to be ruled by irrational fear rather than by reason, which we have the right to demand from our legislators in enacting a law which it is unanimously agreed, drastically cuts into our fundamental rights and freedoms and, at the very least, comes perilously close to offending against the Constitution. (Honychurch 1984, 189)

Less than a month after the Dread Act was passed, the government sought to amend it. Charles became very impatient with the amendment and maintained that the act had to be watched carefully: "We must not allow it to stand on our Statute Books, one day more than is necessary. We must realise that it must be removed as soon as the necessity for it has vanished; may that be at a very early date, Mr Speaker" (Dominica 1974b, 7).

Charles in fact did very little in parliament to see that the legislation was repealed quickly. There were sporadic discussions in the House about the act, for which she was either not present or to which she did not contribute. On 24 July 1975, a bill was introduced by Patrick John to suspend the operation of the Dread Act for a specified time to provide a period of amnesty to attempt to hold discussions with the Dreads and facilitate their readjustment to society. In May 1977, A.A. Casimir, member for the Grandbay constituency, brought a motion stating that the Dread Act had come under attack recently because of a dawn swoop made on some young people which brought the fairness of the operation of the law into doubt in some minds. He argued that it was better to remove the law from the statute books than to have people openly defying it (Dominica 1977a, 19–20). The motion that carried, perversely, was that the government should take the necessary steps to effectively enforce that particular section of the Dread Act dealing with locks. In 1978, in parliament the minister of home affairs described the Dread Act as an "unfortunate piece of legislation" (Hansard, 23 February 1978, 23) and the attorney general promised that it and also other legislation was being re-examined in light of criticisms made locally and internationally about it (Hansard, 23 February 1978, 23).

An Act to Repeal the Dread Act was first read in 1979, soon after the introduction of the interim government, with its second and third readings deferred to facilitate public discussion. The Dread Act was finally repealed in 1981 in Eugenia Charles's first term as prime minister, and the Prevention of Terrorism (Temporary Provisions) Act 1981-10 was introduced. This was consistent with the recommendation of the Special Committee on Dreadism six years earlier in 1975. After two coup attempts it became clear that the Dreads were not the greatest threat and more general anti-terrorist legislation was needed. So for reasons that had little to do with human rights, Eugenia Charles was responsible for removing the Dread Act from the statute books. Charles's handling of the Dread Act signalled her pragmatism – she knew that it would be easily enacted, that there was wide public support for the law and that strong criticism would damage her political goals. It was equally an indication of her veneration of majoritarianism as an expression of the interests of the community, not just as a gauge for political action. It is sobering that no court of law adjudicated on the constitutionality of the law; it was the majoritarian process that produced its intemperance, which inelegantly became the source of its restraint and eventual repeal.

Plain Politics: Running with the Hares and Hunting with the Hounds

Eugenia Charles's unswerving political pragmatism contoured her rights discourse. Her advocacy of rights was often coterminous with her political goals. Her equivocation and variability on the Dread Act – support in one context and criticism in another – was labelled by Patrick John as "running with the hares and hunting with the hounds" (Dominica 1977b, 113). During the debates in 1974 on the Dread Act, Charles said she agreed "entirely" with Patrick John's statement, quoted earlier, that there was a need to fight "fire with fire" in dealing with the Dreads. Seven years later, in 1981, as prime minister, she quoted John's notorious words with disapproval. Charles was then seeking support for an extension of the state of emergency after the coup attempts. She said that this was not a call to "fight fire with fire", but merely an application for more time so that the police could properly do their work (Dominica 1981a, 28). Charles continued: "[H]ad we had the Terrorist Act as part of our legislation from 1975 when it was first recommended by no less a person than Lennox Honychurch, had we had it then, we would not have had the action [the state of emergency] taken that was taken three weeks ago" (Dominica 1981a, 31).

Charles sidestepped her own inaction on the Dread Act and appropriated the more unequivocal position of her colleague, Lennox Honychurch, who was a Freedomite in the House of Assembly and her press secretary. Honychurch was the secretary to the Dreadism Committee, which had recommended in 1975 that the Dread Act be repealed and replaced with more general anti-terrorist legislation.

As Eugenia Charles's functions and position as a politician changed, so did her emphasis on what rights mattered most and what rights meant. After 1968, Charles's opposition transformed from writing letters to newspapers to giving speeches on political platforms and making contributions to debates in parliament. So too did her campaigns about freedom of speech change: they were no longer about the freedom of the press but about access of the opposition to airtime on the government radio station and about pressing for parliamentary proceedings to be broadcast live on the radio. Charles had much to gain for herself and the Freedom Party from both initiatives. She was a formidable force in parliamentary debates and in some way "made her name in Dominica and the Caribbean through the auspices of live broadcast" (Charles 1986, 24). The right of access to radio time for the opposition, she said, was "part and parcel of a democracy" and an entitlement that followed from being a taxpayer (Dominica 1971, 63). Charles strenuously made this point in welcoming the UK delegation in 1978:

> We boast that we have Freedom of Speech but let us examine the reality of the situation. In a country where the only radio is owned and operated by the government and no opposition voices are permitted on that most effective media, can one really say that we believe in Freedom of Speech. When time and time again Ministers of Government and some officials are permitted to abuse persons opposed to the government without the right being given to such persons to explain their side of the matter. . . . Can it be said there is Freedom of Speech? (Dominica 1978b)

As prime minister, her attitude changed and she was severely criticized for restricting live broadcasts of parliamentary proceedings. She countered that the proceedings were carried at night rather than during the day when it would distract people who were working (Charles 1986, 24). She admitted that the later broadcasts were edited but solely for the purpose of removing statements objected to by the Speaker on the basis of parliamentary rules (Charles 1986, 24). In 2002, Charles spoke more plainly, saying that she moved for the restriction of live debates because some were using the forum to abuse others and that she could control her own members but not those on the opposition side (Charles 2002g). Political opportunism, blended with a concern about the larger common good, produced a very meagre miscellany of circumstances in which Charles believed in freedom of speech. It had to be a form of speech or expression she considered worthwhile, and rarely did she think her opponents to have anything sensible to say. Charles reputedly made a statement after victory in the 1985 elections: "I shall not allow the world to hear Patrick John." When asked in an interview about this statement, she bluntly responded: "I did say that the rest of the world did not want to hear this man, and I was right" (Charles 1986, 26).

As prime minister, Charles was often challenged by the opposition about her own human rights record. She was faced with a series of crises on entering office that required strong leadership and firm measures to contain them, namely, the devastating Hurricane David, the coup attempts in which the military and former premier Patrick John were involved, and a number of high-profile kidnappings and the murder of Ted Honychurch. The country was placed under successive periods of public emergency in the first two years of her prime ministership. Parliament enacted a number of laws in response, including the Extradition Act 1980, Foreign Incursions and Mercenaries Act 1980, Detention Review Tribunal Act 1981, Prevention of Terrorism Act 1981, Military Uniform Prohibition Act 1982, State Security Act 1984 and Treason Act 1984.

On the whole she displayed sensitivity to the need to contain the crises with the minimum restrictions on civil liberties, particularly during the emergency periods, and responded ably and comprehensively to many of the criticisms launched by Michael Douglas, the Labour Party representative for Portsmouth, about the measures introduced during the emergency periods. Charles also had a rhetorical rejoinder:

It is the people who are trampling on the rights and freedoms of Dominicans . . .

a small dissident group who want to continue to annoy the larger grouping of Dominicans but seventy-four thousand Dominicans have their human rights and cannot allow five or six dissidents to trample on their human rights. (Charles 1983a)

Majoritarianism and the common good again became the governing precepts.

Some close allies of Eugenia Charles later expressed dismay at the force of her political expediency. In 1993, when Charles was in her third term as prime minister and Honychurch was then pursuing postgraduate studies in Oxford, he wrote to her shortly after the seminal decision of the Privy Council on delay in carrying out the death penalty (*Pratt & Morgan v Attorney General* [1994]). Honychurch's father was a well-known farmer who in 1981 was kidnapped and murdered by Dreads. The Honychurches were viewed as members of the elite "gros bourg". The kidnapping coincided with the crises occasioned by the coup attempts and the hurricane. Charles, who was very vulnerable to criticisms about her wealth and affiliation with Dominica's elite, was at pains to explain to the public that the kidnapping was not the only reason for the declaration of periods of public emergency. The man who murdered Honychurch's father had been convicted and sentenced to death but the sentence had not been carried out (*Joseph v The State of Dominica* [1988]). Honychurch alleged that Charles had dealt less vigorously with this case than with that of the man who orchestrated the coup attempt and threatened the stability of her government (Honychurch 1993). He put it to Charles that the death penalty could be misused by politicians and said this was a case for its abolition. In responding to Honychurch, Charles did not equivocate from her support for capital punishment, but told him that she could not disclose the reasons for the delays in carrying out the death sentence on his father's murderer (Charles 1993).

Charles's robust use of rights discourse was rarely equal to the conceptual understanding of rights or the authenticity displayed by some of her close allies. In retrospect, Phyllis Allfrey's liberal articulation of freedoms and rights in 1968 had only a vague coincidence with Charles's political orientation at that time. Brian Alleyne's forthright and thorough critique of the Dread Act embarrassed Charles's ambivalent and conservative reading of the human rights implications of the law. The advocacy of Lennox Honychurch and the Dreadism Committee for the repeal of the Dread Act and the introduction of more moderate, non-specific anti-terrorist legislation stood in contrast with Charles's unwillingness to decisively press for repeal until the suggested legislation became necessary after coup attempts in her first years as prime minister. A shrewd and sagacious politician, Eugenia Charles carefully chose the moments to adopt the positions of her more liberal colleagues.

Courting Justice: The Limits of the Law

Eugenia Charles's open challenge to the state began in the 1950s in her law practice, well before the 1968 Sedition Bill. By 1968 when she entered formal politics, she was arguably the most prominent lawyer in Dominica (Higbie 1993, 74) and had gained a reputation for fiercely representing clients in disputes with the government. Colonial officials were scared of her. Charles Maynard, a junior clerk in the government in the 1950s and later a cabinet minister in Charles's government, said, "She was blunt, aggressive, clear" (Higbie 1993, 75). Her legal representation and advice to those in conflict with the state continued after 1968; but, thereafter, despite her protests otherwise, law and politics became inextricably intertwined.

The first big contest after the formation of the Freedom Party was the election of the Roseau Town Council in late 1968. The two seats won by the Party in the elections were a modest but important success. Edward Scobie, the newspaper editor, won his seat very narrowly, by two votes. Eugenia Charles successfully represented Scobie in an election petition brought against him by his defeated opponent (*Active v Scobie & Davis* [1969]). A year later Charles represented Scully Lestrade, who had been appointed town clerk of the Roseau Town Council in an action against the council. Relations between Lestrade and the town council deteriorated in 1969, he was suspended and the council appointed a commission of inquiry to determine his future. In a fine set of administrative law arguments before the Court of Appeal, Charles succeeded in establishing that Lestrade was a civil servant and entitled to all the privileges attached thereto and that the appointment of the board of inquiry was invalid (*Lestrade v Roseau Town Council and Another* [1970]).

By the 1970s, Charles was closely linked as a lawyer to both the Employers Federation and the Civil Service Association (CSA), and the latter was increasingly in conflict with the government (Baker 1994, 173). In June 1973, the CSA called a nation-wide strike because of the manner in which a member of the staff at Radio Dominica had been transferred. The chaos and disruption led the government to declare a period of public emergency on 15 June. Notable Freedomites in the CSA were involved and Renwick J. who first heard an action arising out of the state of emergency stated that he was convinced that the strike was politically motivated (*Maximea and others v Attorney General* [unreported] 17 July 1973, at 30). Charles disagreed, insisting that it was an industrial dispute in no way connected with the Freedom Party, and she described the emergency period as "an ill-conceived plan by a power mad man who wished to show that he could manipulate people's lives" (Charles 1977, 1). During the emergency period, the provisions of the Emergency Powers Ordinance (Cap. 244) came into force and the Emergency Powers Regulations 1973 were made under that ordinance. Certain orders were made against Christopher Maximea and Charles Savarin, who were instrumental to the strike action, restricting them from speaking at public meetings unless the speech was previously handed to the commissioner of police and, among other things, from leaving their home without notifying the commissioner of police of their destination.

In her only notable case as a barrister on a constitutional issue, Charles together with K.C. Alleyne, QC, and Brian Alleyne acted as counsel for these men. Legal proceedings were instituted challenging the constitutionality of the ordinance, the regulations and the orders made against them on the grounds that they contravened the constitutional protection of freedom of expression, assembly, association and movement. In the High Court, the men succeeded partially. A regulation that required permission in writing from the commissioner of police to hold a public march or demonstration was declared to be unconstitutional by Renwick J. because it did not afford the commissioner any guidelines as to how his discretionary powers were to be exercised. Aspects of the orders against the men were also struck down because they made the men "virtual prisoners in their own home and seek to cut off communication between each of them and their fellow man" (*Maximea and others v Attorney General* [unreported]

17 July 1973, at 36). Additionally, the judge did not find evidence that such sweeping restrictions were reasonably required. On the larger question of whether the ordinance was constitutional, the men did not succeed in the Court of Appeal (*Maximea and others v Attorney General* [1974]).

Charles often characterized her political activism and her legal work representing those in disputes with the government as autonomous. In 1976 in debates about amendments to the Industrial Relations Act, Premier Patrick John made references to "a certain lady lawyer" who advised employers "don't pay" when the employers were at fault and were willing to compromise (Dominica 1976, 37). Charles in response asserted her right to act as a lawyer and to participate in discussions with her client, the Employers Federation, as their legal adviser. She distinguished this from her political role as leader of the opposition and her views on the legislation in the House (Dominica 1976, 38). The Speaker crudely characterized Charles's comments as meaning she was not a general adviser to the employers "but if from time to time a specific issue presents itself with a 'bread' value she will deal with that point on a fee and deal with it that day" (Dominica 1976, 38).

Law and Politics

The early post-independence period in the Caribbean, the mid-1960s to the late 1970s, which roughly coincided with Eugenia Charles's leadership of the main opposition party in Dominica, saw many upheavals and crises. There were escalating crime and violence, large-scale industrial disputes, mass demonstrations, extra-constitutional regime changes and powerful ideological movements in opposition to the state. Governments responded by intermittently declaring periods of public emergency and by implementing measures, through legislation like the Dread Act, that were akin in their severity to those commonly required in emergency periods, but without formally declaring a state of emergency.[3] In response to the onslaught of measures and laws limiting personal liberty, freedom of expression, assembly and association, and in turn compromising their political viability and effectiveness, political minorities used judicial review proceedings as one of their strategies.

They sought to capitalize on a key premise of the new constitutional regime: that the bill of rights within the constitution, and not the government of the day, had the last word on the scope of enjoyment of civil liberties and human rights. They took their fights with the government to the courts, asking them to stand guardian over the constitution and to impugn repressive laws enacted and state action. But this was not Eugenia Charles's *modus operandi,* despite her skilfulness as a lawyer. In contrast to many political opposition figures of her time, she was not taken with constitutional litigation as a political strategy. Until she became prime minister in 1980, she continued to act as a lawyer on behalf of those in disputes with the state, but rarely did her claims that the state was violating the fundamental rights and freedoms of the citizen rise beyond political argument and action to constitutional litigation.[4]

Notwithstanding this, Charles invoked constitutional litigation as a threat in her political discourse. The reminder to the government that if offensive legislation was both enacted and enforced constitutional litigation would follow added an edge to her political rhetoric. In parliamentary debates a few years after the passage of the Seditious and Unlawful Publications Act, Charles said that the government was very aware that if it attempted to prosecute anyone under the act, "the Law [would] be invoked to prevent a flouting of the Constitution" (Dominica 1973a, 29). Charles was at the time debating two bills to amend the Public Order Ordinance and the Small Charges Act that had been presented to the House of Assembly by the then minister of home affairs, Patrick John, in 1973. In a not entirely convincing argument about the meaning of the word "demonstration", Charles accused the government of planning to make the populace criminals "merely because they use the rights given to them under the Constitution" (Dominica 1973a, 29). Casting her critique in broad constitutional language, Charles warned: "[I]f the Government thinks that the populace is going to sit by and let them play ducks and drakes with their rights, I can assure them that this will not happen" (Dominica 1973a, 29).

The initiatives of Charles's peers who actively used the counter-majoritarian weapon of judicial review during these formative years of nation building had mixed results. The Industrial Stabilisation Act 1965 of Trinidad and Tobago became one of the first pieces of legislation to be challenged in the Caribbean in the post-independence period. Oil workers took their protest at its restrictions on strikes to the courts but failed to convince the Privy Council that the law abridged their freedom of assembly and association (*Collymore and another v Attorney General* [1969]). In the same year, a period of public emergency was declared in Trinidad and Tobago, and there was an unsuccessful challenge to the constitutionality of Emergency Regulations of the same year (*Beckles v Dellamore* [1965]).[5] In 1970 when another period of public emergency was declared in the twin island country, a detainee established that his preventive detention was unconstitutional (*Weekes v Montano and May* [1970]). Another detainee succeeded in proving that his detention in the state of emergency declared in 1971 was unlawful (*Kelshall v Pitt, Munroe and Bernard, ex parte Kelshall* [1971]). On the other hand, A.N.R. Robinson and others were arrested in San Fernando and charged with having taken part in a public march contrary to an amended Summary Offences Act but did not succeed in challenging the constitutionality of these amendments (*Robinson et al. v Sealey* [1974]).

St Kitts–Nevis–Anguilla was a hotbed of constitutional litigation immediately after associated status was achieved in 1967 and the new constitution was introduced. Henry Charles turned to the new constitution to challenge his detention during a period of public emergency declared in the same year (St Christopher Nevis and Anguilla Constitution Order 1967). He succeeded by establishing that emergency law gave the governor dictatorial powers to do what was necessary and expedient instead of permitting objectively what was reasonably justifiable (*Charles v Phillips and Sealy* [1967]). Again in 1967 there was a successful challenge by a number of persons charged with speaking at a public meeting without first having obtained permission from the chief of police (*Chief of Police v Powell, Chief of Police v Thomas* [1968]).[6] A few years later, the Privy Council assessed the Public Meetings and Processions Act 1969-4 when Arthur Francis was charged with using a loudspeaker at a public meeting without permission, contrary to the act. The Privy Council ruled that the absence of guidelines for the chief of police to exercise his powers did not make the law defective, or at any rate not seriously defective (*Francis v Chief of Police* [1973]). The judicial conservatism of this period is nowhere better evidenced than in the *Antigua Times* case (*Attorney General and the Minister of Home Affairs v*

Antigua Times [1975]). In 1971, new legislation was enacted in Antigua and Barbuda that subjected newspapers to an annual licence fee and a large deposit to satisfy any judgement for libel (The Newspapers Registration [Amendment] Act 1971 and the Newspaper Surety Ordinance [Amendment] Act 1971). This legislation was viewed as an attempt to close down the opposition newspapers. The *Antigua Times*, an opposition paper seen as one of the targets of the law (Lent n.d., 57), challenged the constitutionality of these new laws on the grounds that the law contravened the newspaper's freedom of expression as guaranteed by section 10 of the constitution. The newspaper failed before the Privy Council, which ruled that these laws were "reasonably required" for legitimate state objectives.

Many courts during this period gave governments wide latitude to enact restrictive measures pursuant to their power to make laws for the "peace, order and good government" of the nation. I doubt, however, that one can attribute Charles's infrequent resort to judicial review proceedings on the question of civil liberties to an insight about judicial conservatism during that period. Eugenia Charles was a conservative and first and foremost a politician, deeply invested in majoritarian justice and majoritarian processes.

The Law of Politics

The incongruity I keep calling attention to between Eugenia Charles's apparent indifference to constitutional litigation and her indisputable legal acumen derives a good deal of its force from the assumptions in traditional legal thought about the pre-eminence of judicial review in constitutional matters. Eugenia Charles's leadership of the Freedom Fighters and the Freedom Party as a citizen engaged in political life and later as a politician puts the emphasis on the courts in doubt by offering a fuller account of how constitutional vision unfolds over time. Constitutional texts derive meaning not simply from how courts interpret them, but fundamentally from the actions of a bold citizenry and from political agents who challenge unconstitutional state action through political rather than legal processes. They may not do so with the moral clarity or normative framework of judges, but they have in key historical moments played as influential a role as courts in determining the fate of legislation that restricts constitutionally protected rights and freedoms.[7]

Moreover, in periods when courts can do little about the potential abridgement of fundamental rights and freedom, political agents and a bold citizenry have responded with efficacy to what they view as unconstitutional state action. Lawmakers are given a wide degree of autonomy over their own proceedings. Courts are very unwilling to review laws that are being debated in parliament unless the circumstances are extraordinary. Those seeking to challenge the constitutionality of a law in the courts will usually have to wait until the legislation is actually enacted (*Bahamas Methodist Church v Symonette* [2000]). The bill stage of lawmaking is therefore one during which courts can do little about potential abridgement of fundamental rights and freedoms, but political agents can play a decisive role in explicating the terms of the constitution and insisting that they be observed.

The actions of Charles and the Freedom Fighters around the sedition legislation in 1968 played a decisive role in determining the fate of a law that unduly restricted freedom of speech. Charles helped to lead protests of civil society against the legislation that resulted in a *de facto* government moratorium on enforcement of the law and the creation of space for the beginnings of a viable political opposition in Dominica. With the moratorium, judicial review was not as crucial and it may also have been difficult. The courts have no power to address abstract injustice, but are interested only in hearing the very particular claims of those who have been adversely affected by government action which is inconsistent with the constitution. Once a law is enacted, judicial review can proceed only on the existence of a litigant who can show that his or her protected rights are being infringed or are likely to be infringed by the law. In the case of the Sedition Act of 1968, it would have been challenging to find someone whose interests were affected or likely to be affected by a law that had not yet been enforced.

In 1979, the opposition to the offending industrial relations and libel and slander laws led to the demise of the John regime and ultimate repeal of the legislation. Again no court ruled on the constitutionality of these laws. The story of the 1974 Dread Act is different but still instructive. Widespread public support for strong measures to deal with the Dread crisis muted opposition to its excesses. Eugenia Charles supported the act but contributed to modest refinements in the parliamentary debates and it was the parliamentary process that led to a temporary suspension of the act and its ultimate repeal in 1981. It is tempting to hypothesize about how much more definitive a declaration the courts could have made, avoiding the vagaries of majoritarian justice, but the reality is that the Dread Act is no longer law, not because the courts declared it inconsistent with the constitution but because parliament repealed it.

Eugenia Charles participated in influential political action in foundational moments of Dominican constitutionalism. She described 1979 as "a creative manifestation of the genius of a people in using democracy for development" (Charles 1987, 5). The important implication of the mobilization of Charles and the Freedom Fighters in 1968 and 1979 was that "We the People" – the citizenry, not just judges or even other traditional governmental organs, the executive and legislature – have a key role to play in determining the constitutionality of legislation. This serves to remind us of the Freedom Party's first policy statement: "People Before Power. People Before Politicians, People Before Privilege and Things" (Paravisini-Gebert 1996, 233).

Conclusion

Traditional legal thought tends to tell a fantastic story about Caribbean constitutions and the rights and freedoms enshrined in them. The constitution stands as a quiescent colossal, supranational, virtually supernatural law, with a fixedness that is to be preserved by the courts. Within this account, "fundamental rights and freedoms" stand apart from and above politics. On the other hand, Charles seemed to view rights as contestable and politically negotiable over time; rights could be reconfigured and recreated within a majoritarian morality. This is one way of thinking about her support of the Dread Act and her explanation of its necessity in the interests of the common good. In her republican orientation, law and rights were the preconditions for good politics, leading to her insistence on freedom of speech, assembly and association in 1968 and 1979. Conversely, politics was to be respected as the source and main guarantor of rights (Michelman 1988,

1,505). Charles reminded her political opponents that the constitution was a democratically produced document negotiated with participation from all sides (Dominica 1981c, 15).

Charles's version of constitutionalism has us talking almost exclusively about politics; the traditional legal approach has us obsessed with the courts. The flaw in Charles's approach is that it keeps us bound to thinking of human rights only where they are linked to political possibilities, leaving little room to canvass a broader slate of social, economic, cultural, civil and political rights. An overriding common good tied to sentiments of the majority will in many cases, such as the Dread Act, be plainly unacceptable. Still, there is much to learn from the methods of Eugenia Charles. Charles saw virtue in politics as the practice of citizenship. Here I am borrowing from Hanna Pitkin's understanding of politics as "the possibility of a shared, collective, deliberate, active intervention in our fate . . . tak[ing] charge of the history in which we are all constantly engaged" (Pitkin 1981, 344–45).

We often fail to appreciate that the words on the parchment on which constitutional texts are inscribed tell only part of the story. The meaning of constitutional law derives from the tone and rhythm of conversations about the organization of social and political life (Robinson 2003). These conversations happen in fora other than courts. Formal political processes and other arenas of public citizenship, Charles shows us, play an important role, especially in crises, in contesting and articulating constitutional vision. Ours will be an impoverished theory of Caribbean constitutional development if we fail to recognize this. There are crucial limits that the law, particularly the constitution, places on government. By the same token, there are limits to what the law can do, and freedom and justice in the Caribbean cannot be imagined and theorized entirely through legal mechanisms and structures.

Notes

1. The Seditious and Undesirable Publications, Cap. 254, Law Revisions 1961, s. 3 defined seditious intent as including an intention to bring into hatred or contempt or excite disaffection against a member of the government and to raise discontent or disaffection amongst Dominicans. A fine distinction was made: if the publication or speech was intended to point out errors with a view to remedying them, it was not seditious. The punishment for preparing, publishing or uttering seditious words was a term of imprisonment of not more than two years and/or \$480 for a first offence and a term of not more than three years for a subsequent offence.

2. In Trinidad and Tobago, for example, the Sedition Ordinance, Chap. 4:6, was amended in 1971 in response to the Black Power crisis [Sedition (Amendment) Ordinance No. 36 of 1971, s. 4]. New definitions of sedition now included the promotion of feelings of ill-will or hostility towards any class of persons distinguished by race, colour, religion, profession. Also added as sedition was advocating the commission of certain crimes to destroy persons in an identifiable group. In St Kitts–Nevis–Anguilla, the Bradshaw government soon after its re-election in 1971 enacted the Press and Publications Board Act which made it an offence to publish anything intended to malign or injure the reputation of the state or bring the name of the state into contempt, hatred or ridicule [Press and Publications Board Act 1971-27, s. 6(1)(f); White 1977].

3. I have described this elsewhere as *de facto* emergency legislation (Robinson 1994). Another example of *de facto* emergency legislation is the Suppression of Crime (Special Provisions) Act 1974 which gave extraordinary powers to law enforcement officers and the minister of national security to deal with the escalation in crime in Jamaica.

4. The exception is the *Maximea* case arising out of the 1973 period of public emergency, discussed earlier.

5. Judicial review proceedings had been brought by a man charged with having in his possession documents of such a nature that the dissemination of them was likely to cause disaffection among persons in a protected area, contrary to the Emergency Regulations.

6. They challenged the constitutionality of the amended Public Meetings and Processions Ordinance, Cap. 302. The High Court declared that part of this law contravened freedom of expression, assembly and association as protected by the constitution.

7. In 1798 the United States Federalist Congress enacted the Sedition Act; this criminalized criticism of the government and was used against political opponents (Tribe 2000, 724). Thomas Jefferson became president of the United

States in 1800 in an election that was in good measure a referendum on the Sedition Act and he immediately pardoned those convicted under the act and defended the right of the Executive to make determinations on what is unconstitutional (Tribe 2000, 724). His argument was that the executive and legislative branches, not just the judiciary, had the responsibility in their own spheres to decide on the constitutionality of laws.

3

Straight Roads or Bumpy Rides?
Eugenia Charles's Path to Power

CYNTHIA BARROW-GILES

Introduction

This chapter explores the forces that elevated Eugenia Charles, first female prime minister in the Commonwealth Caribbean, to the position of party leader of the Dominica Freedom Party (DFP) and subsequently to the position of prime minister of the Commonwealth of Dominica. An interest in her political durability therefore guides this analysis, particularly in a context of the lack of parity of women in national domestic politics in the region. First, the inquiry is particularly interested in discovering what defined her political ambitions and identifying any early political activity prior to her first official involvement in party politics. It is also concerned with the forces that contributed to her political awakening, and whether other candidates confronted her for leadership of the party. It is also interested in determining what factors and forces motivated her selection as party leader and the challenges she faced as a political candidate running for public office. The manner, nature and extent of her impact on the Dominica Freedom Party are also critical to this analysis.

Given that Eugenia Charles came to the position of prime minister of Dominica during one of the country's most politically turbulent periods, the research will also attempt to understand what motivated her to take up the challenge of national leadership during this period. Finally by 1993 when Eugenia Charles announced that she would not be contesting the constitutionally due elections in 1995, domestically both she and the party had already begun to show clear signs of declining popularity. The inquiry will therefore also attempt to understand what forces contributed to her personal decline and to that of the Dominica Freedom Party by the 1990s. Underlying the analysis are the constraints, challenges and opportunities that the Westminster political arrangements afford potential parliamentary leaders.

The research is partly archival but heavily grounded in interviews. Methodically, therefore, the research utilizes existing published documentation where possible, but heavy reliance is placed on unpublished primary data sources such as party papers, newspaper accounts, speeches, parliamentary discussions and personal interviews with Eugenia Charles, the Dominica Bar Association, party officials and other parliamentarians, including members of the opposition and civil servants who worked with her, particularly during her formative years and in the period of the late 1970s to the 1980s. The documentary research is used to check, particularize and enrich the interviews.

Caribbean Women Are Where Power Is Not

Internationally women are under-represented in national parliaments. This is as true of advanced metamorphosed democracies as it is for newer democracies, and the Commonwealth Caribbean is no exception. In the case of the Commonwealth Caribbean many of the structural obstacles to women's participation in politics have long been eliminated. Women acquired the right to participate in the political system with the advent of universal adult suffrage. Yet for the most part politics and certainly national decision making continue to be dominated by males. Women in the Commonwealth Caribbean have historically been and are still under-represented in government and other political institutions (Barriteau 1998a). Barriteau argues that possessing a de jure right to vote and to stand for elections has not produced a de facto inclusion and representation of women at all levels in Caribbean political systems. It has not transcended national government structures to be a common feature at the level of local government. Women in the Commonwealth Caribbean continue to experience a combination of sub-systemic material and ideological barriers that thwart their full participation in the practices of governance nationally and at the community level. (Barriteau 1998a, 6)

Interestingly, in the last decade of the twentieth century, female participation in national decision making in the United Kingdom and the United States was under 10 per cent. In 2000 it was estimated that on average women comprised only 14 per cent of the national parliaments worldwide. While this figure had doubled since 1975, nonetheless electoral and legislative politics continue to reflect women's under-representation. Many Caribbean countries, however, experience a higher level of female participation in national parliaments than advanced democracies. For example, in the mid-1990s Trinidad and Tobago recorded a 17 per cent representation of women.

By the end of the twentieth century, after nearly fifty years of universal adult suffrage, less than 10 per cent of the candidates contesting general elections were women and fewer have won parliamentary seats.[1] Eugenia Charles's electoral participation, her rise to the level of party leader of the Dominica Freedom Party and her elevation to the post of prime minister as the Commonwealth Caribbean's first and only female prime minister, makes it imperative that we understand that process and the significance of her rise to power. It is indeed a remarkable journey.

Westminster Politics

Cabinet government is government by means of an executive ministry chosen by the chief magistrate – a ministry sitting in the ranks of the legislative majority – a ministry sitting in the legislature and acting as its executive committee; directing its business and leading its debates; representing the same party and the same principles; "bound together by a sense of responsibility and loyalty to the party to which it belongs", and subject to removal whenever it forfeits the confidence and loses the support of the body it represents. (W. Wilson 1992, 72)

The essence of the Westminster model is majority rule and the fusion of legislative and executive authority. The government – that is, the executive – emerges out of the legislative branch and is therefore organically linked to the legislature. Additionally, under the parliamentary Westminster model of government as practised in the Commonwealth Caribbean, constitutionally and politically power is skewed towards the chief executive, the prime minister.[2] The Westminster constitution gives considerable power to the prime minister. For example the constitution of the Commonwealth of Dominica gives the prime minister the right to hire and fire ministers of government, dissolve parliament and call a general election. Constitutionally, the prime minister is therefore given tremendous opportunity for influencing the decisions of his or her cabinet colleagues and, by extension, all members of his or her government. Politics is therefore conducted in an environment in which there is a powerful and potentially autocratic chief executive. It is this highly unequal power relation embedded within the model that has given rise to the view that prime ministers are "elective dictators". Yet the power of the chief executive also rests on political circumstances that are linked, but not limited to, the inclinations of a ruling parliamentary political party. The ability of political circumstances to affect the power of the chief executive is determined by the second key feature of the model, that is, its constitutional flexibility.

The Westminster political arrangement, unlike its democratic competitor,[3] allows for significant flexibility. Not only can government respond to a crisis within its environment; it can take advantage of a favourable political and economic climate by shortening its constitutional term of office and calling an early general election. Moreover, flexibility is imparted into the system as the political model also provides the opportunity for the parliamentary opposition to unseat the government through the no-confidence motion. This is in contrast to the presidential form of government, where it is not obligatory for the members of Congress and the president to constantly seek the confidence of the legislative branch of government. This political model therefore partly rests on the ability of the executive branch of government to constantly seek the support of the legislative arm of government from which it emerges. Parliamentary democracies like those of the Commonwealth Caribbean therefore imply that governments are dependent on parliament. It is this constitutional provision of a vote of no confidence that makes the government theoretically vulnerable. The constitutional provision of the no-confidence motion is therefore a powerful weapon that can be effectively used by opposition parties to harass both the prime minister and the government, especially in a context of governmental tension.[4]

It is that instrument, the no-confidence motion, that leads to yet another critical feature of the Westminster model. To be able to function effectively in a context of the constitutional flexibility of the parliamentary form, parliamentary parties essentially must be disciplined, defined by loyalty, with no cross-voting on the floor of a parliament. To do otherwise would in fact make government unworkable: "In a nutshell, parliament- dependent government implies party-supported government; a support that in turn requires voting discipline along party lines" (Sartori 1997, 193). To ensure that party discipline is upheld requires elements of cohesion, solidarity, self-interest and enforcement. The principle of collective responsibility requires that all ministers as well as all members of the government not only support but also defend government policy even though they may oppose that policy. Giovanni Sartori argues, "When voting along party lines comes 'naturally' or 'rationally', this is all to the good. Nonetheless there is a point at which the party – its secrecy and its directorate – must have the capability of enforcing discipline" (Sartori 1997, 191).

While clearly significant to the overall functioning of the model, the no-confidence motion should not be overestimated. The operation of the model is also backed by a very specific electoral system. The plurality or majoritarian electoral system itself tends to provide fairly strong governments. The combination of the electoral system, the convention of party government, the almost-strict adherence to party discipline and party cohesion should impart governmental stability.[5] While theoretically the model is unstable, the reality suggests otherwise, as few governments have been harried by the parliamentary opposition to the point of resignation. Therefore, most parliamentary governments that begin their administration with a strong parliamentary presence do not easily succumb to the no-confidence motion.

It is this political arrangement that Eugenia Charles inherited when she took office in 1980. While in opposition, she had used the opportunities to harass the Labour government quite successfully. She would find that by the early 1990s it would provide the same opportunities for her political opponents.

Early Influences in Shaping Charles's Future

Mary Eugenia Charles was born in Dominica on 15 May 1919, the fourth of four children to J.B. Charles and Josephine (Delauney) Charles. By the beginning of her formative years, her parents had become quite prosperous, owning several businesses in rural Dominica and in Roseau. From all accounts Eugenia Charles had a privileged upbringing (Higbie 1993). It was a combination of her parents' wealth and in particular her father's respect for education (he himself had little formal education) that eventually led to her entry into the legal profession, although she had shown no great aptitude for intellectual studies.

Beyond the influence of her father in motivating her to acquire a university education, there is little doubt that he was a major political influence, especially in relation to his concern for the plight of poor Dominicans and his belief in the value of education. By the early 1920s, J.B. Charles had achieved tremendous economic success and it was therefore not surprising that he would embark upon a political career. In the 1920s, Dominica, like the other British West Indian territories, was governed under a political arrangement that offered little scope for popular participation in the governmental process. Dominica differed little in terms of the development of a movement that, like the other British colonies, sought political concessions from the British government. The primary demand for political reform in the colonies focused on the relaxation of the structure and functioning of Crown Colony government to permit greater popular participation. That movement provided an opportunity for J.B. Charles. He therefore joined the Dominica Government Association, which was the primary vehicle in the colony challenging the British colonial government for constitutional reform. In 1928 following the Wood Report,[6] which recommended an increase in the elected element to the Dominica Legislative Council, he became a member of that council. National legislative participation was by no means J.B.'s sole excursion into politics. Prior to his election to the Dominica Legislative Council, J.B. had gained some political experience in local government. In 1923 he became a member of the Roseau Town Board, a position that he held for the better part of twenty-five years. J.B. was also elected by the Dominica Legislative Council to the Leeward Island's Federal Council as a senator at the age of eighty-three (Higbie 1993).

Eugenia Charles reflected that from the age of ten she frequently travelled with her father to the east of Dominica and that her father's political activity left an indelible mark upon her. That influence, however, was to surface in the form of active politics only in 1968. In an interview, Charles reminisced that

> My father was a member of Parliament in his time and so . . . at our table we always were talking about the things that mattered in Dominica. You grew up knowing there were things to be done in the country and the people had to do it themselves . . . God wouldn't come and do it for you. (Charles 2002b)

She also recalled that as a result of her travels with her father, she was able to get a glimpse of the less-than-privileged life of the majority of people in the country; this made her realize that she was "fortunate that she was able to go to school every day" (Charles 2002b). Thus her place in a family that was intensely politically involved during her formative years undoubtedly had a major impact on her political personality even though it was to remain dormant for a number of decades.

In 1995 in an interview with Levis Guy, in response to a question on her early influences in politics, Charles credited her father with being her major political influence, though ironically she admitted that he was not her model for politics. According to her, "My influence in the things that I have already done was my father. He never forced us into education but there was always the underlying theme in the house that a profession was yours if you wanted one" (Brill 1995, 136). She also explained in a private interview that her father "[i]n many ways . . . was my guide and my mentor, a very hard-working man, a role model with very little education" (Brill 1995, 136). Despite such acknowledgements of the impact of her father, Charles nonetheless downplayed and rejected his brand of politics in the country. In 1995 she stated, "I didn't plan to go into politics. My father was in politics before me, but he was not my model for politics" (Brill 1995, 137).

In 1942, Eugenia Charles took advantage of a special arrangement with the Canadian government, whereby West Indian students could study in Canada, to enrol at the University of Toronto to read for a legal degree. There is no evidence to suggest that her sojourn in Canada prepared her for a life in politics, and Charles herself admits that she did not become involved politically as she could not afford the distraction of student body politics or political activism. Of her apolitical role in Canada she observed, "I didn't take part in school [meaning student politics]. I was too busy studying" (Charles 2002b).

Nonetheless it was partly as a result of her legal studies and in particular her preparation in constitutional law that she became a leading voice in Dominica. This preceded the "Shut-Your-Mouth Bill" that catapulted her into public life. She challenged the government in her articles to the press and urged Dominicans to pressure government for change in their socio-economic positions. At the same time it was precisely because of her legal practice that she was able to remain connected to the problems of Dominicans, particularly with working-class Dominicans. As she readily admitted, "being a lawyer meant that you were in touch with people, closely, because they come to you with all their problems and they would tell you the things that were happening and they were worried about in their villages, that got you interested in their own problems" (Charles 2002b).

Yet, at another level, her experiences with racism in Canada also partly shaped the personality of Eugenia Charles and perhaps in a very indirect manner prepared her for her eventual entrance into politics. While in Canada, Charles suffered many encounters with racism. These encounters sharpened her resolve and certainly led to the development of a combative, strong and unintimidated personality. This personality had already been honed in Dominica, in a social environment that had imbued her with a strong sense of her social superiority (Higbie 1993). This preparation served her well in her dealings with the local colonial administration on behalf of her clients, as a nominated member to the Legislative Council in 1970, and as prime minister a decade later, even while she suffered negative criticism for her combativeness and determination. The report of one British administrator of Dominica on Eugenia Charles is instructive: "Miss Charles is I am afraid, an unbalanced young woman, an Anglophobe suffering from repression and an inferiority complex" (Higbie 1993, 75).

Freedom Fighters and Political Leadership:
The Makings of a National Leader

The obvious political success of Eugenia Charles can be attributed to a combination of factors. Not only did her formative years have a deep-seated influence in shaping her personality, but her political ascendancy certainly is related to a number of circumstances that were emerging during the 1960s and 1970s. This tumultuous period coincided with her rise to power in Dominica. For one thing her rise to power cannot be dissociated from the 1968 events in the country. The 1968 crisis in Dominica heralded an opportunity for Eugenia Charles to enter active politics in a very decisive manner. It was in fact the first critical step in what can only be described as her meteoric climb to political power in the country. Indeed just twelve years after her entry into electoral politics, she became prime minister of Dominica.

By the mid-1960s, and only one year into the second consecutive term in office of the Dominica Labour Party (DLP), there were a number of disturbing signs of growing authoritarian tendencies. Not least among them was the increasing sensitivity of the Labour government towards escalating criticism from the media and the public of the management of the economy of the country. In the face of serious discontent with the management style and policies of Premier LeBlanc, the Labour Party administration moved decisively to control and curb all opposition to the Labour Party's political rule of the country. Labour's control was based on its two successive electoral victories in 1961 and 1966.[7]

In a context of hostility among the elite to the Labour government, the single-minded determination of LeBlanc and his attorney general led to the decision to muzzle the media through the enactment of the Seditious and Undesirable Publications Bill. The 1968 bill had one dominant aim: to terminate all opposition to the government. It was perhaps somewhat naive for the business and professional elite to expect that the government would not retaliate in some form. Selwyn Ryan notes that LeBlanc himself unapologetically signalled the political intent of the bill by publicly stating, "we are here to rule, and rule we will" (Ryan 1999, 101). Thus the handling of the press by LeBlanc with the controversial Seditious and Undesirable Publications Bill caused a political problem to escalate into a crisis by outraging sections of the population and provoked a series of protests against what was dubbed by the press, political activists and the general public as the "Shut-Your-Mouth Bill".[8]

The bill itself would have considerably intensified the existing colonial legislation on sedition by both widening its scope and increasing the penalties for violations. Proposed by the then attorney general, Leo Austin, the bill made provisions for the attorney general to obtain a court order aimed at the suspension of the publication of any newspaper that printed seditious material, incited violence or animosity, and authorized the government to ban the importation of any publication that it deemed contrary to the public interest.

Moreover, the bill included a provision that was regarded by leading activists in the country as an attempt to stifle all opposition voices, as it essentially made illegal the interpretation not only of the intentions of government officials, but also those of the entire Parliament of Dominica. Further, the bill made criticisms of government officials in other parts of the Commonwealth a criminal act (Higbie 1993, 87). It was this new and sweeping provision that sparked public opposition and mass demonstrations in the country. The ineffectual parliamentary opposition, although unanimously opposed to the bill, was incapable of mounting any serious challenge to it. The leader of the opposition, A. Moise, in strong condemnation of the bill, called for its abandonment:

> Mr Speaker, Honourable members, I can see no other way but that this bill or the amendment must be jettisoned or abandoned as it is. And the reason for saying so, Sir, is because this bill seeks to destroy our liberty and freedom. That is what it will do.
>
> . . . it seeks to promote hatred. It seeks to promote disunity and therefore, Sir, to avoid such conflict, I would suggest that the bill be abandoned altogether and be forgotten. Mr Speaker, we have in this constitution our fundamental right which has been signed and given to us, but today we see that government seeks to rob it from us. (Dominica 1968, 14)

Arguably this marked a turning point in the political life of Dominica and specifically for Eugenia Charles. What began inauspiciously as a Roseau-based protest movement was to lead to the creation of a party which was able, just twelve short years later, to catapult itself into political

office with Eugenia Charles as leader. The act became a powerful symbol of
LeBlanc's authoritarian nature and a focal point for opponents of the
Labour Party. The refusal of the government to entertain opposition and
rescind its decision to limit the freedom of expression in the country led to
new forms of mobilization. The deprivation of civil liberties especially in
the form of the intended curtailment of press freedom via censorship was
to have long-term implications for the party system and party control in
Dominica. It was in this setting that Charles emerged as one of the powerful voices challenging the government. The "Shut-Your-Mouth Bill"
offered Charles a signal opportunity to insert herself into political activism
in a manner that was consistent with her earlier social activism as a barrister. Together with the leading newspaper editors in the country, Eugenia
Charles offered some of the most articulate critiques of the LeBlanc
administration. The seeming indifference of the government to domestic,
regional and international condemnation and pressure to eliminate media
censorship by pressing forward with their plans and rushing through the
enabling legislation, even in the face of public demonstrations, had long-
term damaging implications for the Labour Party.

The importance of the leadership provided by Eugenia Charles outside
parliament against the Seditious and Undesirable Publications Act, 1968
was critical and indeed recognized by the government. The Labour government in an effort to defuse opposition therefore sought to deflect attention away from the act itself and focus on Charles and her fellow Freedom
Fighters. On the occasion of the parliamentary debate on an amendment
to the act in July 1968, Charles was therefore the subject of much criticism
by the government. The minister of communications and work, Ronald
Armour, in reference to the letter of protest written by Eugenia Charles,
referred to her not only as juvenile and rich but also as the protest movement's "eminent professional virgin" (Hansard, 18 January–19 December
1968).

The first response of the bill's opponents was the formation of the
Freedom Fighters as the main political pressure point on the government.[9]
This led to the launching of the Dominica Freedom Party and Charles's
ultimate decision to enter politics as a way of ensuring the defeat of the
politics of LeBlanc.[10] According to Lennox Honychurch, "[A] loosely knit
group calling themselves the Freedom Fighters stomped the country

explaining what this 'shut- your-mouth bill' was all about and calling for its repeal" (Honychurch 1995, 237). As subsequent events would reveal, the uproar over the "Shut-Your-Mouth Bill" would not prove to be sufficient to turn the new party into a major political force in the country and it remained on the political fringes until the late 1970s when the Dominica Labour Party under the administration of Patrick John imploded.

From the Freedom Fighters to the Dominica Freedom Party

Against the backdrop of public protest over the "Shut-Your-Mouth Bill" the Freedom Fighters was formed in 1968 with a core of upper- and middle-class professionals. Eugenia Charles was one of its chief architects. Its formation epitomized a new period of citizen-based political activism in the country.

While the initial political objective of the Freedom Fighters was to repeal the Seditious and Undesirable Publications Act, it soon became apparent that in order to obtain substantial change, political power had to be achieved by the group. While the "Shut- Your-Mouth Bill" provided the immediate impetus towards the formation of the Dominica Freedom Party and Charles's role in that political party, there was some deep-seated animosity to the Labour government. The underlying reason for the opposition to the Labour government stemmed not so much from its increasingly authoritarian rule, but in fact related to the dynamics of class politics in the country. Charles herself noted that her antipathy towards the LeBlanc administration perhaps had as much to do with her rejection of the Seditious and Undesirable Publications Act and her concern over the lack of infrastructural development in the country as it had to do with Labour's class origin, and especially to its neglect of urban Roseau and its people. Indicative of her animosity to the politics of the Labour administration, Charles stated: "They [the LeBlanc administration] were not interested in people in town, they thought people in town were despicable and only the people in the country could be looked after because they themselves were of the country, you know [*sic*]" (Charles 2002b). Labour's politics, however, were, as Riviere puts it, a calculated strategy designed to forestall the possibility of the primarily planter-merchant–dominated Dominica United People's Party (DUPP) from attaining political power (Riviere 1993, 31).

The need to effect some kind of change in the country for the majority of persons seems to have been a concern of Eugenia Charles for most of her political life. Yet her later approach to the politics of the Labour Party is quite contradictory. Despite her frequent statements and rhetoric of empathy with the poor and her view that the Labour Party, whether led by LeBlanc or Patrick John, was not doing much to assist that sector of the society, one is left with the distinct impression that there was never a strong ideological commitment on her part to improving the state of social inequality in the country.

Moreover, in 1968 Dominica did not possess a credible opposition political party. The existing political forces and groups in the country were not sufficiently strong to provide an alternative to the Dominica Labour Party. In October 1968, just three months after the passing of the offensive legislation, the Freedom Party was born. Eugenia Charles was selected in her absence, along with Phyllis Allfrey, Edward Scobie, Loftus Roberts, Elkin Henry and E.C. Loblack, to the party's Steering Committee (Higbie 1993). Charles was elected president of the party in 1969.

The question, however, is why Eugenia Charles, lacking any real political experience, was selected as political leader of the party when there was a core of individuals with tremendous political and parliamentary experience. On this point it is extremely difficult to come to any clear-cut conclusion. However, it is important to note that Charles, although she had opposed the Labour government, did not carry with her the baggage of electoral association with planter-based political parties or candidates. Besides that, she had clearly shown her lack of intimidation, with her fearless and forthright approach to issues. To her advantage she also had the political resource of her father's name and reputation. Her legal profession also provided her with political capital, as she had represented not only big business but also many poor Dominicans who came to her for advice. Her association with the business community, which was opposed to the Labour government, would certainly guarantee her the ability to raise funds that were critical for electoral success. Charles herself conceded that what gave her valuable influence in the new party was her ability to raise funds and her personal financial support for the party. Not only did she provide a location for the national party and raise funds to pay for housing the national organization; she was also an energetic fund-raiser, domestically, regionally and internationally. According to her she was critical to the party because "I can collect, because I am able to do it" (Charles 2002b). It is indicative of her importance to the party's ability to raise funds that Eugenia Charles continued to be a member of the fund-raising committee of the Dominica Freedom Party even after she resigned as party leader and prime minister.

The Dominica Freedom Party itself represented a coalition of multiple and diverse forces, yet socially they shared a common bond. A core component of the group was the remnants of the Dominica United People's Party (DUPP). Founded between 1957 and 1958,[11] it comprised a group of loosely banded, formerly independent candidates who had grouped themselves as the DUPP with Franklin Baron as its political leader.[12] The party came into being for the single purpose of forestalling the possibility of the Dominica Labour Party taking political power (Riviere 1993). By 1966, two years before the formation of the DFP, the DUPP had been dissolved. It re-emerged as the National Democratic Movement following its massive electoral defeat at the hands of the DLP. A second element in the newly formed Freedom Party was one-time founders and dissidents of the Dominica Labour Party itself such as Phyllis Shand Allfrey, a white Dominican who had become increasingly unhappy with LeBlanc's management style and politics. The third force in the new party was, of course, the group of Freedom Fighters, comprising primarily urban professional and business interests.

The composition of the Freedom Fighters and of the early Dominica Freedom Party that emerged to provide the leadership of the anti-Labour forces was therefore quite different from the majority of persons that they hoped to mobilize against the Labour Party. Professing to represent the interests of Dominicans, the DFPs class background was radically different from that of the majority of Dominicans.

The Impact of the Roseau Town Council Dispute

The Roseau Town Council dispute provided another opportunity for Eugenia Charles in the early days of her parliamentary career to emerge as a national political leader. In 1971, the DFP won the Roseau Town Council elections and soon found itself in conflict with the LeBlanc administration. The introduction of the Roseau Town Council Amendment Act in 1971, following the dispute with the government over the acquisition of land to build the Roseau Town Market, provoked another round of public protest against the government. This time Eugenia Charles was in parliament and strongly condemned not only the bill but, in general, the politics of Labour, which she regarded as sinister. Her parliamentary statement on the bill is instructive and reveals her deep-seated frustration with what she felt was government's deliberate and continuing efforts to undermine, silence and stifle political opposition in Roseau. During the first reading of the bill, she stated in parliament:

> They are not interested in village councils, they think they will aggrandise themselves where they think they will win votes. This, Mr Speaker, is well known, and this is of course one of the basic reasons for bringing the Roseau Town Council bill here. The reason for it is that they do not like the fact that Roseau Proper [sic] does not go to the government.
>
> I want to stress again that . . . it is in fact a law which is intended to take away from the Town Council their rights which they had before, and it is seen in every section . . . It also takes away from the Town Council the right to look after its own affairs and matters unless the Minister tells it. And then, Mr Speaker, most interesting of all, whenever a resolution of the Council is passed, it is not to take effect unless or rather – the Minister may inform the Council not to take action on the resolution, and nothing must be done right away. (Hansard, 19 November 1970–23 September 1971, 28–29)

Among other things, and perhaps most disturbing to opponents, was the fact that the Roseau Town Council Amendment Act, 1971, provided for the placement of town council elections in the hands of the local governor, and the empowering of the local government commissioner to conduct inquiries into the workings of the council when requested by the minister, and to provide the minister with the power to request the council from taking action on any resolution for an indefinite period (Hansard, 19 November 1970–23 September 1971, 15). Again LeBlanc's single-minded approach was at work and the Labour government made no attempt to mask the fact that the amendment to the act was aimed not so much at regulating the local government system itself but instead at victimizing and controlling opposition to the government. Clearly this was not only an attempt to render the council impotent but also a deliberate strategy designed to reduce the influence of anti-Labour members on the council and therefore to weaken one of the institutional strengths of anti-Labour and therefore DFP forces in the country. But the DFP's opposition to the act and public protest once again made little difference, as the DFP was to lose the 1975 general elections.

Class, Political Leadership and Representation: Struggle to Shed Old Clothes

An understanding of the class structure and class dynamics of Dominica in the post–World War Two period is critical to an analysis of the political successes and failures of Eugenia Charles. This is particularly crucial if we are to come to terms with her early electoral failures in the twelve years following her decision to embark upon a political career.

Midgett notes that the "Dominica social formation differed significantly from those of its more plantation-based neighbors" (Midgett 1997, 49). In contrast to the socio-economic formation in many former plantation colonies of the British authorities, the Dominican rural landscape was dominated by independent peasants and fishermen. Where plantation labour did exist, many of the communities that supported the plantations remained largely isolated. However, what is clear is that Dominica, like the other plantation societies in the region, was marked by tremendous social cleavages. The socio-economic division in Dominica was primarily between the Roseau-based planter, mercantile mulatto elite (the "gros bourgs") and the professional middle class on the one hand, and the peasant producers, banana merchants, rural black sharecroppers and lumpen urban elements on the other (Ryan 1999). However, Douglas contends that these divisions were not as clear-cut as the above description depicts. Instead, he argues, long after trade unionism had made a distinct break between peasants, agricultural labourers and fishermen on the one hand and the plantocracy on the other, the rural population continued to support the political interests of the plantocracy. In political terms therefore Dominica lagged behind the other British West Indian colonies.

However, by the early 1960s, the Dominica Labour Party, founded in 1955 and now led by E.O. LeBlanc, had established itself as the most popular political party in the country. It owed much of its political appeal and strength to its relationship with the Dominica Trade Union, its association with the West Indies Labour Party and the majority black labour and "petit bourgs" population as well as to the personality of E.O. LeBlanc, whom Ryan describes as "a radical populist who sought to govern Dominica on behalf of the black masses. He was a man of the people and a leader to whom the masses and the petit bourgs had ready access and who could speak their language" (Ryan 1999, 103).

The hostility and suspicion directed at the Freedom Fighters and later the Dominica Freedom Party had as much to do with the class leadership of the early protest movement as it did with the location of the movement and the new party. To a large extent the Freedom Fighters' locus of support was the Roseau area and it therefore required that the leadership of the movement broaden its political base if it was serious about sustained polit-ical pressure on the LeBlanc administration, albeit initially on a single issue. Conceived as a primarily urban-based movement and party, its opposition to the LeBlanc administration under the circumstances could not prove sufficient to destroy the base of support for the Labour government among the lower, primarily rural, classes in the country. In fact if the movement and then the party felt that it could make political capital out of the "Shut-Your-Mouth Bill" and in so doing discredit the Labour government, it proved to be highly optimistic. For the class of people who formed the core support of the movement lacked political leverage to force political change in the context of 1960s Dominica. So while there was increasing dissatisfaction with the management style and politics of the Dominica Labour Party, the socio-economic location of the members of the Freedom Fighters did not augur well for their political ambitions. The working classes' dislike of the strong advocacy of the Freedom Fighters led them to view the group with tremendous suspicion. LeBlanc and the Labour Party had built a formidable organization in terms of its support among the working classes in rural Dominica. As noted by both Honychurch and Higbie, in 1968 there were tremendous obstacles facing the newly formed DFP. In fact Honychurch argues:

> From its inception the DFP had major hurdles to overcome, not least of which was the very origins of the party itself and the nature and social background of the

people who led it. The fact that its power base was in Roseau and that its leadership for the most part was of the "mulatto gros bourgs" gave Labour party spokesmen a large, obvious and easy target for refuting every criticism made by the DFP . . . it was natural that the mass of the people would not leap to enfold a party associated with urban-based "elite". People of that class had in many ways only themselves to blame for their reputation. In most cases these people were seen to be negative and unadventurous in enterprise, warily protective of their property and businesses, watching askance the new people filling places of prestige and influence (Honychurch 1995, 238).

For Higbie, "Most formidable of all was the Freedom Party's image as Roseau-orientated, wealthy, elitist, light-skinned and uncaring. That image was to bar Charles and her party from government for 12 years" (Higbie 1993, 98). Thus in the context of the time, LeBlanc went on to win the next general election in the country.

To be sure, the personal support of LeBlanc himself was critical to the inability of opposition groups to dislodge an increasingly internally embattled Dominica Labour Party, as the period preceding the 1970 election was to prove. By 1970, it was clear that the political management style of LeBlanc, which Midgett (1997) describes as "increasingly autocratic", was having a negative impact on parliamentary members, and open conflict emerged between LeBlanc and party bosses. The internal schisms eventually led to the splitting of the party on the eve of the elections. Days before the 1970 general elections LeBlanc founded a rival Labour party, which in the style typified by some of the early nationalist leaders in the Caribbean, like Alexander Bustamante, he named the LeBlanc Labour Party (LLP). This provided an opportunity for alternative political parties, including the Dominica Freedom Party, to displace the DLP. However, the result of the 1970 general elections represented a personal victory for LeBlanc and therefore presented a formidable challenge to all existing political parties and certainly to the two-year-old Dominica Freedom Party. The LLP won eight of the eleven parliamentary seats with 49.9 per cent of the votes cast, with the DLP taking only one seat and the DFP two seats (Midgett 1997). LeBlanc delivered a crushing defeat not only to the DLP but also to the DFP, which had promised to rid Dominica of the arrogance of his administration.

It is clear that from the outset Eugenia Charles recognized the liability represented by her class background and that of the new party for her burgeoning political aspirations and those of the DFP. She therefore moved to counter the suspicions of large sections of the Dominican population, particularly in the rural areas where Labour was strongest. Integral to her political strategy was the deliberate attempt to downplay her social origins, to deflect criticism and to make contact with the people. During the island-wide mobilization efforts by the Freedom Fighters to harness support against the "Shut-Your-Mouth Bill", one strategy used by Eugenia Charles and also by her associates was to dress informally in an attempt to mask the group's strong identification with particular social classes in the island. They also tried to develop an intimate communication with the people, given the cultural predisposition of Caribbean people to lean towards public speeches of politicians, born from both the lack of other forms of affordable communications and also the state of illiteracy at the time. Higbie notes, "In the country, she wore a blouse and shorts, occasionally with her hair in rollers. The Freedom Fighters spoke in creole if they could, although Charles, who had difficulty speaking the language since she was a child, found it difficult to use in political speeches at first" (Higbie 1993, 90).

However, the initial lack of depth in support for the group and for the new Dominica Freedom Party because of its easy identification with special interests in Dominican society proved to be extremely difficult for Charles and her associates to overcome. It remained the single most important national challenge for the party. To win political power, the party leadership not only had to strategize in order to effect a broader coalition of social forces to avoid the risk of remaining a permanent opposition, but it also had to try to expose LeBlanc himself and by extension possibly the DLP as bad for the governance of the country. In the absence of this crucial two-pronged approach to wresting political power from Labour, the Dominica Freedom Party would not be able to garner sufficient votes in any electoral contest to play a significant role in the political life of Dominica.

As circumstances would have it, it remained for LeBlanc, to whom the 1970 general elections had given unquestionable political supremacy over his detractors, to exit electoral politics, thereby creating a political vacuum into which the DFP and Eugenia Charles could step. That opportunity did not arrive until the resignation of the premier in 1974 and even then, as the 1975 elections showed, the DLP remained central to the politics of Dominica.[13]

First Foray into National Electoral and Parliamentary Politics

Prior to her entrance into electoral politics in 1970, Eugenia Charles had already gained some experience in national politics, even though this was for a very brief period. In 1952, she sat on the Legislative Council for a five-month period.[14] However it was only after 1968 that Charles made her entry into party and therefore elective politics. From 1968 to 1970 Eugenia Charles campaigned for a seat in the national legislature. As events were to prove she had little realistic chance of success and the constituency results strongly suggest that the DFP and Eugenia Charles were rejected by the people. While her first electoral venture resulted in her personal defeat and that of the DFP at the hands of newcomer Patrick John in Roseau North, nonetheless the election result did indicate that there was strong support for the party nationally. Indeed the DFP may have taken only two seats in the national parliament yet it had significant national support, receiving 38.3 per cent of the popular vote (Emmanuel 1992).

Defeat left Eugenia Charles undaunted, and her leadership of the Dominica Freedom Party gave her the possibility of representing the interest of the party in parliament, not as an elected official but as a nominated member. In October 1970, following her defeat at the polls, she became one of the three nominated members of parliament.[15]

Undeterred by the personal setback of her electoral defeat in a constituency that offered her the best possibility for electoral success, the next five years saw Eugenia Charles and the Dominica Freedom Party offering a critical challenge to the Labour government. She and the Freedom Party in the immediate aftermath of the party's resounding defeat played an important role in the increasing politicization of the Dominican people. She was to be given another opportunity in 1975 to enter parliament on her own electoral strength.

Her 1975 electoral success, however, did not occur in a vacuum. The

DFP suffered yet another massive defeat at the hands of the Dominica Labour Party, now led by Patrick John. Even though she was castigated by the DLP as the "Danger Lady", childless and husbandless, Charles experienced personal victory in that election. However, the party's loss was seen as a result of the hostility directed at Eugenia Charles. In the aftermath of the defeat of the party, Charles faced a challenge to her leadership of the DFP (Savarin 2002a). However, even in the face of internal criticism, the party was not convinced that there was, within the party itself, a credible alternative to her (Higbie 1993). Thus, Eugenia survived her first real leadership test.

Having survived a leadership challenge, Charles and the Dominica Freedom Party set about to strengthen the support of the party. Among other things, the party understood that it needed not only to widen its support base among the rural and urban poor, but also to mobilize the youth population. In that regard the formation of the Young Freedom Movement in 1977 was critical. Not only was the group instrumental in organizing activities for the party but it was pivotal to the creation of a network of village branches that strengthened the DFPs support in the rural constituencies. Additionally, Charles's elevation to the position of leader of the opposition afforded her the opportunity to serve on one of the standing committees of parliament. This was the Public Accounts Committee. She used the position effectively to score political points against Patrick John's administration (Higbie 1993).

"Déjà Vu": Political Crisis and the Committee for National Salvation

A series of events in Dominica, beginning with the racial riots in 1974 and eventually culminating in the disintegration of Patrick John's administration, was to prove highly advantageous to the Dominica Freedom Party and to Eugenia Charles herself (Higbie 1993; Honychurch 1995). The period between 1971 and 1980 was perhaps the most tumultuous in the modern period of Dominica's history. Labour was at its peak, having defeated the DFP in two successive general elections. Yet the personal ambitions of Patrick John, poor political judgement on his part and corruption were to lead to a series of crises and ultimately to the political demise of the party. To consolidate his political command of the party, guided by his personal ambitions, Patrick John ruthlessly sought to destroy Ronald Armour. Armour, a long-time Labourite, cabinet member and deputy premier was seen as the logical successor to LeBlanc (Honychurch 1995). The handling of Dominica in the context of Black Power radicalism and John's relationship to Sydney Burnett-Alleyne[16] also led to Labour's undoing. These factors, in combination with concerns over the lack of development of the country and Labour's increasing flirtation with socialist ideology, could only provide an opportunity for the DFP to exploit. It was also clear that under Patrick John's administration there was a growing rift between the Labour Party and the trade unions that had provided mass support for the party. By all accounts the amendment to the Industrial Relations Act under John's administration only served to heighten the increasingly tense situation in Dominica. The amendment itself sought to prevent civil servants and other workers in the essential services from organizing and participating in any strike action (Smith 1979a). It also sought to prevent financial contributions to striking unions and workers. These developments were detrimental to the survivability of Patrick John's administration. Indeed, during this period, Dominica experienced two major civil disturbances and the shooting of several individuals at the hands of the Dominica Defence Force (Higbie 1993).

The rift with the trade unions was significant as it brought in its wake a new wave of confrontational politics in the country. The Dominica Labour Party's success had hinged not only on populist charismatic political leaders but also partly on its ability to control the labour unions. Under Patrick John's administration, relations with trade unions began to change. In particular, the government's relationship with the Dominica Public Service was instructive. The public service had a number of grievances with the administration led by Patrick John. These included victimization, threats from the government, a "politically loaded" Public Service Commission, an unpopular Civil Service Act that, among other things, sought to criminalize illegitimacy and strained wage negotiations (Honychurch 1995). Combined, these ultimately led to a series of industrial actions in 1973, 1976 and 1977, the last of which lasted some forty-seven days and paralysed the country. In May 1979 the industrial dispute re-emerged following the Industrial Relations (Amendment) Act and the Libel and Slander Act. The Libel and Slander Act sought to further frustrate the press by providing for newspapers to disclose the names of anonymous writers who criticized professionals. Both acts therefore would have considerably increased and strengthened the hands of the government while simultaneously limiting the rights of Dominican citizens. It appeared that the newer Labour government had not learned from the mistakes of the 1968 Labour government, or from its earlier confrontation with the powerful Public Service Union. In a repeat of history, Eugenia Charles was one of the strong voices raised against the actions of government. This time around, however, there was one discernible and crucial difference. Patrick John's administration had considerably strengthened the coercive apparatus of the state with the creation of the defence force. On this occasion, the defence force, controlled by John, opened fire on protestors, killing one individual and injuring twelve others (Savarin 2002a). In the immediate aftermath, the workers took the decision to go on an indefinite strike until the government resigned from office (Savarin 2002a). The strike lasted for twenty-two days at the end of which several ministers of government, beginning with Oliver Seraphin, individually resigned (Savarin 2002a). The spillover from the unrest created by the movement against the Labour Party left the Freedom Party as the only credible alternative. Before the DFP could enjoy the fruits of the large-scale protest from the workers, however, an interim government was formed.

As a direct result of the May 1979 events and the constitutional crisis that was unleashed, a twenty-eight person Committee for National Salvation (CNS) was established. Eugenia Charles and Brian Alleyne represented the Dominica Freedom Party on the committee, with Charles acting as its secretary. The CNS itself was symptomatic of the politics of convenience and a pragmatic non-ideological approach to the problems of the country. It represented various political, economic, philosophical and economic interests. Hastily pulled together, it was a motley collection of persons with differing agendas but with a common and prime concern – the immediate departure of Patrick John's administration. Not surprisingly, the CNS was itself divided on the question of where Dominica should go. One proposal that emerged was that a revolutionary government of Dominica should be formed. The idea for the establishment of a revolu-

tionary government did not find favour among the majority of the committee members. Many of its members opted instead for the proposal to
form a constitutional assembly under the prime ministership of Oliver
Seraphin. Seraphin had distanced himself from John's politics by resigning
from the DLP government. His action enhanced his chances of heading a
new administration in the post-John period. This heralded the end of
Patrick John's administration, and John was removed from office upon los-
ing the confidence of parliament.

In what later would turn out to be a brilliant political move on her part,
though she was offered the post of interim prime minister, Eugenia
Charles took the decision not to participate in the interim government.
She opted instead to await the opportunity to fight a national election
some time in the future. Her party colleague Brian Alleyne became the
attorney general of the interim administration.

The interim government was given the single mandate by the CNS of
preparing for elections within a six-month time period (Savarin 2002a). In
any event, with different political viewpoints, personal ambitions and interests, and with constitutional requirements that elections be held by 1980,
the interim government could not survive for long. If these were not sufficient reasons for failure, then the devastation of Hurricane David[17] and its
handling by the Seraphin administration delivered a fatal blow to the
interim government. By then, too, Seraphin had openly sought to consolidate his political position and had moved to contain Brian Alleyne and
Charles Maynard, two of the leaders in the government. By early 1980,
under the weight of internal schisms, lack of direction and political
manoeuvring, the hastily put-together interim government collapsed.
Maynard himself, in a letter of resignation to Seraphin, had been critical of
the management of Dominica's affairs by the Seraphin administration. He
was also critical of the handling of Robert Ross and the Ross University
School of Medicine, which were to be critical issues that dogged Eugenia
Charles's administration.[18] Meanwhile Charles, untarnished by failure of
the interim government and the squabbles that had emerged, was therefore
set to lead the Dominica Freedom Party to electoral victory, even though
not under the best economic and sociopolitical circumstances. It meant
having to deal with the urgent question of reconstruction, bringing back
the people's confidence in government and creating a stable sociopolitical

environment, not to speak of having to deal with the vexing issue of the defence force created by Patrick John. Not one to dodge issues, Eugenia Charles showed both her flexibility and her rigidity: in one of her first tasks as prime minister, she sought to consolidate her position with the defence force by trimming the force of its political bias.

Prime Ministership and Management of Her Colleagues: No Time to Spare

Eugenia Charles became prime minister of Dominica without having served a lengthy apprenticeship in party and national politics. She came to power in the midst of profound crisis in the country, against the backdrop of a number of structural developments that threatened to destabilize the newly independent democracy.

The circumstances of Charles's coming to power in 1980 were directly related to the intensity of anti-government, anti-John sentiments in the country. In the political turmoil that followed the May 1979 events, with the failings of the interim government and with no other existing credible political alternative, the Dominica Freedom Party was able to make effective political mileage of the events. Dominicans totally rejected the Labour government and attempts by Seraphin to challenge the Freedom Party with the formation of a Dem–Lab coalition. In 1980, following the collapse of the interim government, the Dominica Democratic Labour Party (DDLP) led by Oliver Seraphin was formed. Its formation was also a manifestation of the continuing internal divisions and struggles within the Dominica Labour Party. The long dominant but now troubled Dominica Labour Party disintegrated. Campaigning on a platform against corruption and the mismanagement of the economy, and calling for an end to instability, victimization and repression, the Dominica Freedom Party was able to take maximum advantage of Labour's confusion and the obvious disillusionment of the Dominican people. In the absence of these events it is doubtful that Eugenia Charles would have become the prime minister of Dominica, and certainly not in 1980. The result of the 1980 elections and her elevation to the post of prime minister of the newly independent country did not occur by chance nor was it the end result of a carefully thought-out electoral strategy on her part. Yet it is also clear that Eugenia

Charles had worked consistently towards political leadership. It is clear that issues of legitimacy and support of her political rule were central to her. It is for that reason that she had made the decision to reject the offer of the CNS to serve as interim prime minister.

Without dismissing efforts to mobilize support island-wide, her victory and her prime ministership were related to a series of events in the country linked to the failures of the DLP which ended with Charles enjoying the fruits of Labour's problems. In the midst of the profound crisis in the country following the May 1979 fiasco, Eugenia Charles and the Dominica Freedom Party strolled to its first electoral victory in 1980 in Dominica's eighth general election. There were in fact no serious challengers to the Dominica Freedom Party as other political parties were by then afflicted by allegations of corruption and/or internal dissension. That victory also occurred in the context of the changing nature of international politics.[19]

In the 1980 elections the DFP took seventeen of the twenty-one parliamentary seats, increasing the party's 1975 parliamentary presence from three. Independent candidates secured two parliamentary seats and other parties two (Emmanuel 1992). Eugenia Charles, who was at the peak of her popular appeal, took 77 per cent of the votes in her constituency (Higbie 1993). That victory signalled the start of a political career as prime minister of Dominica that catapulted her into history as the first female head of government in the region. It also signalled the beginning of a career as chief executive that was to surpass that of any other chief executive in Dominica in the modern era. Charles's 1980 triumph came only a decade after her first electoral competition but by then she had experienced nearly two decades of political activism and involvement in national political debate.

While there was little doubt that the DFP would form the government, the 1980 victory would prove a test of her leadership capacity. Yet that victory confirmed Charles's control of the party. Since 1975 she had been challenged by Ronan David for political leadership of the party (Savarin 2002a). However, the party's second constitution precluded any real possibility of a successful challenge because it required that the political leader be also a sitting, elected member of parliament. David's unelected status prior to 1980 afforded him little prospect of a successful challenge to her leadership. Though David went on to contest the 1980 elections successfully, by then the formidable electoral victory of the party did not offer any prospect of a successful challenge. In the aftermath of the 1980 elections, Charles proved to be too strong to be challenged. In assessing her political strength then, Savarin opined that "her grip on the party was absolute" (Savarin 2002a).

This, however, is not to suggest that Eugenia Charles did not face opposition in cabinet. Just three years into her administration the possibility of trouble among her colleagues reared its head. Her management of that potential source of conflict reveals not only her willingness to confront issues but also her determination to win. Savarin noted that one such occasion concerned the issue of citizenship. When the issue of automatic sponsorship of citizenship to spouses of Dominicans emerged, Eugenia Charles declared her intention to amend the constitution to withhold such sponsorship (Savarin 2002a). According to Savarin, Charles was quite prepared to discipline cabinet members who opposed her and in anticipation of opposition from the front bench she made plans to reshuffle her cabinet.[20] As prime minister, Eugenia Charles expected a high degree of loyalty from her ministers. The risk of exclusion from cabinet was ever present during her first administration as Charles had a strong enough parliamentary presence to effect cabinet changes. It was a whip she dangled over the heads of her cabinet colleagues. This is a power that has in fact come under tremendous scrutiny throughout the region. Savarin stated, "She told me that I should stand by to be brought into Cabinet because if anyone opposed the bill, they would be removed from the Cabinet" (Savarin 2002a).

Although overall Charles's relationship with her colleagues was good, further examination of their views of her personality suggests that during her period in office as prime minister, there were some definite differences among them. First, her sex set her apart from the rest of the group. While she herself often discounted the significance of gender differences, given the dominant political role that she was to play in a parliamentary democracy that typically centres around the prime minister, it is clear that she was perceived as an outsider. Charles Savarin, a former cabinet colleague of Charles, explained:

> Eugenia is not a cuddly person. She was highly respected but it was not the kind of old boy . . . First of all she is a woman . . . she was not the kind of person who went out to a social evening . . . she would not sit at a bar . . . She was not a

chummy type of person. You could be very close, but not the "huggly" chummy
type of relationship that can develop between colleagues. (Savarin 2002a)

Indeed her personality exhibited strong paradoxes that were perhaps
partly responsible for the alienation that Charles experienced with respect
to her cabinet colleagues. She had emerged on the national political scene
as a consequence of the deeply felt antagonism to LeBlanc's growing brash
authoritarianism, yet during her reign as prime minister, Charles was often
impatient with open debate and opposition. Her impatience, her uncom-
promising nature and her strong will very often left her cabinet colleagues
with little option but to adhere to her wishes and to follow her. She very
often took positions that members of the cabinet were uncomfortable with
(Maynard 2002a). Nothing perhaps illustrates this inclination to dominance and intolerance better than the following statements by Charles
about her approach to the business of parliament: "I didn't care who [was]
doing the damn nonsense, I'm going to find fault with it. I didn't go into
parliament to waste my time, to have rubbish done. I didn't have time to
spare for that" (Charles 2002b).

Second, in commenting on the souring of relations between Brian
Alleyne, Charles Maynard and Eugenia Charles, Savarin noted that the animosity directed at these two cabinet members by the early 1990s was in no
small way related to the prime minister's need to control her colleagues
and the priority that she gave to personal loyalty. Therefore, she saw their
disagreement with her over the Public Service Commission as the ultimate
betrayal. She is reported to have told Savarin privately that she was aware of
their leadership ambitions and that she would not support them: they
would succeed her as political leader of the party "over her dead body"
(Savarin 2002a).

Outside parliament itself she faced an attempted overthrow of her
administration in 1981. That aborted attempt led to the creation of a state
of emergency in the country (Higbie 1993; Honychurch 1995). It was also
clear that some of the structural problems that had bedeviled the Labour
and interim governments were never effectively resolved by Charles's
administration. Problems with the police and the trade unions remained
and the new administration showed its inability to deal effectively with
these matters.

Disillusionment and Decline

In 1980 Eugenia Charles and the Dominica Freedom Party were at their zenith. Yet, as Table 3.1 clearly demonstrates, by 1990 the DFP was just barely able to cling to political power. General elections in 1990 saw a very marginal victory for the DFP. The party narrowly defeated the opposition, securing only eleven of the twenty-one parliamentary seats and polling 35.81 per cent of the popular vote – thus falling below the level of support it had achieved in the first elections it contested in 1970. There was no disguising this fact and by 1995, with only five parliamentary seats, the bad news for the party was clear. What accounts for the gravity of the electoral situation for the DFP and Eugenia Charles by the early 1990s and ultimately the shifting balance of political support in the country? Why and how did the DFP move from a position of dominance to minority status in the country? The changed political fortunes of the party were partly related to the underlying core of support of the DLP, which was beginning to return to its natural position in the country. It was also related to the rise of the United Workers Party and its displacement of the DFP as a credible alternative, and also to a series of domestic and international events.

From the start of Charles's third term in office it was clear that she no longer could rule the party and the cabinet with the iron fist that her previous election results had enabled her to do. If the 1980s was her golden period, then the 1990s was certainly the end of the gold rush as it was for all intents and purposes a troubling period for her. Individual members of her cabinet and the party felt that she could be successfully challenged and intra-cabinet relations were therefore not harmonious (Savarin 2002a). She increasing felt isolated. She also felt deeply threatened and betrayed by senior cabinet members such as Charles Maynard and Brian Alleyne with whom she had broken over negotiations with the Public Service Commission. But it was Jenner Armour who was seen as committing the worst form of betrayal. Armour had served as president during the period of the interim government. He had resigned that post to contest the general elections of 1980. Armour had been brought into the party by Eugenia Charles in the post-1980 period. She had rewarded him with the position of attorney general of Dominica and in many ways she expected complete loyalty from him. In late 1992 and early 1993 Armour's stance

TABLE 3.1   Dominican Election Results 1970–2000: Seats Won and Votes Cast

Year of Elections	DFP		UWP		DLP		Other Parties and Independents	
	Seats (no.)	Votes (%)	Seats (no.)	Votes (%)	Seats (no.)	Votes (%)	Seats (no.)	Votes (%)
1970[1]	2	38.30	–	–	8	50.00	1	11.70
1975	3	32.40	–	–	16	49.30	2	18.30
1980	17	51.30	–	–	0	16.80	4	31.90
1985	15	56.70	–	–	5	39.10	1	4.20
1990	11	49.40	6	26.90	4	23.50	0	0.20
1995	5	35.81	11	34.36	5	29.75	0	0.22
2000	2	13.57	9	43.44	10	42.91	–	–

[1]In the 1970 elections, there were only eleven constituencies. This number was increased to twenty-one for the 1975 elections. The United Workers Party was only formed in time for the 1990 elections.

and public statements on the Ross university affair not only exposed the corruption within the government but also embroiled the party in public quarrels.[21]

In 1978 the Government of Dominica, led by Patrick John, entered into an agreement with Robert Ross and others to establish an offshore medical school in the country. The agreement was considerably generous to Ross, who was granted resident status personally as well as work permits for foreign personnel, and who in addition received duty-free concessions on all medical supplies and equipment. He also secured the right to repatriate the salaries of foreign employees, the repatriation of 80 per cent of the medical school's profits and tax relief. In return Ross undertook to pay the Government of Dominica US$500 for each student enrolled at the university per semester. He also agreed to assist in the upgrading of the local hospital, and to award ten medical scholarships a year for Dominicans in a school of the government's choice. This was the situation that the new DFP government inherited in 1980. From the start of the new government's administration, the Ross medical university had appealed the terms and conditions of the initial agreement. The medical university not only requested, but received cabinet's approval for, a reduction in the agreed fees as well as other concessions. The Charles administration responded with several favourable amendments to the initial agreement. These included a reduction in the payable fees and in the number of scholarships to be offered by Ross, which was reduced to five scholarships. In spite of repeated concessions, however, Ross continued to renege on his promised agreement (*New Chronicle* 1993a, 1). One consequence of Ross's failure was that several Dominican students who were studying at the University of the West Indies were denied entry into classes for nonpayment of fees (*New Chronicle* 1993a, 2).

By 1985, frustrated in its efforts to collect from Ross and facing embarrassment over the fate of Dominican students at the University of the West Indies, the prime minister took a hard-line position with respect to Ross. In a bold and courageous move, Eugenia Charles publicly accused him of reneging on his agreement with the Government of Dominica and exploiting the country. The government therefore demanded that Ross's debt of $4 million to the government be paid in keeping with the terms of the agreement. As the prime minister explained:

> Government has had to pursue Ross at every turn to attempt to get payment from him. He has persistently refused to pay. When he has made arrangements to pay, instead of making good his promise, he will issue cheques and then ensure that there is no money in the account to meet payment of these cheques. (*New Chronicle* 1993a, 2)

In her written statement to the press on the Ross imbroglio, the prime minister explained further that

> I have told Ross that he must not try to take advantage of Dominica. If he wants changes made to the agreement he must come straight and deal with honesty with his request. Because he has demonstrated that he intends to cheat us of our rights under the agreement, we are standing fast to the terms of the agreement. We have ceased to expect him to do what he had said he was going to do, that is, enhance the Medical care and facilities of Dominica. He has not even given us a broken thermometer! ... We cannot allow one foreign investor to hold us to ransom ... as if we were inferior beings to be pushed around and to beg to be kicked further. (*New Chronicle* 1993a, 2)

While it was clear that within the inner circles of cabinet there were dis-agreements on the appropriate course of action that government should take with respect to Ross, Charles displayed the strength of her character. Tension immediately surfaced within the cabinet. In what was to be the start of a public disagreement played out in the national newspapers, Jenner Armour openly criticized the government, expressing his disagreement with the government's position (*New Chronicle* 1993a, 1). His very public pronouncements on the Ross affair were therefore seen as a personal betrayal, one that Charles was powerless to deal with. For, in the context of waning public support as shown in Table 3.1, Charles lacked the capacity to discipline cabinet members. Indeed the open rift between Charles and her attorney general was portentous and easily capitalized on by the young but increasingly popular United Workers Party. Yet Charles remained deter-mined to force Ross to satisfy the government's demands.

The Ross affair therefore exposed a number of problems within the government. It revealed the danger of Westminster-style politics with its potential to destabilize a government when the notion of collective responsibility fails. It also exposed the fragility of the notion of collective responsibility and therefore the assumption of solidarity within the Cabinet of ministers. It also highlighted the obvious conflict of interest and lack of transparency of the national political system given the fact that Attorney General Armour was also the legal representative of Ross and the Dominica medical school.

Ironically, just as the legislative actions of Patrick John's administration had given Eugenia Charles the opportunity to mount an effective parlia-mentary campaign against his administration in 1979, the parliamentary opposition now resorted to similar effective action against her administra-tion. The leader of that party, Edison James, called for the resignation of Charles as prime minister. While she had experienced challenges to her party leadership, this was the first-ever challenge to her parliamentary lead-ership (*New Chronicle* 1993a). James argued that the public disagreement between Charles and Armour constituted instability of government. He further argued that the only responsible course of action would be the res-ignation of the government. In criticizing the government and the public row over the concessions given to Ross, James contended that the dis-agreement "highlighted the instability of the present administration . . . This instability has created a crisis of confidence throughout the country" (*New Chronicle* 1993a, 1).

Arguably the Ross affair contributed to the loss of credibility of the DFP because it exposed corruption and schisms within the party. These two factors were played upon by the media and contributed to the growing public distrust of the DFP. They also reinforced the public's perception that Charles had weakened considerably. Of course it could not be expected that the cabinet of ministers would always agree. However, prior to the Ross affair, for the most part internal differences had been kept hidden from the public. Whereas at the peak of her political career Charles was able to control her cabinet privately, internalizing disagreements, now internal disagreements became publicly visible. The seeming solidarity of the party and the government broke down. Charles had not faced a resignation from cabinet, though she had fired one minister from her cabinet. She now faced a revolt from Jenner Armour over the Ross affair. In any event the 1990 performance of the party did not afford Charles the same opportunity for disciplining her colleagues in the way that her earlier victories had automatically assured her. Indeed the threat of dismissal was ever present during her first ten years as prime minister even though she seldom resorted to it. Now she found herself with only a bare working majority in parliament, not a position sufficiently strong to use the only means of disciplining her colleagues, that of dismissal from the cabinet. However, even while exposing the weaknesses of the government, the manner in which the affair was brought to a conclusion represented a small victory for Charles and a personal moral victory over Armour. It is true that damage was done to the party, as internal difficulties of the government were exposed, but in the end Robert Ross capitulated to Charles's demands. Ross transferred all the land held by title in his name of that of the university to the Government of Dominica. In return it was agreed that the land would be leased to Ross at an annual fee of US$42,000 (*New Chronicle* 1993a, 2).

The Ross episode represents quite simply a change in the fortunes of Eugenia Charles. While she survived the no-confidence call, forced the capitulation of Ross, survived what she considered Armour's betrayal and indeed was victorious over Armour, it all seemed rather hollow. In the wake of the confrontation with her attorney general, her first open and public struggle with a member of her cabinet, she clearly had no more appetite for elective and parliamentary politics. While as early as November 1988 she had announced that it would be her last term in office, undeniably her authority had been undermined by the travail of the Ross affair. In an article entitled "Who Will Inherit the Crown?" in July 1993 (*New Chronicle* 1993b), Honychurch paid tribute to Eugenia Charles, suggesting that "one of her greatest political achievements is keeping up the appearance that all is peace, love and unity within the cabinet".[22] The Ross affair exposed the lie of it all. In 1993, two years before the constitutionally due elections, she resigned not only as prime minister but also from parliament before the completion of her third consecutive term in office.

Political issues aside, there was an amalgam of other factors in the post-1985 period that focused on the credibility of the DFP administration, not least among which was the impact of an accumulation of international events that impacted Dominica and indeed the entire Caribbean. If the decade of the 1970s was a period of radicalism, by contrast the 1980s was defined by its conservatism. Eugenia Charles, who had shown a marked antipathy towards socialism and communism, was ideally suited for the climate of that period. Indeed her antipathy towards socialism and radical politics found favour in Washington and she benefited from the assistance of the US administration of Ronald Reagan. However, by the end of the 1980s and early 1990s, the special relationship between Dominica and Eugenia Charles changed. Coinciding with this change was the declining fortune of the banana industry, the lifeline of the Dominican economy.

Conclusion

As highlighted above, there is no single dynamic that explains the political emergence of Eugenia Charles in the 1960s and her domination of Dominica's politics between 1980 and 1993. Clearly her success cannot be explained simply in terms of her personal traits, that is, her personality, her ability to raise funds and her forthrightness. However, we can conclude that her personality, the political immaturity of some of her political rivals, the internal schisms of the Dominica Labour Party and, later, its political corruption, authoritarianism, poor leadership, political extremism and privilege all combined to produce the opportunity for Eugenia Charles to make her mark, not only at home but also on the international scene. To be sure, therefore, much of her political success was aided by good fortune and by failings on the part of her political opponents. Yet as Honychurch pointed out in 1993:

> Filling the place left by Dame Mary Eugenia Charles, as Prime Minister will not be an easy task, even under the best of circumstances. It is a combination of parentage, upbringing, education and experience in one human being linked to a twenty-five year period of our history which resulted in the uniqueness of her leadership. (*New Chronicle* 1993b, 5)

Eugenia Charles therefore left an indelible impression on the political history not only of Dominica but of the entire Caribbean. The significance of her role is dramatized when we place her in the context of the political milieu of the Caribbean, which has been and continues to be almost exclusively dominated by males.

Notes

1. The late Patrick Emmanuel did some excellent work on the status of women in electoral politics. Though his study of 1991 needs to be updated, it remains the best single source of data on the electoral candidacy of women in the Commonwealth Caribbean (Emmanuel 1992).

2. Some constitutionalist and political scientists have argued that the use of the term "Westminster model" to describe the constitutional form in the Commonwealth Caribbean is a misnomer. This view rests largely on two issues: first, that there are fundamental differences between the parent model and that of the Caribbean and second, that Caribbean independence constitutions are mere orders in council, drafted primarily with the input of British civil servants at Whitehall. As such the political system of the Commonwealth Caribbean, it is argued, should be more appropriately called the "Whitehall model" of government (Barrow-Giles 2002).

3. Reference is made to the presidential political form. The two most popular democratic political models are the presidential and parliamentary forms of government. Two of the defining characteristics of a presidency as a political form are its rigidity, given the constitutionally fixed term of office enjoyed by both the executive and legislative arms of government, and its separation of power among the three branches of government.

4. While the no-confidence motion is not unusual in the region, only rarely has it been used to effect the ultimate undermining of government. The best-known examples are the successful no-confidence motion against the St Lucia Labour Party in 1981 and the defeat of the Sandiford-led Democratic Labour Party government in Barbados in 1994.

5. It is often argued that the plurality or "majoritarian" electoral system in the region tends to overestimate the support of the winning political party and that very often it produces a government whose parliamentary support does not match its national support. This discrepancy or disproportionality is repeated throughout the electoral history of the region. In effect then the electoral system produces strong governments (that is, government with a strong working majority) with few exceptions. Infrequently governments with bare working majorities, minority governments and stalemated parliaments (hung parliaments) do emerge. While these are not a common feature in the region, weak governments have led to interesting post-election scenarios. In the 2002 general elections in Dominica, for example, the DUWP, DFP and DLP won nine, two and ten seats, respectively, forcing the DLP to form a coalition government with the DFP with which it has historically been opposed. See Patrick Emmanuel (1992) for election results from 1944 to 1991 in the Commonwealth Caribbean.

6.   In 1921, the British government appointed Major E.F.L. Wood (later Lord
      Halifax), then parliamentary secretary for the British colonies, to undertake a
      study of constitutional reform in the British West Indies. The British decision
      came in the context of repeated demands for reform of the colonial administra-
      tions. For the most part colonial administration was dominated by the plantoc-
      racy and excluded the growing middle classes from electoral and nominated
      council politics (Bolland 2001).

7.   Prior to 1961, party politics in Dominica was relatively undeveloped with inde-
      pendent candidates winning the majority of legislative seats in parliament. It
      was not until 1961 that the Dominica Labour Party, led by Edward LeBlanc,
      won a decisive mandate and was able to manage the affairs of the country with-
      out the previous coalition support of independent candidates. In the 1966 elec-
      tions the Dominica Labour Party had increased its electoral support, taking ten
      of the eleven legislative seats.

8.   It was Eugenia Charles who nicknamed the bill the "Shut-Your-Mouth Bill".

9.   In fact the meeting place of the Freedom Fighters was the legal office of
      Eugenia Charles.

10.   For further details on the protest movement against the "Shut-Your-Mouth
      Bill" see Janet Higbie (1993).

11.   There is some dispute as to the origins of the DUPP. Bill Riviere (1993) claims
      that the DUPP was formed by five victorious independent candidates in the
      1957 elections, while Douglas Midgett (1997) claims that the DUPP comprised
      two successful PNM candidates who had resigned from the party in protest
      over moves by the PNM to form a coalition with the DLP and three independ-
      ent candidates. Perhaps, therefore, to quote Higbie (1993), "non- labour legisla-
      tors" is a more fitting description.

12.   Baron, Dominica's first chief minister, was later to become Eugenia Charles's
      major financier, organizing election funds for the DFP until her resignation as
      its political leader.

13.   Several explanations have been advanced for the resignation of LeBlanc.
      Midgett (1997) argues that it had much to do with global economic events
      emanating from the oil crisis of the early 1970s, while others have argued that
      his demise has much to do with the impact of radical politics in the form of the
      youth and Rastafarian movements on the island. A third thesis, however, views
      the decline of both the LeBlanc administration and the DLP as an effect of the
      politics of colonialism.

14.   She replaced a member of the Legislative Council who was away from
      Dominica for five months (Higbie 1993).

15.   In 1970 she replaced Elkin Henry as the third nominated member of parlia-
      ment (Hansard, 19 November 1970–23 September 1971).

16. Sydney Burnett-Alleyne, a Barbadian, reputed mercenary and gunrunner, entered into an agreement with Patrick John to assist in the development of the country. In 1975 Patrick John and Burnett-Alleyne entered into an agreement in which Burnett-Alleyne's Mercantile Bank undertook to establish the Dominica Development Corporation and a subsidiary branch of the Mercantile Bank. The subsidiary of Mercantile Bank agreed to provide funds for the construction of an international airport at Point Crompton. In return John agreed to grant to the bank the right to set up an oil refinery and subsidiary industries. Burnett-Alleyne also agreed to pay EC$50 million dollars a year to Dominica. The deal never materialized. For further information see Smith 1979a. Alleyne was implicated in two abortive coup attempts to overthrow the Government of Barbados under two administrations, those of Errol Barrow and Tom Adams.

17. In August 1980, Hurricane David swept across the country, almost totally destroying the local economy and leaving in its wake incalculable socio-economic problems.

18. In a letter to the interim prime minister on 1 January 1980, Charles Maynard indicated his disenchantment with the manner in which the public business was conducted, which he claimed was increasing the ineffectiveness of the government and the position of the Ross University School of Medicine. Also see below for more discussions on Ross.

19. By 1980, the humanistic approach to politics of President Jimmy Carter of the United States had been defeated with the victory of conservative Ronald Reagan, which strengthened the conservative global swing that had begun with the victory of Margaret Thatcher in Britain.

20. Henry Dyer, married to a Barbadian, had defeated Patrick John in the 1980 election and was the only cabinet minister to be dismissed by Prime Minister Eugenia Charles.

21. The attorney general's legal company, Armour, Armour and Harris, in which he was a partner, represented Robert Ross and the medical school in Dominica.

22. In that same article Honychurch criticized the prime minister for what he saw as her failure to provide the Dominican public with the opportunity to become familiar with the new leader of the party and the prime minister.

4

"We Are Kith and Kin"
Eugenia Charles, Caribbean Integration and the Grenada Invasion

ALAN COBLEY

Introduction

As prime minister of the Commonwealth of Dominica between 1980 and 1995 Dame Eugenia Charles was often highly critical of the Caribbean Community (CARICOM) and repeatedly expressed scepticism about the potential for political unity in the Commonwealth Caribbean. Yet in 1971 she had been a signatory to the Joint Statement of Opposition Parties in the Eastern Caribbean which called for the creation of "an independent, living and viable Caribbean nation" (Higbie 1993), and, during her years in office as prime minister, she was a pivotal figure in the promotion of political and other forms of unity between the peoples of the "Inner Caribbean", as one of the driving forces behind the Organization of Eastern Caribbean States (OECS) formed in 1981. This chapter explores this apparent paradox by examining her specific contributions to the Caribbean integration movement during her political career.

The Making of a Caribbean Leader

In October 1932 political leaders from a number of West Indian territories gathered in Roseau to discuss the future of the region. The seventeen delegates who attended the Dominica Conference were frustrated by the experience of Crown Colony status within the British Empire. This had protected the entrenched privileges of the (mostly white) plantocracy at the expense of the (largely black) majority, and had led to economic stagnation, endemic poverty and deplorable social conditions throughout the islands (Macmillan 1936). They hoped to rally support for a self-governing West Indian confederation – under the slogan "Educate! Agitate! Federate!" – prior to the arrival of the Closer Union Commission appointed by the British government, which visited Dominica a couple of months later. The delegates included the Trinidadian labour leader Arthur Cipriani. Also present was a local farmer and businessman named J.B. Charles, the father of future Dominican prime minister Mary Eugenia Charles (Honychurch 1975, 91–92). The young Eugenia, then thirteen years old, went after school to sit among the audience and listen to the discussions during the conference (Higbie 1993, 33).

J.B. Charles was born into a peasant family and left school at the age of fourteen to train as a mason. However, beginning with a small plot of land at Pointe Michel, just outside Roseau, he gradually accumulated property, wealth and status in Dominican society through a combination of successful farming and business enterprises. By the time of the 1932 conference he had served on the Town Board, as mayor of Roseau and as a member of the island's Legislative Council. He was considered a member of the local mulatto elite, dubbed in local parlance the "gwoh bougs". Later he served as a senator representing Dominica in the parliament of the short-lived West Indies Federation (1958–62). While "J.B." was a supporter of greater West Indian integration, as a self-made man he also tended to be pragmatic and politically conservative by instinct. His heroes were George Washington Carver and Booker T. Washington, rather than the radical Marcus Garvey (Higbie 1993, 32–34).

Politics in the British West Indies in the period immediately prior to and immediately following independence is hardly explicable without reference to the emergence of a small black (or, more often, brown) elite in many island societies during the late colonial era, of which men such as J.B. Charles and his family were a part. Their presence provided for a smooth transition (notwithstanding the hiccough of federation) to formal independence and the emergence of many small island states in the

Caribbean in the 1960s and 1970s, not least because some of the more effective political leaders across the Caribbean were drawn from their ranks. As Ralph Gonsalves wrote in a book published in 1994, "It is interesting to note that those Caribbean leaders who seem to wear the mantle of power with the greatest ease are the so-called 'local aristocrats', that is to say, persons whose antecedents prepared them for governance" (Gonsalves 1994, 74). His list of examples included Norman and Michael Manley in Jamaica, Errol Barrow and Tom Adams in Barbados, and Eugenia Charles in Dominica. It is instructive to note that in the same passage, Gonsalves suggests that much of the post-independence politics in the Caribbean has been marked by "authoritarian leadership of the post-colonial type" (Gonsalves 1994, 74–88). Arguably, this patrician style (often, though not always, accompanied by a conservative ideological orientation) was also a legacy of the peculiar social, economic and racial milieu of late colonial Caribbean society.

Both her biographer, Janet Higbie, and Eugenia Charles herself report lively political discussions over the dinner table as a standard part of the Charles family home life in her formative years, and it seems uncontroversial to suggest that the future prime minister would have derived some of her attitudes, if not her political views, from her father. However, when asked whether his specific views on regional integration had influenced her, Charles replied: "His views did not influence us; his influence made us forthright in conversation" (Charles 2002a). Nevertheless, one important observation on regionalism that had been derived from her father's experience in this period concerned the reasons for the failure of the West Indies Federation: "I don't think that at that time the parliament was thinking about it as a region; each island had its own point of view of what they wanted for their island, so I don't think we were talking regionally at that time ourselves" (Charles 2002c). It was also clear to Charles from conversations with J.B. that the smaller islands of the Leewards had worked together more effectively than they had with the larger islands: "We had the same problems, we were quarrelling about the same things" (Charles 2002a). This also was a lesson for the future. For her own part Charles felt "it was necessary for us to be able to get together because . . . we were too far apart and we didn't have one voice to speak from . . . the great thing is that we must speak with one voice" (Charles 2002a). Yet it was evident that she did not espouse regional integration on the basis of any vaulting pan-Caribbean ideology or philosophical position; she viewed integration primarily as a platform for development, as cooperation in pursuit of common goals. This practical view of integration was at the heart of her support for the pro-integration statement issued by political opposition leaders in the Caribbean in 1971:

> We had something that was unique to us and we should build on that and develop that so we could make something out of ourselves ... Also I think that Britain was listening more to us as a grouping. I suppose we felt that if we talked the same language we might more likely get the things we wanted. (Charles 2002a)

Her attitude to regionalism was also shaped profoundly by the historical relationships that had developed between Dominica and its neighbours. Dominica's geographic and cultural proximity to the French territories of Martinique and Guadeloupe, for instance, influenced her views on links with the other English-speaking islands:

> We had a good relationship with the two French islands – better than the other islands had, because we spoke the patois, and our people went across there to work a lot; a lot of labourers went across to Martinique and Guadeloupe ... So I think we had a close association with the French islands ... and they came over here, I mean, every night a boat was coming across from Guadeloupe and dropping off people, you know ... We were closer to Guadeloupe and Martinique than we were to Antigua, for instance, not only in distance but in thinking. (Charles 2002a)

Thus, when CARICOM was formed, with the signing of the Treaty of Chaguaramas on 4 July 1973, Eugenia Charles, then still in political opposition in Dominica, was an interested observer. She supported the move because she felt it was important "that we should get together and understand each other's problems; that we might be able to solve these problems if we thought along those lines" (Charles 2002). However, she did not agree with the distinction drawn between the larger and smaller islands in the treaty, which spoke of "more developed countries" (MDCs) and "less developed countries" (LDCs):[1] "I didn't agree with them; I thought all of us were important. I thought Dominica was the most important of all of them, I mean! [Laughs]" (Charles 2002a). Later this distinction would be seen as increasingly artificial and discriminatory. As John Osbourne, chief minister of Montserrat, warned at the Sixth Heads of Government Conference of the Caribbean Community in Barbados in July 1985:

> CARICOM must earn the goodwill of all its constituent territories. This is only possible as all are allowed to taste the fruits of integration. More especially I am indicating that we must aim at a more equitable sharing of the benefits of integration. We must reduce wide gaps and disparities and ultimately abandon the concept of MDCs and LDCs. (Hall 2000, xix)

She also felt that insufficient attention was paid at the outset to education, a long-standing concern of her father's, and to other cultural issues:

> Cricket was the most binding thing between us. I didn't agree that cricket was an important thing – I didn't play cricket! But I thought that it brought about a unification among people, I mean, they thought the same thing. And I thought that was the way we should have gone on. We should have gone like that with education too.
>
> [Question: So things like the Common External Tariff and so on, these were perhaps necessary, but perhaps not so important?]
>
> No. Cricket was more important. There is more unification in talking cricket than there is in talking money. (Charles 2002a)

Her interest in the regional integration movement, such as it was, however, was overshadowed in the 1970s by the dramatic events that unfolded much closer to home in Dominica during that decade. These events culminated in a series of political crises that eventually brought her to power as the country's leader in 1980. The catalyst for these crises was the accession to power of Patrick John as prime minister in 1974, followed by the passage of the controversial Prohibited and Unlawful Societies Act (the "Dread Act") at John's insistence in November of that year. For the remainder of the decade the Dominican state was locked in a struggle characterized by Gabriel Christian as "a small, undeclared and semi-secret war" with the local Rastafarian community, or "Dreads" as they were known (Andre and Christian 1992, 32). In the process Patrick John's leadership of Dominica became increasingly erratic and authoritarian, symbolized by his decision to establish a Dominica Defence Force, and then to dub himself "Colonel". By the time of independence in November 1978, he had first nurtured, then discarded, a group of young left-wing radicals, led by Rosie Douglas, and was at the same time increasingly at odds with the private sector and propertied classes, as well as the labour unions who formed the core support for his Dominica Labour Party. The devastation of the island's banana crop by leaf spot in late 1978 and early 1979, coupled with rumours about various shady business deals undertaken at this time by John with outside investors (evidently in a desperate effort on his part to find a quick infusion of cash to prop up the country's economy), pushed Dominica to the edge of economic collapse. Popular demonstrations against his government followed, culminating in a full-fledged riot and the fatal shooting of one demonstrator by soldiers on the streets of Roseau on 29 May 1979. In the wake of these tumultuous events, the political forces alienated by him over the years at last coalesced into an effective anti-John coalition that formed the Committee for National Salvation to force him out of office in June 1979 (Andre and Christian 1992, chap.1).

By the time the Dominica Freedom Party led by Eugenia Charles came to power in the elections of 20 July 1980, the country had suffered further devastation and serious loss of life from Hurricane David on 29 August 1979 and was still on its knees in economic terms. The economic problems were compounded by Hurricane Allen, which hit just one week after she took office and undid much of the recovery work undertaken since the previous storm. Meanwhile, even as Eugenia Charles was being sworn in as the Commonwealth Caribbean's first woman prime minister, her old adversary Patrick John was plotting a coup that aimed to return him to power with the help of an invasion by right-wing mercenaries from the United States. Although the plot was exposed and John was arrested in March 1981, a number of disgruntled former soldiers from the now-disbanded Dominica Defence Force, led by their former commander, Frederick Newton, tried to release John by force of arms and to stage a coup of their own in December of that year. One policeman was killed and several injured in an attack on police headquarters. The general climate of instability was also fuelled by continued armed clashes with the Dreads, including the kidnapping and killing of Ted Honychurch in February 1981 (Andre and Christian 1992).

A flavour of these challenging times in Dominica is conveyed in Eugenia Charles's message to the nation on the third anniversary of independence in November 1981:

We were beset with security problems which could bring all the work we had undertaken to reconstruct and reorganise the services of our nation and give it new direction, to naught. In spite of the heavy weight and burden which these security matters brought to bear upon our time and our resources we continued with the herculean task of reconstruction and reorganisation. However, we dealt very firmly with the problem not seeking to make ourselves popular by the actions we were obliged to take, but carrying out our duty of ensuring the safety of the citizens. (Charles 1981)

These events would prove to be a watershed in Dominica's relations with the region and the wider world. As Andre comments:

The attempted invasion [of 1981] exposed the vulnerability of the island and its reliance on the comity between states for the preservation of its democratic institutions. The reliance on US intelligence for information about the attempted coup initiated the process whereby the island's foreign policy would be closely allied with the United States. (Andre and Christian 1992, 169)

They also unexpectedly thrust Eugenia Charles, the country's plain-speaking and plain-dealing prime minister, into the forefront of the regional integration movement.

Regional Integration and the Security of Small Island States

The circumstances in which Eugenia Charles had acceded to power in Dominica, as well as the mortal threats she had faced in her first months in office, undoubtedly influenced her thinking about the nature of regional integration. It is well to remember, however, that the experience of Dominica in these years was by no means unique. During the same period, the Barbados Labour Party government in Barbados had been threatened by two coup plots led by Sydney Burnett-Alleyne, in November 1976 and December 1978, the latter with the backing of Patrick John from Dominica; Prime Minister Eric Gairy had been overthrown by a popular uprising in Grenada on 13 March 1979; and the newly elected government of Milton Cato in St Vincent and the Grenadines had faced an uprising by Rastafarians on Union Island in December 1979 (Serbin 1990, 76–79).[2] Henceforward, the issue of cooperation for security in small island states would be an important theme in any discussion of regional integration of which Charles was part.

While mutual security was a prominent issue for all those concerned in the drafting of the Treaty of Basseterre of 18 June 1981, which established the Organization of Eastern Caribbean States (OECS), as chairperson of the organization for its first three years Charles was central to the early development of this strand of OECS policy. Indeed, such was her high profile as leader of OECS in the early years that it was the subject of criticism by her political opponents in Dominica, as she explained to her OECS colleagues when handing over the chairmanship to John Osbourne of Montserrat in 1984:

> In ending, I wish to share with you an amusing saying coming from the lips of my Opposition at home nearing the end of 1983. They informed the public that the initials "O.E.C.S." means "Only Eugenia Charles Speaks". I wish to go home and remind them that "Osborne Etcetera Can Speak" – indicating that the OECS is no one-man show but a genuine coming together of States for the benefit of all our peoples. (Charles 1984a)

Article Three of the Treaty of Basseterre included the following as objectives of the OECS: "Cooperation among the Member States; the promotion of unity and solidarity; the defence of their sovereignty, territorial integrity and independence; common representation vis-a-vis the international community, e.g. through the harmonisation of foreign policy, joint overseas representation abroad; and the promotion of economic integration" (Müllerleile 1996, 137). Security issues were also highlighted in Article 8, which established the Defence and Security Committee as one of the Organization's standing committees. In Section 3 of the article, the committee's role was defined as advising the OECS on defence and security matters, while Section 4 spoke of

> coordinating the efforts of Member States for collective defence and the preservation of peace and security against external aggression . . . including measures to combat the activities of mercenaries, operating with or without the support of internal or national elements, in the exercise of the inherent right of individual or collective self-defence recognised by Article 51 of the Charter of the United Nations. (Müllerleile 1996, 137; Gilmore 1984, app. 2)

This latter clause, which gave the right to the OECS to intervene to defend democratically elected member governments from violent over-throw, had been drafted in the light of the recent experience of Dominica and other Eastern Caribbean states, and was clearly intended to meet the possibility of a threat in which external forces were involved. However, it would soon be invoked, amidst much controversy, to justify military inter-vention in an internal political crisis in Grenada.

A year after the founding of the OECS, in October 1982, the govern-ments of Dominica, Antigua and Barbuda, St Lucia, St Vincent and the Grenadines and Barbados were signatories to the Roseau Security Memorandum, which went further still in committing the four govern-ments to the establishment of the Regional Defence and Security System, including a combined defence force with headquarters in Barbados capable of launching combined operations under a common command structure. They agreed "[t]o assist one another on request in national emergencies, prevention of smuggling, search and rescue, immigration control, policing duties, protection of offshore installations, pollution control, natural and other disasters and threats to national security" (Gilmore 1984, app. 4).

The central role played by Barbados in the new Regional Defence and Security System reflected a perception in Bridgetown in these years that instability in the sub-region was a direct threat to the security of Barbados – a perception reinforced by the unsuccessful Burnett-Alleyne coup plots of the late 1970s. It also illustrated the extent to which security dominated the discourse on regionalism among conservative Caribbean leaders by the early 1980s. Prime Minister Tom Adams of Barbados became the chief advocate for a wider, multinational security force to protect the sovereignty of eastern Caribbean states, a policy which became known as the Adams Doctrine, while Edward Seaga, whose Jamaica Labour Party had acceded to power in Jamaica in the elections of October 1980, carried the banner for a CARICOM-wide defence system (Serbin 1990, 81).

Together, Adams, Seaga and Charles formed a powerful neoconservative, pro-capitalist, authoritarian bloc against socialist and communist influences in the region in the early 1980s and, as a result, they enjoyed good relations with the right-wing administration of US president Ronald Reagan. Not surprisingly, they were also vilified by those on the left in the Caribbean who had nurtured the hope during the 1970s that Fidel Castro in Cuba,

Forbes Burnham in Guyana, Michael Manley in Jamaica and, latterly, Maurice Bishop in Grenada would be able to forge an alternative, socialist, path to development for Caribbean peoples. The gospel of regional integration had thus evolved into two polar versions by the early 1980s; for the conservative right it had become a vehicle for mutual security, a platform for capitalist development and a bulwark against communism; for the radical left it was the sine qua non for an end to neocolonialism, dependency, social exclusion and economic injustice. It was only the periodic bouts of high-flown political rhetoric at meetings of regional organizations, as well as the continuing affirmations of a common Caribbean heritage and identity at a cultural level, that papered over these deep ideological fissures in the integration movement during the rest of that stormy decade.

The OECS: Integration on a Cost-Effective Basis

The signing of the Treaty of Basseterre in 1981 was an important moment in the history of sub-regional integration but it was by no means the first step towards greater unity in the Inner Caribbean. Prior to the formation of the short-lived West Indian Federation in 1958, a Leewards Islands Federation had been in existence for several years. After the collapse of the West Indian Federation in 1962, a number of key institutions were put in place to promote greater cooperation between the various smaller Eastern Caribbean territories. These included the Eastern Caribbean Currency Authority, set up in 1965, which established the basis for a common currency; the West Indies Associated States Council of Ministers, constituted by five Eastern Caribbean territories in 1966 to act as an advisory body on economic and other forms of cooperation; the West Indian Associated States Supreme Court, established in 1967; and the Eastern Caribbean Common Market, created in 1968 (Müllerleile 1996, 136–39).

After the OECS came into being, the member states linked their economic destiny even more closely together with the formation of the Eastern Caribbean Central Bank (1983), while the Eastern Caribbean Supreme Court replaced the West Indian Associated States Supreme Court as the region's highest court around the same time. An OECS Central Secretariat was also established to oversee various developmental projects within the member states: while the salaries of the core staff were paid by the constituent governments, most of the projects were funded by major international donor agencies.

According to Müllerleile, the OECS owed its existence largely to discontentment among the member states about the slow progress towards integration in CARICOM. A feeling that they were being discriminated against by the larger CARICOM member states because of their status as less developed countries also played a part. However, in the final analysis there is no doubt that the prospects for effective integration were much greater among the territories of the Inner Caribbean than elsewhere: "The similarity of the economic and social problems, geographic proximity, common foreign policy and security interests, favour closer co-operation, which from the beginning was not limited only to the economic sector, but which also did not exclude [the possibility of] political union" (Müllerleile 1996, 136–37).

At the meeting of ministers held in June 1981 to discuss the establishment of the OECS, Charles made it plain that she had little time for high-sounding words, and that her views on integration left little room for delusions of grandeur or unrealistic expectations:

> We are small and we must take advantage of our smallness. We must ensure that we fashion the integration movement so that it fits into our limited resources. True, we may obtain aid to assist us in this integration movement but we must recognise that we seek aid for the purpose of putting us in a position of ceasing to be aid seekers . . . We can only succeed if we are completely honest–honest with ourselves, honest with each other, honest with our electorate. We can only succeed if we cease to be foolishly sensitive. In short, we can only succeed if we have the dedicated will to make it succeed and we are prepared to compromise with and understand each. [West Indies (Associated States) 1981, Annex IV]

Three years later, reflecting on the early history of the Organization as she prepared to hand over the chairmanship to John Osbourne of Montserrat, Charles recalled the primary motives behind its formation: "It was mainly due to the need for the provision of a more effective instrument for the rapid development of our member states and the preservation of our security that this sub-regional integration movement was perceived and came into being" (Charles 1984a). However, she emphasized the particular benefits that she felt collective action through the OECS could bring to the smaller islands:

> This Organisation is the last to be set up in a series of efforts to bring the English-speaking Caribbean together so that certain essential services and expertise can be provided to the smaller and less fortunate countries on a cost-effective basis. This means that we should be able to act together to solve common problems where it would be costly, if not impossible for an individual country to do so on its own. Our small and fragile economies with too little available trained and experienced manpower to engage in essential activities and services of our independent countries, coupled with our limited public sector revenue base on which the demands are great and competing, make it even more vital for us to seek to work together in many common and priority areas. (Charles 1984a)

Ultimately, she concluded, the success or failure of the OECS "will be measured by our citizens on the manner in which we tackle the day-to-day bread and butter issues of development which affect their progress in life" (Charles 1984a).

Twenty years later, in light of these statements, Charles was asked to comment on whether the OECS had achieved any notable successes during her time in government (1980–95). She replied, initially at least, in characteristically dismissive style: "No, I don't think so. Nobody had any money. How can you say you were successful ? [laughs]" (Charles 2002a). However, she went on to qualify this bald statement by pointing to the practical benefits that had accrued to ordinary people from membership in the Organization:

> But we did have an exchange of people. A lot of people went to work in different islands and felt quite at home doing it, you know . . . And we were interested in people's problems. We were interested in what was happening in Montserrat, for instance . . . And we exchanged teachers. A lot of our teachers at grammar school came from Antigua or somewhere like that . . . I thought that was a good thing because it made us learn about the other islands, you know. (Charles 2002a)

The 1980s were difficult times for Caribbean states, as many faced painful structural adjustment programmes proposed by the International Monetary Fund and the World Bank. Money was tight. However, the survival of the OECS through this difficult period suggests that it was a relatively robust infant in economic, as well as in other terms. The EC dollar proved to be a particular success; by the mid-1990s it had become one of the most stable currencies in the region. But Charles's comments point especially to the effectiveness and sustainability of the Organization as a vehicle for regional integration at the grass-roots level.

One of her own particular interests in the early years was the Eastern Caribbean Primary Textbook Project, a project designed to develop and distribute common textbooks throughout the primary schools of the member states. It could be said to have embodied her views about the form regional integration should take, in that the goals of the project were modest, practical and achievable, and above all accorded a central role to education in the process of development. As she later explained, "I thought that would bring about a closeness" (Charles 2002a).

Another critical issue for Charles in the formative years of the OECS, as noted earlier, was security. Her experience of instability in Dominica was behind her strong support for efforts to bring the police forces from the various member states together for training and to improve cooperation between them under a common leadership structure. Barbados, although not a member of the Organization, was already playing an important part as headquarters of the Regional Security System established in 1982; it also played a role in supporting this aspect of OECS activities as the site of the Regional Police Training College (Charles 2002a; Serbin 1990, 81).

Probably the high-water mark for the Organization in the 1980s came in June 1986 when William Demas, president of the Caribbean Development Bank, called for a political union of English-speaking countries in the Eastern Caribbean, beginning with the OECS. OECS leaders debated the idea at their annual meeting in 1987 but opinion was split, with James Mitchell of St Vincent and the Grenadines leading the pro-union lobby versus Vere Bird, Sr, of Antigua and Barbuda, who was strongly opposed. For her part, Eugenia Charles felt that any union would be stillborn without popular support, so she launched a series of public consultations around Dominica during 1987 and 1988 to explain the proposal and test public opinion. Eventually, in November 1988, she committed Dominica to the idea of a political union, together with the governments of St Vincent and the Grenadines, St Lucia and Grenada. The moment had passed, however, and little progress was made subsequently towards implementing the plan (Higbie 1993, 269–70).

Does CARICOM Have Any Meaning? Integration and the Wider Caribbean

The relative success of the OECS in the 1980s contrasted sharply with the frustration many of the smaller islands felt with CARICOM. This growing frustration was evident in the comments made by Eugenia Charles during the course of that decade. At the first Heads of Government meeting of CARICOM that she attended, in Ocho Rios, Jamaica, in July 1982, she spoke hopefully about the future of the Caribbean Community:

> To our people in this region, Member States must be able to answer the question loudly and clearly when asked, "does CARICOM have any meaning?" We must be prepared to bear in mind the *reality* of the Caribbean Community and we must be able to see the potential of the Movement. But are we able to see beyond the trials and errors and see CARICOM as an article of faith – an ideal, not sterile, but vibrant and meaningful?
>
> ...This Meeting must be seen as an opportunity for the Region to reaffirm our commitment to and continued support for the Integration Movement of the Commonwealth Caribbean. (Hall 2000, 431–33)

But if her comments in 1982 suggested a measure of idealism, tempered with realism, by 1984 she was already beginning to sound a more discordant note. This was reflected in her remarks during an interview for *CARICOM Perspectives,* when she was asked what benefits Dominica had received from its membership of CARICOM:

> When I first came in, I found if I wanted personnel to help us, they could help us at very short notice. We have also had a number of studies and workshops which were very helpful in that way.
>
> With CARICOM I have one quarrel. I think we meet too often. There are so many sub-organisations, so many committees of Ministers that take up a lot of time. I'm not saying that we should not meet, but we should concentrate on the things that brought us together, the industry part, the trade part. (*CARICOM Perspectives* 1984, 4–5)

By the time of the Eighth Conference of Heads of Government of the Caribbean Community in St Lucia in 1987, Charles was in the midst of her second term as prime minister of Dominica and had earned a reputation as one of the most outspoken critics of the Organization. In light of this she admitted to being reluctant even to speak publicly at the opening ceremony:

> However, because I have always made it very clear that CARICOM is too loath to consider the needs, the aspirations, the ideas and the suffering of the people of all our States, perhaps it is right that I should express some of my views at this session of our Eighth meeting. (Hall 2000, 299–302)

Citing examples from the agenda for the meeting, she highlighted the failure to make "very high sounding principles, ideas, motions and aspirations" into reality and noted "with great sorrow, that the cost factor is usually left out of all calculations. This may have been possible in the old days when we had oil-rich Trinidad and Tobago and bauxite-rich Jamaica and Guyana. But perhaps even then it was misguided" (Hall 2000, 299–302). She went on to question the cost and relevance of many of the "desks, agencies and organizations" set up by CARICOM and called for regular reviews of their activities.[3] She also lambasted those governments that had not implemented previous CARICOM decisions, and complained about poor communication between governments and with the people of the region. In the end, her message was simple:

> I am of the firm opinion that CARICOM must continue to exist, but it must exist for the purpose of improving the quality of life of our people. If it does not succeed in doing this, then we must abandon it. We must emphasize that we are not in CARICOM merely to show that there is "unity" among us in the English-speaking Caribbean – no, we are in CARICOM because the unity it aims at achieving will bring benefits to all our people. Therefore, we must work hard at making CARICOM what it should be, what it was meant to be, what in our dignified and formal speeches we (with tongue in cheek) say that it is. (Hall 2000, 299–302)

It would be unjust to suggest that no progress was made by CARICOM during these years. After years of wrangling, tariffs on most products produced within CARICOM were abolished in October 1988, while efforts to establish a common external tariff regime had also begun to bear fruit. Yet by the early 1990s, few CARICOM leaders and officials had been spared the rough side of Charles's tongue as she continued to rail against what she saw as examples of waste and unrealistically grandiose schemes within the Organization. It was evident that some CARICOM leaders increasingly regarded her as though she were an irascible older aunt, outside the mainstream of thinking on regional integration. This perception, together with her own growing weariness with politics both internationally and at home in Dominica, where she was in her third term as prime minister, meant that her influence in the inner councils of the regional movement began to wane.

Grenada and the Politics of Intervention

During the long period in which Eugenia Charles held office as prime minister of Dominica, no single issue combined her innate political conservatism with her emotional commitment towards regional integration more clearly than her role in the events surrounding the intervention in Grenada by United States forces in October 1983. It was to be the defining moment of her career as a Caribbean leader. The final section of this chapter is therefore dedicated to this episode.

Maurice Bishop's "New Jewel Movement" had come to power in Grenada via a bloodless coup in March 1979.[4] Few lamented the fall from power of the eccentric Eric Gairy, and for the most part the new "People's Revolutionary Government" was greeted calmly by Grenada's neighbours. The left-leaning Oliver Seraphin, head of the interim government in Dominica after the fall of Patrick John in June 1979, met Bishop and Allan Louisy of St Lucia at the Grenada Summit on 14–15 July and pledged closer ties between the three countries as they worked towards "the liquidation of all traces of colonialism in and out of the Caribbean" (Andre and Christian 1992, 47–48). As always, the politically conservative Eugenia Charles had taken a pragmatic view: "We felt we had to work together . . . We didn't think that we would agree with the things he was doing but we felt that we had to work together if these islands were going to get anywhere" (Charles 2002a).

So far as the fledgling OECS was concerned, she recognized Bishop as an enthusiastic ally in its development, even if their approaches were very different: "I was very practical about it. He was up in the sky dreaming dreams" (Charles 2002a). At a meeting of ministers which discussed the establishment of the OECS prior to the signing of the formal Treaty in Basseterre in June 1981, Charles (in remarks cited earlier) had sought to lower the expectations of those present and to focus on practical issues. Bishop, by contrast, opted for the rhetorical high road:

> The People's Revolutionary Government of Grenada . . . is totally committed to regional integration. We are equally committed to sub-regional cooperation and integration . . . We believe that the OECS is a testament to our people and our people's determination moving through a conquest and settlement and slavery and colonialism and now independence for many of us, a testament to the struggles of our people and to the desire of our people for closer unity and greater cooperation. We believe that the ties of blood, the ties of family, of history, of geography, of tradition, of culture, of trade, of friendship are ties which no one or no force can ever break or destroy. That is always going to be so. . . .([West Indies [Associated States] 1981, Annex V, "Address by Hon. Maurice Bishop, Prime Minister of Grenada")

When news broke on Friday 13 October 1983 that Bishop had been overthrown and was under house arrest in St Georges, Charles was on her way to a speaking engagement in Jamaica and was not unduly concerned by the development. She told her biographer that her initial feeling was that it was a matter for the people of Grenada: "[I]t's their business, not mine." According to Higbie, Charles had been estranged from Bishop since 1980, when he had made a much-quoted remark about "Uncle Tom Adams" and other "yard fowls" in the region who attacked his left-wing policies at the bidding of US President Ronald Reagan; she interpreted this as an attack on her, among other political conservatives in the region. Now, in his moment of extremis, she was not inclined to rush to his defence publicly, or in any other way. However, on the following Wednesday, 19 October, the radio reported Bishop's summary execution and a number of other fatal shootings in Grenada following a botched rescue attempt by a crowd of his supporters. Her government was among several to issue statements deploring the violence and the ensuing military takeover, and to call for a rapid return to democracy in Grenada (Higbie 1993, 227–28).[5]

It was John Compton of St Lucia who took the lead in calling for emergency meetings of the OECS and CARICOM to discuss some form of regional intervention in the crisis in Grenada. He received strong backing from Tom Adams of Barbados ("Address to the Barbadian People by Prime Minister Adams [Extracts] of 26th October 1983", app. 11 in Gilmore 1984, 102–5). When the OECS leaders met in Barbados on Friday 21 October under Charles's chairmanship, they quickly agreed that action was required and drew up a list of sanctions against Grenada that could be implemented immediately. The idea of military intervention seems to have been raised first outside the Organization, by Prime Minister Adams of Barbados. Once it had been broached, however, Adams quickly arranged for Charles to meet with the US ambassador to the Eastern Caribbean, Milan Bish, to discuss the possibility of US military assistance. The following day the leaders travelled to Trinidad for the emergency CARICOM meeting, where the option of military intervention was the subject of heated discussion. The role of the United States during these few days – whether as instigator or facilitator of the military option – has been the subject of much controversy, both at the time and in the years since. Certainly, President Reagan had been saying for months prior to these events that he considered Cuban involvement in Grenada a threat to US security. Whatever the truth about the role of the United States, by the time Charles returned to Barbados on Sunday, 23 October, she was carrying a formal note requesting assistance from the United States under Article 8 of the OECS Treaty in her capacity as chairman of the Organization.[6] It was this formal request that gave the United States a legal justification for the military invasion of Grenada, code named "Operation Urgent Fury", that was launched in the early hours of Tuesday, 25 October 1983.

Part of the controversy over the US military action in Grenada related to the question of the legality of the intervention in terms of Article 8 of the OECS Treaty, with its emphasis on "external threats" to national security rather than internal disorder. A second issue was the legitimacy of an intervention without a formal request from the member state itself. The response to the latter point, conveyed by Charles in a speech to the UN Security Council, was that the OECS had received a secret request for intervention from the governor general of Grenada, Sir Paul Scoon, at its meeting in Barbados on 21 October. A written version of this request surfaced later (Dominique 1984, app. F).[7]

International reaction to the US-led invasion was almost uniformly hostile. In Latin America, the Mexican newspaper *El Universal* asked: "With what sort of moral authority can the US Government condemn the Soviet invasion of Afghanistan if it acts in the same way in its own hemisphere?"; while *The Times* of London, normally a bastion of conservative reaction, declared roundly that "the US and its Caribbean allies are in breach of international law and the Charter of the UN" (Andre and Christian 1992, 193). At a subsequent session of the UN General Assembly the invasion was condemned as illegal by a vote of 108 to 9.

For Eugenia Charles, however, these appeared to be relatively unimportant details. It was characteristic of her that she never expressed any doubt about the course of action taken, and she often became exasperated when asked to justify the military intervention. For her it was more personal than a simple question of regional solidarity; it was a family matter – a point she made publicly at the first available opportunity, as she stood beside President Reagan at a White House press conference on the morning of the invasion:

> I think we were all very horrified at the events which took place recently in Grenada. We, as part of the Organisation of Eastern Caribbean States, realised that we are, of course, one region; we belong to each other; we are kith and kin. We all have members of our states living in Grenada. (Dominique 1984, 30–31)

For both Janet Higbie and Anthony Maingot, "kith and kin" was the key phrase in her justification of events. Higbie expresses it thus:

> The "family of nations" is a cliché that is usually applied to the United Nations. In the case of the OECS the description happens to fit, though it is a distinctively West Indian family, outside children and all. Britain's cast-off Eastern Caribbean islands quarrel constantly, often over money. Nevertheless they feel a kinship that has less to do with the technicalities of a formal legal relationship than a shared sense of brotherhood that came from centuries of colonial oppression and neglect. (Higbie 1993, 234)

Maingot argues in similar vein that Charles "expressed well the nature of

West Indian diffuse reciprocity when she spoke of 'our kith and kin' ". He suggests that Charles's remarks caught the popular mood throughout much of the West Indies, which was overwhelmingly supportive of the intervention on emotional, if not political, grounds:

> The immense popularity of the Grenada intervention – even in those nations such as Trinidad which did not participate – spoke more clearly about the nature of inter–West Indian bonds and solidarity than all the official texts, treaties and rhetoric. The same sentiments and values of reciprocal understanding that had led West Indians to cooperate with a "deviant" PRG [People's Revolutionary Government] led to the support for action against behavior generally regarded as totally outside anything West Indians had witnessed at least since the days of slavery. West Indians had responded to the fait accompli of Maurice Bishop in March 1979 partly for personal reasons. This was, in October 1983, also a part of their reactions to his murder. (Maingot 1989, 287)

In Jamaica, a public opinion poll by Carl Stone a week after the invasion found support for the action was overwhelming, while in Barbados, Prime Minister Adams commented in a radio address that he had been surprised by the degree of unanimity seen in the islands for such a potentially controversial action (Müllerleile 1996, 163; Gilmore 1984, app. 11). In such an atmosphere, anguished debates about compromised sovereignty or the niceties of international law cut little ice. Eugenia Charles emerged, albeit briefly and somewhat to her own surprise, as a popular leader in this moment of crisis because she reflected the sense of deep emotional engagement with events in Grenada that was being felt across a wide spectrum of Caribbean society.[8]

For the Caribbean Left, the collapse of the revolution in Grenada and the invasion that followed was a devastating experience; it marked the end of an era in which progressive alternatives to the hegemonic power of the West had flourished. The charismatic figure of Maurice Bishop had embodied the hopes of a radical generation; his summary execution at the hands of his former comrades in October 1983 dealt those hopes a crushing blow.[9] The political scientist Brian Meeks, who had been working with Bishop and the People's Revolutionary Government in Grenada as a consultant on media and political education only a matter of weeks before Bishop's death, sums it up this way:

> For my generation, radicalized in the popular awakening that accompanied the
> Black Power movement in the late 1960s, our hopes for a different, more equal
> and more just Caribbean were at first raised and then dashed by the course of
> events in the following decade and a half. Grenada was the last nail in the coffin,
> but before that deadening seal there had been the revelation of the corrupt
> Burnham regime in Guyana and the death by assassination of the country's first
> son Walter Rodney and the running to ground of the Manley Government in
> Jamaica by a brutal, relentless process of financial, psychological and military
> destabilization. (Meeks and Lindahl 2001, ix)

As left-wing politics in the Caribbean descended into disarray, anger
and recrimination in the mid-1980s, the enduring image of a martyred
Maurice Bishop was juxtaposed in the minds of many with the austere,
unbending figure of Eugenia Charles. Her pragmatic, conservative policies
during that decade were the very antithesis of Bishop's idealistic socialism.
Thus, while he was excused perhaps too readily by leftist intellectuals of
any responsibility for the chaotic end to the socialist experiment in
Grenada, she was blamed perhaps too easily for her willingness to compromise the sovereignty of the small island states of the Caribbean through her
support for the Grenada invasion and in her subsequent relentless pursuit
of Western development aid. In the process an important lesson about the
nature of the Caribbean integration movement was lost.

Conclusion

In an era when political conservatism was in the ascendant, the image of
Eugenia Charles standing shoulder to shoulder with Ronald Reagan at the
White House on the morning of the invasion of Grenada made her a star.
She was portrayed as a bastion against the spread of communism in the
Caribbean – the Caribbean's own "Iron Lady" to set alongside Britain's
Margaret Thatcher. She parlayed this image into major international aid for
Dominica from Western donors over the next few years. The effect was
most evident in the upgrading of infrastructure in Dominica, including
improved roads and upgraded airport facilities, as well as new schools and
other public buildings. Such was the nature and pace of this development
that Dominicans joked about her unnatural love for concrete. But her

stance was not without negative consequences for cooperation between Caribbean governments; some had opposed the Grenada intervention, and continued to object to what they saw as growing US interference in the region. Responding to heated criticism of her stance from Forbes Burnham of Guyana, Charles went so far as to suggest that Guyana should be expelled from CARICOM, and, failing that, proposed moving the Secretariat away from Guyana to "a more central location". Burnham retaliated by halting exports of rice to Dominica, but Charles declared that her country could buy the commodity cheaper elsewhere, and, in any case, Dominica was still awaiting payment due from Guyana for sales of soap (Dominique 1984, 83–84). Immensely popular at home in Dominica and fêted abroad, she did not feel the need to compromise or court popularity in her stinging critiques of regional integration efforts in the decade that followed.

Asked in 2002 to define her philosophy or guiding principles, Charles was typically down to earth: "I come from a family that's always grown things, so I think that is the answer – for people to grow things. But they must have a market to sell them in, otherwise there's no point growing them" (Charles 2002a). Her regional politics were essentially an expression of her own character, marked by strong doses of pragmatism, honesty, plain speaking and intolerance to criticism. Throughout her career she abhorred "big government" in any form and remained hostile to any notion of ideology, even refusing to call herself a Caribbean nationalist: "No, I'm not a nationalist at all. I just belong to Dominica . . . I'm not interested in making a Caribbean nation. I want Dominica to do better than it's doing, and everyone in Dominica being able to make a living out of what they are doing" (Charles 2002a). Yet, notwithstanding her innate conservatism and often articulated scepticism about the prospect for effective political integration in the Caribbean, in her practical contributions to the development of the OECS in its formative years on the one hand, and in her instinctive reaction to the Grenada crisis on the other, Eugenia Charles had exposed and articulated a powerful, visceral commitment to regional integration among Caribbean people.

Notes

1.   The less developed countries included the seven smaller island territories of the Eastern Caribbean (excluding Barbados) and Belize (Müllerleile 1996, 141–42).

2.   St Lucia went through its own period of instability in 1981–1983, culminating in a claim by Prime Minister John Compton that Libya had been training local terrorists to destabilize the island, while in the same period the government of Vere Bird, Sr, in Antigua and Barbuda had been hit by a secessionist movement in Barbuda and by a series of allegations about government involvement in drug running, the operation of criminal syndicates and gun-running to South Africa.

3.   The request for a review of programmes had already been conveyed by the Government of Dominica to the secretariat prior to the meeting, and a briefing paper had been prepared which proposed reviews under six main headings: trade development, agricultural development, industrial development, functional cooperation, foreign policy coordination, and the service sector (information and communication) (Caribbean Community Secretariat, "Review of Programmes of the Community as Administered by the Secretariat", 29 June 1987).

4.   For a detailed discussion of the events leading to the revolution in Grenada, see Meeks (1993, 138–57).

5.   For a discussion of the reasons for the implosion of the Grenada revolution, see Meeks (1993, chapter 4).

6.   A copy of this note is preserved as Appendix E in Dominique (1984, 107).

7.   An exhaustive discussion of the legal arguments surrounding this episode is contained in Beck (1993).

8.   One of the more striking ironies of this episode is that in her remarks about "kith and kin" Charles was, probably unconsciously, echoing part of the rationale for integration offered by Maurice Bishop at the launching of the OECS two years earlier [West Indies (Associated States) 1981, Annex V, "Address by Hon. Maurice Bishop, Prime Minister of Grenada"].

9.   For an interesting, if sometimes superficial discussion of the role of "charisma" in Caribbean political leadership, including a comparative study of Gairy and Bishop in Grenada, see Allahar (2001).

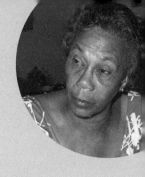

PART 3

The Psychology

of Personalized

Leadership

5

Eugenia Charles and the Psychology of Leadership

JOAN CUFFIE

Introduction

Social psychologists have always been interested in and intrigued by the topic of leadership. Research on leadership has been a major focus for social psychologists. The earlier researchers concentrated on questions such as "Who becomes a leader?" and "Do personality traits determine who becomes a leader and who does not?" Observations of political leaders such as Abraham Lincoln, Queen Elizabeth I, John F. Kennedy or Martin Luther King, Jr, have suggested that these leaders possessed attributes that ordinary individuals did not. As a result, researchers formulated the *great person theory* of leadership, which postulated that there were certain key traits great leaders displayed. However, the research findings showed little evidence to verify this theory, as it proved difficult to compile a list of personality characteristics shared by all great leaders. Nevertheless, in recent years, some researchers have suggested that there are special traits that separate leaders from others. Kirkpatrick and Locke (1991) found that leaders rate higher on traits such as "drive, self-confidence, creativity, leadership motivation (the desire to be in charge and exercise authority over others), and a high level of flexibility".

While this research indicates that personality characteristics are important in determining who is likely to become a leader and who is likely to succeed as a leader, this is simply one perspective on the nature of leadership within a social context. In the political arena in particular, leadership has "significant costs as well as benefits" (Kenrick, Neuberg and Cialdini 1999, 460); therefore, not everyone seeks leadership. Consequently, it is important to discuss leadership in terms of motivations – what kind of person is motivated to lead an organization, an institution, or a country? According to McClelland (1995), people who aspire to leadership are motivated by the *need for power* – the desire to acquire prestige, status and power over others, or by the *need for achievement* – the desire to do something exceptionally well for its own sake. Thus, for example, it can be argued that the US president John F. Kennedy was motivated by the need for power, while President Jimmy Carter was motivated by the need for achievement. Whether leaders are motivated by the need for power or the need for achievement, it is apparent that they are all highly ambitious, highly energetic and able and willing to work hard (Hogan and Hogan 1991; Simonton 1994).

Situational factors also determine who assumes leadership roles. Circumstances provide opportunities for individuals who may possess leadership ambitions but who are reluctant to display their ambitions until distinct possibilities are presented. One such situational factor is what Kenrick, Neuberg and Cialdini (1999, 462) refer to as "voids at the top". They point out that leadership prospects become available when current leaders die or leave the group, or when the groups become too large and new leadership positions are created. Openings are also created when groups become dissatisfied with the leader and other ambitious individuals are willing to accept the challenge to displace the existing leader. Such was the case with Margaret Thatcher, who became a vocal critic of Edward Heath when it was obvious that the people were dissatisfied with his policies and leadership. Thatcher seized the opportunity to show her leadership ambitions when she recognized that there might be a "void at the top" (Kenrick, Neuberg and Cialdini 1999).

It is also important to acknowledge that some individuals are better situated than others to gain access to leadership. They occupy certain positions in the workplace and are linked to particular social and political networks that increase their chances of being selected as leader. In addition, their personal connections could also improve their chances of attaining leadership. In the case of Eugenia Charles, her father's involvement in politics and the people he associated with apparently offered her a network of individuals from which she could draw in terms of expertise and experience as she entered the political sphere in Dominica. Similarly, Margaret Thatcher's ascent to political leader was aided by her father's role as mayor of their home town and her personal connections to politicians such as Airey Neave and Keith Joseph (Kenrick, Neuberg and Cialdini 1999, 462).

Social psychologists have also examined another group of leaders that they refer to as *transformational* or *charismatic* leaders. According to Baron and Byrne (2002, 558), these leaders "exerted powerful effects on many millions of persons and by so doing, changed their societies". Anton Allahar (2001), employing a Weberian notion of charisma, explores the characteristics of a select group of Caribbean charismatic leaders, such as Forbes Burnham, Maurice Bishop, Michael Manley, Errol Barrow, Eric Williams, Eric Gairy, Cheddi Jagan and Fidel Castro, and how their charisma impacted on their societies and helped to shape Caribbean history. Like social psychologists, Allahar recognizes the difficulty involved in attempting to define "charisma", but he, similar to others, can identify it when it exists (Allahar 2001, 1).

In spite of the difficulty associated with the definition of charisma, there are definite characteristics observed in charismatic or transformational leaders. According to Judge and Bono, transformational leaders possess four major characteristics: idealized influence, intellectual stimulation, inspirational motivation and individual consideration (Baron and Byrne 2002, 559). These leaders inspire high levels of motivation and commitment in their followers by articulating their vision clearly and, additionally, by providing some insight into implementing and achieving the vision. Transformational leaders also engage in what Conger terms "framing: defining the goals for their followers in a way that gives extra meaning and purpose to the goals and actions needed to attain them" (Baron and Byrne 2002, 559). Transformational leaders also display high levels of self-confidence, are exceptional communicators, and present a personal style that is difficult to resist. Allahar attests to the "oratorical skills" of charismatic leaders, and points out that there is often more emphasis on form than content. He singles out Fidel Castro, Forbes Burnham and Michael Manley as exceptional orators in the Caribbean (Allahar 2001, 8).

Eudine Barriteau adds another dimension to the discussion of this style of leadership when she refers to women's transformational leadership. She proposes that women who utilize this style of leadership should comprehend and analyse power and power relations. She states:

> Transformational leadership is concerned with where power exists, how it is used, for what purposes and who benefits. The woman who practices transformational leadership is reflective. It is a process that requires the individual to evaluate her or his behaviour and actions against the principles and values of justice and democracy. (Barriteau 2003c, 16)

It is obvious from the theoretical perspectives advanced above that transformational leaders alter the motivations, viewpoints and behaviours of their followers whereby their followers perceive a personal stake in the successful achievement of the leader's goals and realization of her or his vision. But women who employ this style of leadership must go beyond the limits so as to transform not only the followers' actions and behaviours, but also their way of thinking, by accommodating alternatives perspectives and actions; that is, "to alter the conventional practices and experiences of authority and power" (Barriteau 2003c, 16).

The Caribbean has encountered a number of political leaders throughout its history who displayed a wide range of leadership styles. While some were transformational or charismatic leaders, others have been more autocratic than democratic. Situational factors, at times, have determined the leadership styles that they have adopted. Eugenia Charles was the first and only female political leader in the Caribbean region. She entered a realm that was dominated and controlled by men, and as a result, she faced and encountered a number of challenges and barriers that her male colleagues may not have experienced. She therefore needed to adopt a leadership style that would consolidate her position as prime minister, especially as she attained leadership in the midst of some turbulent forces.

As Selwyn Ryan remarked, in Dominica at this time, "political crisis followed upon political crisis" (Ryan 1999, 114). As prime minister, Charles was confronted with insurrection from the Defence Force, whose members remained loyal to the previous administration; the kidnapping of Ted

Honychurch by Dreads and an attempted coup by Patrick John. In this difficult political and social environment, she had to adopt an autocratic, dictatorial stance, not only to restore some semblance of order in the country, but also to ensure her survival as political leader.

Charles was a strong woman and a forceful leader who took unyielding positions on a number of issues. She was a political leader who could not be ignored and who stamped her authority on any situation, issue or group that she encountered. It could be said that she exhibited some elements of transformational leadership, in terms of her self-confidence and a personal, dramatic style that showed the diversity of her character. But according to Selwyn Ryan, she failed to transfer and translate her vision for Dominica to the populace (Ryan 1999, 116). It appears that there was a "disconnection" between Charles and the masses in Dominica; I examine some reasons for this in the chapter.

The Impact of Early Influences on Eugenia Charles's Political Leadership

Mary Eugenia Charles grew up in a family and a household where politics and politicians occupied a central place. Her father was a parliamentarian and a strong influence in her life. More importantly, however, her parents encouraged and supported the development of their children's full potentialities. Charles recalled that her father told her that the "sky's the limit" (Higbie 1993, 29). From very early in their lives, Eugenia and her siblings were told about the significance of education and of attaining a profession. So she grew up with the belief and the expectation that she had the capacity and capability to become whatever she chose and to accomplish whatever she wished in public life.

One of her early influences was her father, who seemed to loom large in her life as well as in the history of Dominica. Although Charles stated that both her parents were "powerful influences" in her life, it was her father that she credited as the person who had the greatest impact on her. She stated:

> My influence in the things that I have already done was my father. He never
> forced us into education but there was an underlying theme in the house that a

profession was yours if you wanted one. Not that he was a wealthy man, but I think that he spent his money on the things that interested him, and educating his children was one of them. Two sons were doctors, and when my turn came he asked what I intended to pursue. I replied nursing, and he remarked, "A nurse?" and that was all that was said. He never said yes or no. (Brill 1995, 136)

J.B. Charles, politician and businessman, fostered in his children a sense of responsibility and commitment to themselves, their community and country. They were encouraged, as part of their daily routine, to discuss issues related mainly to current affairs, politics and business. The children were expected to have a point of view on these issues and to express their views. Charles recalled, "You knew what was happening, you heard views, and I remember that we didn't always agree with my father's views and we had arguments but it was expected of you to take part and to argue and to express yourself and hopefully you listened to others" (Higbie 1993, 40–41). It is therefore not surprising that she formed her own opinions about issues and situations in her country and other countries, and made decisions that may not always have been shared or popular with others. She grew up knowing that it was her right to question, challenge and confront situations, individuals and groups that concerned her. She felt at ease interacting with people at the international and regional levels as she did with Dominicans. She related an incident with a representative from the World Bank who told her that the Bank would give her "Cadillac roads". Charles retorted, "I do not want Cadillac roads as I have no Cadillac, instead I want roads that a donkey could ride on" (Charles 2002e). Needless to say, she obtained the money to build the roads that were appropriate for Dominica.

An upbringing as a member of the privileged class known as the "mulatto gros bourg" (Honychurch 1995, 238) not only provided Charles with a voice and the self-perception that she could be accomplished, but also afforded her the opportunities to pursue a profession and political leadership. Both of her parents ensured that she maximized these opportunities, particularly the educational ones. Her mother in particular, when she recognized that Eugenia was not utilizing her educational opportunities appropriately, taught her a lesson that subsequently brought about a marked improvement in her school performance. The episode is recorded in Higbie (1993, 38):

One day when Eugenia was 10 years old and in the third form, Mrs Charles took her daughter for a walk to the old Roseau Girls School, a government primary school. Standing outside, they could hear the monotonous singsong of the children reciting their multiplication tables. "I could hear the children singing, 'Twice 2 are 4! Twice 4 are 8! Twice 8 are 16!' and so on, out loud", Charles said. "And I couldn't stand it! And she said, 'That's what you're going to if you don't do better work at school!' And I tell you, I never looked back again after that, boy!" (Higbie 1993, 38)

The message of the importance of education was so deeply ingrained in all the children that Charles placed tremendous emphasis on its significance. In her interview, she spoke of the fact that education was critical for the people of Dominica. Her commitment to the education of Dominicans was evident in the fact that she provided scholarships to a number of individuals (Maynard 2002b).

Personality Characteristics, Skills and Capabilities

While Charles's early socialization and upbringing, as well as her educational opportunities, paved the way for her entry into the political arena, her personality attributes cannot be disregarded. She has been described as "strong-willed, determined, and not easily deterred" (Edwards 2002a) and as "known to be a blunt, straightforward person, given to strong positions . . . a forceful person" (Maynard 2002b). As a young girl, she was considered troublesome and rebellious, battling constantly with authority. Her self-description included a notion of strength and a pride in this strength:

[T]he Charles children grew up with a sense that they came from people who were stronger, smarter and more hard-working than the people around them. "Look at them", Charles told an *Ebony* reporter in 1981, as she showed him framed photographs of her mother, father and grandparents that hang on the wall of her home. "Look at how they hold their mouths. Look at the thrust of their jaws. You can see the toughness in them, can't you? That's where I get mine." (Higbie 1993, 22–23)

This strength and toughness had both positive and negative effects for her during her period in office as prime minister. Charles's tenacity enabled her to remain in the opposition for a number of years, enduring biting verbal attacks from members of government and their supporters. Her motivation to continue in the political arena stemmed from her conviction and that of the other members of the Dominica Freedom Party that there was hope for a better Dominica – a place where the citizens enjoyed all human rights, particularly the right to freedom of speech.

In addition to the above qualities, Charles possessed skills that allowed her to provide political leadership to Dominicans. Her career as a lawyer cultivated a number of skills, such as her problem solving, listening and negotiating abilities, that she drew on during her political career, and she believed that it encouraged dialogue between the people and herself. In an interview with Levis Guy (reproduced in Brill 1995, 136–40), she stated: "I enjoyed my chosen career; I loved what I did as a lawyer, enjoyed it thoroughly. I enjoyed solving problems – not so much the court aspect, but that people came to me for advice. They'd tell me their problems and I would give them solutions."

This need to help and care for others has been reiterated by those close to her,[1] but it has also been identified as her other face, her private side to which she did not call attention (Honychurch 1995, 238). Charles summed it up perfectly in her interview with Levis Guy:

> Even before I came to politics officially the things that I was primarily interested in were young people, children, education, and caring for the elderly and the infirm. I did not think of this as social work; I thought I had the capability to serve my country. It may be because I was a woman or it may be my upbringing, but my family influence and background dictated that the best was always expected. Dominica was a relatively poor place and self-sufficiency was expected. I think self-sufficiency is the most important factor in life, taking what you have and making something beneficial of it. (Brill 1995, 140)

Charles herself spoke of her listening skills in her interview with the author, placing tremendous emphasis on the need to listen to others and her capacity to do so. She also believed that "people had a right to know what you were thinking, the direction you were taking, so they would be aware of what you were doing for them" (Charles 2002e). As a result, she encouraged weekly meetings at her law office in Roseau where she discussed critical issues affecting Dominica and the people. Charles Maynard, former minister in Charles's government, reported that she went to all the communities when she got elected (Maynard 2002b). For Charles, contact with the populace was important and she maintained this contact in simple ways; for example, by attending church services in a different village every Sunday. This was in contrast to the perception that she was far removed from the people, cold and aloof, which resulted in part from the *Educator's* portrayal of her as the "Danger Lady", "a cold, unloving person, incapable of caring for ordinary Dominicans" (Higbie 1993, 132).

Eugenia Charles's ability to negotiate served her well during her law career and as prime minister. These skills were very evident early in life when as head girl of her school she negotiated half-days off for cricket for the students.[2] In her first year as political leader, she was inundated with the country's economic hardships, devastations from hurricanes, unemployment and the need for the "restoration of confidence, discipline, pride, and an overall sense of national purpose among all Dominicans" (Honychurch 1995, 275). Her leadership skills were evident to her critics when, as Honychurch stated,

> Within months after the election Miss Charles had galvanized the Caribbean into taking a new opinion of Dominica and Dominicans and was steadily cementing international friendships so that by the middle of the 1980s Dominica and its Prime Minister Eugenia Charles had secured a position of high esteem within the councils of world affairs. (Honychurch 1995, 275)

There was a lighter side to Eugenia Charles that was proof of the diverse nature of her character. Friends and colleagues have related accounts of her sense of humour and the manner in which she dismissed people in a way that was humorous to everyone except the person to whom it was directed. Charles Maynard recounted some of her transactions with representatives of international agencies. He recalled an experience with an adviser from the United States Agency for International Development who made three quick trips to Dominica after Hurricane David to assess needs. Charles asked the adviser how much money he had spent on each trip; then she pointed out that with that money they could have built a school. She concluded by telling him that he should not return to Dominica unless he intended to provide aid. The adviser told Maynard that no one had ever spoken to him in that manner before. However, a grant from the agency arrived in Dominica within forty-eight hours (Maynard 2002b).

Motivational Factors and Charles's Entry into Politics

A number of Charles's friends, political allies and supporters have expressed the view that her entry into politics was accidental and unplanned. Her long-time friend and business associate Daphne Agar stated that "she entered politics because of desperation, somebody had to do something" (Agar 2002). However, her political career was no accident. This path had been paved a long time ago. It began during her childhood and continued throughout her formative years. Her family background, socialization and the educational preparation and opportunities she received all contributed to her selection of a political career. Her personality characteristics, those of being strong, forceful, formidable, caring, confident, outspoken, empowered her to examine and analyse situations in her environmental context that did not produce the kind of development that she believed Dominica needed. Higbie shared a similar perspective:

> Charles's political debut was in all likelihood less spontaneous than it is usually described. From the days when she sat as a schoolgirl at the dinner table at the Old Street house listening to J.B. talk about what he had told whom on the Legislative Council, her life had prepared her for politics. The stream of letters to the Editor in the 1950s and 1960s is proof that she had firm opinions on how the island's affairs should be run. (Higbie 1993, 94)

There were situational factors that motivated Charles to enter politics. She was motivated by the need to achieve change within her country. In her estimation, something had to be done to protect the rights of the citizens of Dominica. One such right was the right to publicly express one's view on any issue, whether or not it pertained to government and governmental matters. Miss Charles strongly opposed the Seditious and Undesirable Publications Act proposed by the LeBlanc administration, known as the "Shut-Your-Mouth Bill". This began her political activism with the Freedom Fighters, a group that included "a number of political independents drawn into the debate over press freedom as well as a number of DUPP survivors and former Labour Party members" (Higbie 1993, 89).[3]

Charles's strong sense of social justice not only propelled her into active politics, it also characterized her interactions both regionally and internationally. After soliciting the help of the US government in the Grenada invasion, Charles was asked by President Ronald Reagan to attend the press conference with him prior to the invasion. She recounted that they (US officials) were quite impressed with her "performance" with the US press. According to her, "I wasn't performing, quite frankly. I was being quite sincere and quite honest and answering the questions. I felt *people had the right to know, that was the important thing*" (Higbie 1993, 236).

Charles seemed to be motivated by the need to ensure that people's rights were protected and assured. At times, this motivation brought her into conflict with authorities and officials, but this never intimidated her. While at university overseas, she experienced racial discrimination while travelling or attempting to eat in restaurants. Unaccustomed to such treatment, Charles, without thinking of the consequences, would immediately confront the individuals involved.

A number of situational factors continued to motivate Charles during her ten-year period in the opposition, as she had to contend with a government characterized by shifting ideological positions.[4] She also had to confront numerous challenges: corruption and mismanagement of government funds, leadership issues within the Dominica Labour Party, the economic hardships facing Dominicans, social unrest and violence, to name a few. Her strength of character came into play during her long period in the opposition, as she had to endure verbal abuse from members of the government and suffer from the perception that she was elitist, manipulative and exploitative, and therefore should not be trusted to run the government. Throughout her public life, she showed that she was never afraid of a fight or an attack. So she never knew about retreating as an option and therefore returned as much abuse as she got.

Women and Gender Issues: The Impact of Eugenia Charles's Political Leadership

Throughout her political career and even in recent times, Eugenia Charles insisted that she was not a feminist and that she was simply a political leader who was a woman. In Dominica, there was also the perception that she did not focus on women and their issues and concerns. However, an examination of her political leadership revealed that she was aware of the differences in the operational styles of men and women and in the treatment that both groups received. She also recognized that male and female political leaders differed in the ideas that they pursued and the viewpoints they expressed. She acknowledged that being a woman made it more difficult, at times, for her to exercise her political leadership and exposed her to abuse and ridicule, particularly about her choice to remain unmarried and bear no children. Like other women in various top positions in different occupational areas, Charles had to tolerate questions about marriage and children, which were issues and questions that were never posed to male leaders.

Charles always made it clear that she had the interests of vulnerable groups at the centre of her activism. In the interview with Levis Guy, Charles was asked about her willingness to battle for the defenceless and the underprivileged. She responded, "I think it may be the instinctive part of womanhood. She thinks that she can teach and help people to care for themselves, to show them alternatives" (Brill 1995, 140).

Although Charles did not perceive that she had a major role as political leader to address women's and gender issues, she nevertheless promoted women, particularly women in the civil service. At one time during her time in office, Dominica had a female Speaker of the House, a female High Court judge and a female mayor of Roseau (Higbie 1993, 217). She acknowledged that women approached situations differently and as a result seemed to be more effective. She stated:

> I think women, and I have noticed it, in women not only in leadership but in the civil service, and in medical professions, are more detailed than men. Men have broad ideas and expect them to be carried out, but women have ideas and stick to it and try to do every little part themselves. They are more painstaking than men in that respect. (Brill 1995, 137)

In that interview with Levis Guy (Brill 1995), she further pointed out that

> Gender has no influence on a decision, though as I indicated before I think women have a more detailed and painstaking approach. We tend to take a lot more advice and research into things before a decision is made. I don't deliberately say I want a woman to do a particular job. I usually say I want the best person there is to do this job and quite often it is a woman. (quoted in Brill 1995, 139)

Charles appreciated the attributes that women brought to the job and conceded that female leadership, in many instances, resulted in greater attention being paid to social issues and problems, particularly those pertaining to women and children (Brill 1995). But she was not willing to engage in institutional change that would have minimized the number of obstacles and barriers that women encountered. She claimed that women in Dominica were not at a disadvantage as their salaries were equal to those of men and as they owned their properties. Women, she stated, could receive child support from men through the legal system (Higbie 1993, 218). However, her analysis was limited to certain groups of women, whose upbringing and class position afforded them the opportunities and tools to surmount some of these barriers. But even these women and Charles suffered gender discrimination because they operated in a context that suggested that women had specific roles and occupations to perform. As a political leader she experienced abuse and ridicule because she was expected to adhere to certain gender norms and rules. However, Charles dared to defy these rules and norms and entered a domain reserved for men. She was able to do this mainly because of her personality characteristics and her self-confidence. Although she emerged from a family environment that suggested that the children could become whatever they chose, it was organized along traditional gender lines – the mother was the homemaker and the father ran the business. Being a product of her upbringing, Charles understood the importance of power and traditional values. She publicly modelled her father's values and behaviours. He was the most influential person in her life, "[s]o in many ways he was my guide and mentor, a very hard-working man, a role model with very little education. I can now appreciate what he did for us" (Brill 1995, 136).

Charles's political leadership was generally described as autocratic and dictatorial. She was considered to be a firm, strong and outspoken leader who at times made harsh, unpopular decisions. As some of her political associates could attest, she took some strong decisions and positions on situations and individuals, which were necessary most of the time (Maynard 2002b; Edwards 2002a; Honychurch 2002b):

> As a leader you make decisions and you don't vary. Such is my personality. I listen
> very carefully to what is said. People think I don't listen, but I am able to make

decisions quickly, but I listen and weigh the statements and I am able to come to a decision promptly, and others may think that because of this I don't listen, but as I said before when you have listened you weigh statements and make a decision. If I am wrong I am quite happy to change. I am not stubborn about that, but I don't weigh things for one hundred years. I arrive at my decisions quickly. (Brill 1995, 138)

Eugenia Charles took over the leadership when Dominicans' faith and confidence in their leaders had to be restored. The country was suffering from a number of economic and social problems, corruption and mismanagement at top management level, wastage of government funds and devastation from natural disasters. Charles therefore had to rule with a firm hand. As Honychurch stated:

Miss Charles' detractors have accused her of an abrasive attitude towards resolving matters of state but the situation facing Dominica when she took office in 1980 could not have been tackled by excessive "sweet-talk" and a faint heart. It required strength and perseverance, which Miss Charles had learned the hard way during over ten years in opposition. For this reason she tends to be impatient with those people who do not share her capacity for strenuous resolve. (Honychurch 1995, 284)

As prime minister, Charles enhanced the landscape of Dominica by sponsoring road repairs, providing electricity, telephones and cable television, building new schools and implementing other national projects. She exposed Dominica to the international world and gained the respect of international leaders worldwide. This enabled Dominicans to take pride once again in their country and their leaders. But she was not fully able to achieve one of her most important developmental goals, that of "self-sufficiency". As Lennox Honychurch (1995) remarked, Charles "did not bring about a change in thinking in the people". She relied so heavily on foreign aid to improve the conditions for Dominicans and had to battle so constantly with the opposition that she could not concentrate on translating her larger vision for the country into action. Higbie (1993) summed up the situation perfectly when she wrote that Charles "remained committed to the mechanics of constitutional democracy", but what was missing was the "spirit of a democracy, the feeling that ordinary people had the right to ask questions and be consulted on government decisions".

Conclusion

To say that Eugenia Charles was born to be a leader would be somewhat clichéd. She was certainly born into a family and circumstances that allowed her to develop her leadership abilities, qualities and skills. Charles's background and upbringing, and her life in two contrasting places, Pointe Michel and Roseau, enabled her to experience different facets of her being. On one hand, she lived a very simple life, not given to excesses, and therefore she could identify with the people in the villages and appreciate and understand their needs and wants. On the other hand, she was sophisticated, well spoken, confident and ready to interact or battle with the best of them. She was a lawyer and this allowed her to connect with a wide range of individuals, but this career also provided her with the knowledge and tools necessary for political life and leadership. As a political leader, she provided a role model for all females who displayed an interest in politics and who had the potential for political leadership. Although she refuted the notion that she was a feminist, her years in opposition and the spirit of her leadership reflected some of the ideals of feminism and an appreciation of how the power differentials impact on vulnerable groups, particularly women.

Eugenia Charles entered politics at a time when males dominated the political sphere and she was therefore exposed to a masculine, autocratic model of leadership that she emulated. It could be stated that some of her personality characteristics predisposed her to adopt this leadership style, but the situational factors promoted her continued use of the autocratic leadership style.

Notes

1. All those interviewed by the author commented on the fact that she was moti-
    vated by the need to help others, but there was the perception in the wider
    society that she was unfeeling and did not care about the welfare of those in the
    working class.
2. Janet Higbie (1993) provided evidence that Charles's leadership and negotiating
    abilities were formed early in her life.
3. This refers to the Dominica United People's Party (DUPP) which was led by
    Frank Baron, who became Dominica's first chief minister in 1960 (Honychurch
    1995, 230).
4. According to Honychurch (1984; 1995), foreign observers were puzzled by
    Patrick John's government because he seemed to be supporting left-wing
    Caribbean politics as represented by Cuba and Guyana, yet dismissed two
    cabinet ministers after accusing them of communist tendencies.

6

Mary, Mary, Quite Contrary
Calypso Images of Eugenia Charles

KETURAH CECILIA BABB

Introduction

Public debate has often charged Caribbean constitutions with granting excessive powers to prime ministers. The constitution of the Commonwealth of Dominica, like that of many other Caribbean states, confers a wide range of powers on the office of the prime minister. Mary Eugenia Charles, prime minister of Dominica from 1980 to 1995, proved to be comfortable with the fullest exercise of the powers vested in that office. Charles's absolute self-assurance may well have ascribed impeccability to her actions, but many of these were controversial and did not endear her to a significant number of Dominicans at home and abroad.

Daring, decisive, acutely conscious of her personal power and ready to show the world that she was fearless, Eugenia Charles led the Dominica Freedom Party for two and a half decades without any serious challenge to her leadership. She retired from elective politics at the end of her third term as prime minister, preserving her powerful public image. At home she was a serious "Mama"; outside Dominica she was known as the "Iron Lady" of the Caribbean.

As we try to capture the story of Caribbean politics, where exactly should this woman prime minister be placed in the pantheon of Caribbean women who are catalysts for change? What was her contribution to societal or political transformation? I am a RastafarI[1] woman who was born in Dominica and resided there until 1987 when I relocated to Barbados. I am interested in exploring Charles's personal use of power and I am preoccupied with the meanings of power. When a person is described as powerful, what does that really mean? Is it the degree to which one imposes personal will upon immediate situations? Is it the degree to which people with whom one works and interacts on a daily basis are intimidated by one's personality, and afraid of expressing their point of view? Is it the extent to which one can transform people's lives for the better: the extent to which one enables others to achieve? Is it the degree of long-term positive change one is able to bring about in a society and nation, or the extent to which one's presence is noted? Is a powerful person at once fearsome and empowering or are these two aspects of power mutually exclusive? I attempt to clarify Charles's legacy to Dominicans, as a means of finding out exactly why the only woman prime minister of the region to date is invariably described as powerful.

From the moment Charles appeared on international television beside then US President Ronald Reagan, fielding questions about the military intervention in Grenada, she was dubbed the "Iron Lady", and the word "powerful" became indelibly attached to her name.[2] I try to use an empowerment paradigm to evaluate the ways in which Eugenia Charles was powerful. I analyse her leadership in relation to her impact on Dominicans in general and search for the sites of people's empowerment during her fifteen years of formal political leadership at the highest level of decision making. I do this primarily by examining how local calypsos portrayed her during those years.

I do not clearly recall when or how I first became aware of Eugenia Charles. Her nomination to the House of Assembly in 1970[3] does not stand out in my mind since the woman whose presence in politics first impressed me was Mrs Mable Moir James.[4] I first paid attention to Charles after the passage of the "Dread Act". The act had dreadful implications for my life, and its passage led me to contemplate the meaning and use of state power. The events of 29 May 1979 in Dominica heightened my reflections on power, and the role of Dominica's prime minister in "resolving" the political events that unfolded in Grenada in October 1983 made my questions about the use of power even more acute.

My inquiry is preoccupied with the prime minister's record of good governance, an issue that was at the heart of political change when she came into office. Mary Eugenia Charles is among the last of an era of charismatic leaders in the Caribbean. These were people who led by personal appeal rather than a record of performance. However, this investigation is pertinent to a leader who was elected at a moment when governance had been severely fractured and the nation sought the best prospects for its repair. Her task was to return the country to civic stability, to validate the citizen's right to choose and to dissent, to restore honour to political leadership and to stabilize the economy.

Charles's speeches reveal a full understanding of her citizens' expectations. She often espoused her personal philosophy of good governance and her intention to allow Dominicans to participate in the governance of the nation. In this chapter I share the evidence, or lack thereof, as found in local calypsos, of Charles's delivery of those promises.

Power to the People?

Dominica was one of the participating countries in the 1999 Citizens and Governance Programme of the Commonwealth Foundation. The exercise found that all over the Commonwealth citizens now want the opportunity for strong, healthy connections between them and their governments. They are of the view that state, private sector and citizens have a role in human development. Citizens want a strong state as well as a strong civil society. They want a deepened democracy and democratic culture: a compact involving citizens, the state and intermediary organizations (Commonwealth Foundation 2002, 5).

These ideas are not entirely new to the Caribbean. Kenneth Valley, minister of trade in the Government of Trinidad and Tobago, reminded participants at a seminar in 2003 of the prominent role of civil society in the labour and nationalist struggles of the region.[5] He recalled that Caribbean history is replete with examples of ways in which citizens, through "pressure groups", have sought to impact the governance of their countries. They have written letters to newspapers, or through other media, demanding to be heard. At different moments since Emancipation, friendly societies, Garveyite groups, trade unions, youth groups, social groups, church groups, Black Power organizations, consumer groups and housewives' associations have been channels through which ordinary people demanded greater involvement in national affairs. During the twentieth century, the first generation to enjoy universal adult suffrage may have been content to allow elected governments to function undisturbed, but since independence the masses have felt entitled to know what governments are doing for their country and to express their views and make suggestions. In addition to demands for the satisfaction of basic needs, good health, a sound education for their children and the enjoyment of peace and security, people have also clung to the belief that they ought to be able to express their views on the ruling government without fear of victimization. And they have rebelled whenever they felt too cut off from national affairs. Often the calypso was the first vehicle for launching protest.

When Eugenia Charles came into office it was common to speak, in the language of the time, of leaders who "raised people's consciousness" and "Black Power", rather than "empowerment". However, consciousness embodies the acquisition of knowledge and a drive to action – the elements of empowerment. When the state regularly shares information with its citizens in a timely fashion, listens to their views on national issues and provides resources that enable them to implement collective decisions, it is sharing its power with the nation. When leaders make room for all citizens to participate in national decision-making processes, empowerment takes place at all levels, institutional capacity grows and positive social change occurs.

A former prime minister of Jamaica, in contemplating power, observed, "politics is the business of power, its acquisition and its use" (Manley 1974, 15). He noted three main approaches to the use of power: tyrannical, pragmatic and idealistic. Tyrants exercise power at the expense of everyone else and are therefore liable to sudden and violent elimination. The pragmatic politician is content to make marginal adjustments in the organization of society for the purpose of relieving discontent and removing points of pressure. Idealistic politicians are concerned with change, but they must articulate the moral foundations for political change and action (Manley 1974, 16). Manley was convinced of the need for political change that would make people a part of the decision-making processes of government. He considered decentralization to be one of the keys to achieving a sense of popular involvement in national governance.

William Demas examined power in the national context.[6] He defined power as the ability on the part of an individual or group or country to make decisions affecting them and others (Demas 1975, 6). Aware that the limits of relative power between two parties are not immutably fixed, he differentiated between latent power and actual power, and advised that the latent power of a group can be mobilized only to the extent that capacity, consciousness, discipline and organization are present. He explained that actual power may often be accompanied by the use of force, either actual or threatened. However, compliance with the dictates of those in power may be secured because the wielder of power possesses authority, and in that sense, power as control of the state machinery may be achieved without violence. Power in that case arises from the consciousness of the people, who can be mobilized to realize their potential. In the Caribbean context the spread of formal democratic institutions internally and the attainment of political independence externally opened space for people to acquire some degree of power. Later, as Demas deliberated on change and renewal in the Caribbean, he acknowledged the need to "re-appraise systems and styles of government and authority with a view to providing for greater participation and for the free airing of rational dissent" (Demas 1975, 56).

On page 1 of its Constitution, Eugenia Charles's Dominica Freedom Party proclaimed, "People before Power, People before Politicians, People before Privilege and Things." While in office she professed that she understood the exercise of power to be a reciprocal relationship "in which claims of authority are respected and obeyed on condition that authority respects the claims of the common good and promotes human welfare" (Charles 1987, 4). Charles stressed to the people of Dominica "the need for vigilance, the need to ensure that the reins of Government are only entrusted to persons who can be trusted" (Dominica 1981d, 4). She wanted Dominicans to have the drive to take decisions and to implement their decisions, because she wanted to provide opportunities for all Dominicans to participate in the development process at community and national levels. She planned to welcome foreign investors only on condition that their activities and plans were consonant with national plans and objectives. To her, people were the most important of the three resources that Dominica possessed (Dominica 1983b, 6–12), and she felt a special responsibility to nurture and train the youth population to play their part in building the economy.

Charles marked out her parameters for good governance in her speeches to the nation. From the start she invited all citizens to participate in the efforts of government to build and develop the nation (Dominica 1981d, 18). She promised involvement of the community in the promotion and development of its own health care. She encouraged the public to comment on a bill before it became law (Dominica 1982b, 5–7). She declared popular participation in local development activities a policy of the Government of Dominica. This meant having activities identified from the outset by the people in the community to be served. Active participation by all Dominicans included giving the grower a more active role in the banana industry (Dominica 1982a, 3–5). It also meant setting up two committees: one to assist in clearing difficulties that sometimes arise, and the other to give the private sector the opportunity to comment on and to assist in moulding government policy (Dominica 1983a, 6).

These promises were renewed during her second term of office, and by the time she addressed the Philadelphia Bar Association in 1987, she claimed that she had been able to instil in Dominicans "a sense of involvement and participation in the development process at all levels and thereby buttress their commitment to the democratic ideals" (Charles 1987, 7). Eugenia Charles expanded her promises even further during her third term of office: "We will continue to respond to whatever valid and intelligent proposals that are put forward by the Opposition or the public at large for improvements in our policies or the development strategies that we employ" (Dominica 1992a, 10–11). She also reiterated, "the banana farmer must be given the facilities to become a stakeholder of the industry" (Charles 1993, 11).

Charles's address to the nation at the sixteenth anniversary of independence could not hold any more promises. It was her last address in the capacity of prime minister. She had already made public her decision not to contest the next general election. She had already enumerated, in the previous year, what she considered to have been her successes achieved "through firm and decisive governance" (Dominica 1994c, 9). In her parting address she asserted, "never before in our history have our people been given the opportunity for self-development as they have over the past ten years" (Dominica 1994c, 15–16).

The calypsonian "General Natty" did not agree.[7] At the first opportunity, he highlighted a number of instances where good governance was lacking: issues about which, "before she go, I'll ask her" (General Natty 1995). His renderings were in the same vein as those of "DBS", the calypsonian who sought a messenger to "Tell Eugenia" that he wanted "things better" (DBS 1994). The many calypsos that addressed the leadership of Mary Eugenia Charles do not chronicle her as having delivered on the promises to involve people in the governance of the country. Many calypsos highlight her failure to do so. The lyrics of the calypso "Viva Mama Eugenia", which may have promoted her even before the general election that chose her as leader, could not be obtained; neither could the identity of the calypsonian who sang it be verified. The three praise songs of Carnival 1981 with which the nation welcomed her as prime minister gave way to songs of disquiet and criticism even before her first term was completed. Subsequent calypsos about her spoke to the pain that she caused former admirers. Later calypsos went on to warn her about "wrong things" (Loblack 1984; Aaron 1984; Cyrille 1986), advised her to desist and sometimes even condemned her: "I will make de girl mad, mad, mad" (DBS 1994).

The Voices of the People

Calypsos are said to be historically related to West African songs of derision, exemplified in the practice of Halo among the Ewes of the Gold Coast, modern-day Ghana (Roberts 1988, 165). The calypso art form is a product of the creole society that emerged in the Caribbean as a result of Spanish, French and British occupation from the fifteenth century onwards, in a colonization sustained by African slavery and the indentured labour of other ethnic groups. The calypso form is constantly undergoing change. There are vast differences between its more obscure early origins and the calypso of the late twentieth and early twenty-first centuries. The calypso in Trinidad society also represented the verbal outrage and declarations of a group who were virtually powerless in the scheme of things, emerging initially out of slavery and colonialism as entertainment combined with social protest: "Calypso relies on rhetoric, humor, and clever wit to bring the message home. Eloquence and verbal skill became . . . power" (Mohammed 2003).

Through double entendre, the singer conveyed ideas of rebellion and resistance to the indignities of slavery and post-slave society, disguising his or her outspokenness behind laughter and innuendo. As an art form the calypso continued to offer the singer, generally men in the earlier days of the twentieth century, the space from which they could articulate the grievances of the class or community to which the singer belonged. The success of the calypso depended on the extent to which the singer or songwriter had tapped into the shared sentiments or popular ideas of people in the society (Mohammed 2003).

The actual shifts which may occur in the form of the calypso result from the events of different historical times and from the changes in economic conditions. As one would expect in a creative musical form, it is also continuously influenced by changes in musical ideas and instrumentation. The calypso as an art form is versatile and resilient within the culture, particularly because it is also in continuous dialogue with itself (Mohammed 2003). One of the modern idioms of calypso is "Soca", a combination of soul and calypso. There is also a variant called "Ragga Soca".

In essence, calypsos are one manifestation of people's power – cultural power that they have forged for themselves as part of their psychological survival. Borrowed from Dominica's neighbour, Trinidad, the calypso in Dominican culture is regarded as the voice of the people. Calypsos are highly prized for exposing national issues and events to public scrutiny and reflection. The calypsonian is a social commentator in the oral tradition who has the freedom to speak out on issues.[8] Calypsos are presented during the season of Carnival, previously Masquerade, that takes place in either February or March each year before the start of Lent. A formal calypso competition is held, a monarch is crowned and prizes are awarded to competitors. Written and performed by nationals, and usually intended primarily for the local setting, calypso is an authentic record of popular sentiment. Each calypsonian usually adopts a stage name, which is intended to convey a particular bias or mission. For example, the calypsonian who adopted "DBS" as a sobriquet was sending the message that his role was to inform the nation. "DBS" is the acronym for "Dominica Broadcasting Services".

More than twenty calypsos were performed about Eugenia Charles during her tenure, with at least one more after she stepped down.[9] There are other calypsos that obliquely refer to her or mention her but are not primarily about her leadership. The calypsonian Pat Aaron, who sings under the stage name "Musician" and commented on the lady prime minister in at least three calypsos, explained why singing about her was so topical: "She scared away all opposition. Only the calypsonians were not afraid of her" (Aaron 2002). "Musician" admitted that Dame Eugenia had some of the qualities necessary for leading a nation. She inspired respect and fear. He credited her with stabilizing the economy and the security situation in the country. During her tenure there were "no gangs, a good Police Force, and both the public and private sector respected her" (Aaron 2002). However, there was much in the personality of Eugenia Charles that alienated many sections of the population as her tenure progressed. Contrary to her often-repeated promise to facilitate citizen's participation, "she was not a consultative person" (Aaron 2002).

Calypsos performed at Carnival the year following Charles's election in 1980 showed that her popularity was at an all-time high. The calypsonian "Element" first named her "Lady of the Year" in the junior competition. The calypso was so well received that he performed it in the Monarch Competition under the title "Eugie the Highest". The calypso paid homage directly to the prime minister, then explained to the audience why she was deserving of the honour bestowed. No specific events were mentioned in the calypso because its sole purpose was to award praise, to endear, to elevate:

> *Lady of the Year Eugie the Highest*
>
> Shine on, Shine on
> Shine on little lady
> Shine bright, shine bright
> Shine bright your majesty
> Some were not looking up to you
> Admiring the things you do
> Though you wont believe it

Yes, it's true
You are the hardest
You are the baddest
Eugenia Charles
You are the Woman of the Year . . .

While "Element" ascribed many virtues to Eugenia Charles due to her attaining the status of becoming "the first woman of the Caribbean ever to be head of any country" without providing a historical context, two other calypsonians, "Checker" and "Zeye", make more direct references to the events which propelled her to power. "Checker" was happy to see the end of Patrick John's government:

For twenty long years we have been getting blows
They wanted to sell Dominica to South Africa
We ain't want to see . . .
Nor John, nor Austin
So now I'm singing Soca for my new Prime Minister
Brave strong Eugenia, is now my new leader.

"Zeye" was more than happy. In "Hold Dem Down Miss Eugie" he celebrated Charles's election to the highest office by the fact that she was using her power. He urged her on:

All those that want to crook,
Are now being stalk by the Freedom hook.
I tell you hold dem down
Eugie say hold dem down
Oh, ho ho hold dem down
She say give dem till de Judgment Day
Oh, ho ho hold dem down
Ms Mary say hold dem down

The new prime minister, according to the calypsonian, was already demonstrating her power. She has "sentenced" the offenders of good governance to the fullest extent possible. "Zeye" was comfortable with Eugenia Charles's exercise of power in 1981 and attributed her position to divine intervention: "Oh me Lord you put a hand on Election Day." Similarly he returned in 1982 to rejoice that she had survived the two attempts to topple her government. Again he thought that this was divine intervention: "De Lord help us and put a helping hand / We won't fall by de gun."

That same year the calypsonian "Spide" also approved of the prime minister's use of power. He too made allusions to divine interventions, for he was inspired while praying for "solutions to heal Dominica . . . / Go tell Eugenia and Rhonan David" that they should not procrastinate in writing their will concerning the guilty and that these persons should be condemned. If the prime minister and her attorney general did not act quickly enough, the very Lord, "Spider" implied, would be "coming soon" to deal with the matter.

After 1982 there are apparently no praise songs for Eugenia Charles. By Carnival 1983 the calypsonian "Tronada" was uneasy about the Freedom Fighters. As far as he was concerned Dominicans seemed headed towards bondage: "Once you were free to fight / Now you must fight to be free". In 1984 Levi Loblack sang "Mother Mary" under his own name (Levi) and employed satire to warn Dominicans that he could no longer endorse some of the ways that Eugenia Charles used her power. Her role in the invasion of Grenada was the main theme of his calypso:

Chorus
Mother Mary you a terror
Mother Mary you act like a saviour
You and Ronald Reagan join hands in a invasion
To destroy de leftist plans
They call dem son-of-a-gun.
Oh Mother Mary
Yeah, you got personality
Oh Mother Mary
Yeah, you impress me on TV

In the first verse Levi cautioned Eugenia Charles that her use of power in that event was misguided, though there would be short-term gain in her involvement in a struggle between two superpowers (America and Russia) for world supremacy. In the second verse he exposed what he saw as her gullibility:

I never know you could convince de White House so
De mission was such a positive step I know

> But all de time de president know
> Arms accumulating for Caribbean overthrow
> You see, Reagan's defence minister always watching his radar
> Grenada was always covered . . .

According to Levi, Charles was also a busybody and an opportunist. Levi offered a few suggestions about how she might better use her power at home:

> . . . not to forget your cleaning
> Factories in the stadium is a wrong 'ting
> Our 'ting, our 'ting
> You see de nation is watching you constructing
> You see they see mamie rising
> Keeping dem wondering
> If there will be a next colonel, or a general
> I hear is bumble bee

The young Levi spoke for all the youth who lamented the prime minister's construction of factory sheds on the site of the sports stadium in Canefield. The seats and amenities of the former stadium had been damaged by Hurricane David in 1979, but much of the wall was left standing. Charles chose to build factories there as part of the incentive package for attracting foreign investment. This was definitely not an occasion when she consulted the relevant stakeholders.

She also did not consult them about resource allocations to the police force at the expense of other needy sectors: "I see you training de policeman doh."

The former prime minister had styled himself an army colonel. Eugenia Charles's behaviour in relation to the political events in Grenada worried Levi. He had believed that she was a genuinely better choice than Patrick John, until the moment when he saw Aston Benjamin[10] give himself up to the police. The police were seeking out members of the Defence Force who had been involved in the attempted coup, yet Benjamin was shot dead in full view of bystanders.

> Boy, that Saturday morning, when I see Benjie bleeding
> Is when I realize what I believing
> Although he surrender like a fish under plunder

Once de army want you
They'll execute you . . .

When Levi saw the lady prime minister align herself with others to invade
Grenada he felt that this also was a "wrong ting". He could no longer sup-
press his misgivings about the way she was using her power. Ashton
Benjamin was not among those who, as Eugenia Charles applauded her
democratic practice in Philadelphia, "were brought to justice and imprisoned" (Charles 1987, 6).

Pat "Musician" Aaron also used a slow satire to lodge a number of complaints about the prime minister's office in 1984. The idea and initial lyrics
for "Mama" were suggested to him by another calypsonian, Cleve Jean
Jacques, who sings under the name "Hurricane". Once "Musician" was
drawn to the idea, they worked together to complete the calypso. "Mama"
was sung in the same competition in which Levi appealed to "Mother
Mary" not to convert the police force to another army. Levi and
"Musician" shared several concerns, but "Musician" sang about much more
than the invasion of Grenada.

I have a strict strict mama
She is the most serious mother in the universe
My robust looking mama
Any problem, anywhere, she could solve it first
She still running de house at de old age of 60
Who working, who going to school, and who have baby
She command respect from everybody
She is a woman of great vigour and personality
She too robust: indeed, she controlling all de money
Imagine, she does control daddy
By de time I'm through with this melody
You sure to see, why our whole life in misery

Chorus
Can't you see times are changing
De rules and regulations you make in de house
Will drive us crazy
Respect we have for you mamie
But de wrong things we see we must say
So things could go right in de family

Discipline we know we need to build de future
But dat doh mean you should go on like a monster
If I had a choice to stay with you mama, or leave Dominica
I'd take a pui-pui to Africa, anywhere, not here![11]

"Musician" emphasized several failures: "the family" was not happy.
Although Mama was capable, Mama was respected, Mama was in control,
Mama was doing "wrong things" in steadfastly implementing the structural
adjustment policies and prioritizing debt repayment. It pained the nation
that while she urged wage restraint, she used her constitutional powers to
raise the salaries of parliamentarians early in her first and second terms of
office. He also highlighted that emigration to neighbouring islands and
places further away was one response to the disappointment felt over several breaches of good governance. Deep demoralization surfaces in verse
two. Charles did not consult; in fact, not even cabinet members could
speak their minds; civil servants dared not offer advice in their areas of
expertise; farmers' views were not taken into account. Meanwhile, upgrading the police force continued to be a priority for government expenditure
while nurses' needs were neglected, sports facilities were left to decay and
the public was denied information.

In the chorus that followed, "Musician" contemplates slipping into
Guadeloupe, illegally if necessary. His next desperate idea is migration to
Cuba to find a job cutting sugar cane. In addition to not rebuilding the stadium, Mama ignored other sports facilities. "Mama" had abandoned the
values enshrined in the national anthem. The level of people's empowerment in Dominica was low.

"Musician" sang "Mama" during Carnival 1984. The next general elections took place on 1 July 1985. Salary increases were negotiated for civil
servants just prior to the election (Dominica 1986, 7). The Freedom Party
was returned to power with fifteen seats, and the prime minister received
the second highest number of votes within her party. "Musician" seemed
not to reflect the popular sentiment when it is considered that 75.56 per
cent of the total registered voters made their mark one year after he sang
his calypso.

Just nine months after Eugenia Charles received that major vote of confidence from the electorate, Morris "Ency" Cyrille took up the role of

spokesperson for the nation during Carnival 1986. He warned Charles, "Doh Rock de Boat". He reported on the degree to which she failed to empower her people and affirmed that Dominicans wanted to give her their support, but there were "things you do wrong" that should be highlighted:

> Mamo I would like you to lend an ear
> Let's talk about some other things I hear
> People are grumbling, showing signs of discontent
> They claim you treating them with contempt
> Ma, they say you are now beginning to practice
> All those low-down tricks
> Against which you preach
> They say you become so arrogant, ruthless and a tyrant
> Stuck up by your importance

This was very strong language. "Element had pointed out in 1981 that the prime minister was not an "idealist": this had been widely interpreted then to mean that she was a pragmatist. But by 1986 "Ency" was reporting that some of her citizens saw her as a "tyrant", the most negative manifestation of her use of power. He provided what he saw as evidence in the next verse:

> But you have been lapsing very badly of late
> Policemen feel misused, civil servants humbled
> Your very supporters, dem you have subdued . . .

"Ency" implored the prime minister to listen to the people's demands, respect her citizens and surround herself with good advice; otherwise, he warned, "de Freedom Party will sink before 1990". In 1986 "Musician" was by no means silent. Lamenting the loss of values and practices long accepted because "It's Traditional", he grew bitter in the last verse: "woman in government / . . . when she is in authority / she lacks human sympathy." Yet another calypsonian, Artherley "Venturer" Winston, was of the same opinion. Also singing in 1986 he explained:

> When I assess conditions in Parliament
> De men and dem they ain't worth a cent
> De ays have it, and they must agree
> Otherwise they marching home shamefully

A fourth calypsonian, "Rabbit", added to the list of those with grievances that year. He admitted to eavesdropping on "My Grandmother's
Prayer". Among many other woes, his grandmother recalled:

> . . . remember Eugenia as Opposition Leader
> back illegal strike to overthrow PJ
> Now we strike for her to pay
> De same Mamo shouting, no way![12]

This was a reference to loss of pay by striking civil servants and spoke to
one of the major ways in which Dominicans were disempowered by the
leader in whom so much confidence had been vested. Charles had built
strong alliances with the local labour movement during her years in opposition. This close relationship proved to be the movement's undoing during
the period of her administration. Rabbit's grandmother did not single out
the prime minister for criticism. She admonished each politician – past and
present, administration and opposition – that only "Papa Bon Dieu" (God
the Father) really had power. But she reserved her last words to comment
again on Eugenia Charles's use of her power. Grandmother told Rabbit
about

> . . . Thomas Baptiste son
> Government wanted to make him a magistrate
> But de John Rose Lindsay case
> Turn their love for him now to hate.

The youth with dreadlocks, John Rose Lindsay, had been arrested one
Saturday afternoon in front of the Carib Cinema, on lower Kennedy
Avenue, Roseau, in full view of the crowd of persons purchasing movie
tickets. His body was seen floating down the Layou River on the next day,
Sunday. The fate of the young lawyer who pursued the case on behalf of
Lindsay's family is referred to above.

"Rabbit" did not need his grandmother's memory to inform his presentation in 1988. His "Three Percent Calypso" commented on the fact that
the public were not consulted before ministers of government "sign all
kind of treaty" which subjected the poor to "levy" and "taxing continually". He also demanded information:

> I hearing 'bout big scandal
> Bob Woodward say hundred 'thou'

Bring the story to light
Before OECS can unite

Bob Woodward reported that Eugenia Charles received a payoff of US$100,000 for her role in the invasion of Grenada (Report of the Americas 1990, 36; Woodward 1987). "General Natty" also asked for clarification on that allegation in 1995. The prime minister's integrity was called into question for several years over that claim. In 1981 she had promised that her government would not "deprive the revenue of its fair share" (Charles 1981, 4). According to Bob Woodward, she had done so by 1983. Since she acted in her capacity as prime minister of Dominica when she intervened in Grenada, any "aid" belonged to the treasury.

Sources at Kairi FM Radio informed that Cleve Jean Jacque ("Hurricane") complained one year that rising prices brought on "Utility Pressure". Another calypsonian had exposed the plight of anyone unfortunate enough to be "Farmer Banana", meaning that the banana controlled the farmer. The lyrics of these calypsos were not found; neither were those of other calypsonians such as "President Lilly", "Black Ghost", "Superior Picky" and "Scrunter" who also commented on Eugenia Charles (Allen 2002).

Eugenia Charles's leadership continued to be a subject for calypsonians during her third term. Albert Mendes, "De Man Himself", sang "Iron Lady" in 1990:

Iron Lady we admire you
Only good things that you say and do
Iron Lady you so rough
Iron Lady you so tough
Iron Lady you try all your best
And your country really need progress

Chorus
Even though they talk
Even though they mock
You solid, solid as a rock ...

The results of the subsequent 1990 general election, three months after he sang, did not show Eugenia Charles to be "solid as a rock". She received 1,245 votes, 395 fewer than the 1,640 votes received in the 1985 general election. Voter participation had dropped in 1990 to 66.64 per cent of the registered electorate, almost 8 per cent less than in 1985 (Dominica 1990b, 11,15). In 1990, Charles received fewer votes than three colleagues within her party. It was also the year that her opponent in the general election gained 717 votes, the highest number ever scored against her. Did "De Man Himself" set out to deride the prime minister or was he a genuine admirer? The use of "Iron Lady" in Dominica to refer to Charles suggests the former, because it is out of step with the common names by which the prime minister was called. Dominicans do not call Eugenia Charles "Iron Lady". It was never used in the many other calypsos that criticized her immediately after the events which led to her being dubbed "Iron Lady". In recalling that name in the Dominican context "Iron Lady" ridiculed rather than affirmed Eugenia Charles.

From the 1980 praise song "Viva Mama Eugenia" to the 1995 critique "I'll Ask Her", the prime minister is variously addressed as Eugie, Mama, Mother, Mamie, Mamo, and even a plaintive Ma and Mamaah. "Eugie" fits within accepted local culture in which endearment is sometimes expressed by contracting a person's real name to a shortened form known as a "pet name", so that Eugenia becomes Eugie. "Mama" is the local patois word used to address one's mother. The shortened "Ma" is a form of endearment, used to express affection or to appeal to a mother's affection. If one is really begging and pleading with "Mama", the drawn-out form – "Mamaah" – comes into use. "Ma" is also a term of respect for addressing any woman assumed to be of one's mother's age group. Nationally Eugenia Charles was embraced and respected as the typical Mama who held family life together, especially when Papa proved reprobate, delinquent and a vagabond.

"Mamo" is an unusual variant of "Mama". "Musician" explained that Vic Riviere, of the Labour Party, first used the word "Mamo" at a political meeting in the eastern village of La Plaine. Acoustically, "Mamo" was more effective in an open-air meeting than "Mama", since the sound of "o" carries much further than the sound of "a" (Aaron 2002). Corruption of "Mama" to "Mamo" effectively conveyed political opposition and the word is only used in that sense. The use of "Iron Lady" before a Dominican audience went beyond political opposition or literary satire to full-fledged ridicule. This was an indication of how far Eugenia Charles's popularity had declined in some quarters during her ten years in office. However, if "De Man Himself" was indeed expressing admiration and support for Eugenia Charles in his calypso "Iron Lady", then I must conclude that he admired her in her "military" aspect.

Governance in Dominica continued to be worrisome to calypsonians. In 1994 "DBS" needed someone to "Tell Eugenia" that "last year was harder, this year I want it better". His song dealt with the rising cost of living and the challenges to the banana grower. "General Natty" was more direct. He could not be quiet.

> I say you gone too far
> Inciting hatred instead of love
> . . . division keep floating higher . . .

"General Natty" spoke of the economic hardships, decline of bananas, rising prices, mass migration, the pain of watching brothers and sisters try to cope. The material hardships were bad enough but that situation was made intolerable by the prime minister's attitude:

> Everyone do make mistake
> Apologies we will accept
> Why each time you do some wrong
> On it you playing barjan [bad John]
> Mamaah, Mamaah . . .

He was disappointed with the standard of governance: "I see in de house where they playing cat and mouse." He wanted the prime minister to share information and clear the rumours about "plots and counter plots". "General Natty" wanted to know the truth about Woodward's disclosure. He also wanted to know whether life would be paradise if Dominicans accepted Eugenia Charles's chosen successor. Charles had opposed the Party's choices for leadership and had publicly campaigned for her choice (Maynard 2002c; Sorhaindo 2002; Jno Charles 2002). "General Natty" was really hurt:

> . . . But I am telling you frankly
> You pin distress on we.

The calypsos indict Charles as not having fulfilled her many promises of good governance. In the opinion of the calypsonians she did not use her power to include the people in the affairs of the country. She withheld information from citizens and refused to admit errors in judgement, and over time her name became attached to acts not of the highest integrity. The verdict of many of the calypsonians is that Charles hurt, disappointed and disrespected Dominicans. Her breaches of good governance disempowered them and the calypsos were their means of telling her where she erred. But are these calypso images of the prime minister authentic? Were the men who mounted the calypso stage to sing about Charles merely being "macho" towards the woman prime minister, as in Artherley Winston's "Woman Taking Over" or Pat Aaron's "It's Traditional"? Are the accusations leveled at her true? Did the calypsos indeed reflect public concern?

The art form of calypso found a place in Dominican culture as an English crossover from the tradition of Creole patois contests, riddles and maxims embedded in slave, maroon and Carib folklore and forms of entertainment. The Caribs of Dominica have a rich lore of tales and legends which have all but disappeared with the loss of the Carib languages. Some of them were told by older people and were recorded as they were given in local French Creole between 1938 and 1941. There were celestial myths, local legends and tales told purely for entertainment (Taylor 1972, 44). The villages of Westley and Marigot are distinct for their cocoy 'torie, stories told in a dialect distinct from Creole patois and Carib languages. Dominica had an ingrained culture of large families gathering to tell stories around the dim light of kerosene lamps, or villagers visiting each other on moonlit nights and telling "jumbie stories" late into the night. It is within this cultural bedrock that calypso found an easy home among its relatives.

During slavery the enslaved gathered on Sundays and holidays to play music, sing and dance. Among other features there were children's play songs, songs for wakes, work-songs, songs of sadness and songs of joy, religion and celebration (Honychurch 1975, 45). With Emancipation, the freed people brought the festival of Masquerade – strongly Afro-French – into the streets. Bands from neighbouring villages joined to flout and tear down the standards of the upper class. Chantuelles led in singing the *chanté mas* while the people sang the *lavway*. For a long period Masquerade was a brief annual revolt of the Dominican masses against a society which, for the rest of the year, demanded their obedience. The best chanson exposed a social scandal, or a social personality or a piece of injustice (Honychurch 1975, 94). The Chantuelles were the lead female singers, *chanté mas* was the most popular song of the Masquerade and the chansons were the various songs, while the *lavway* was the chorus. Singing and storytelling in Dominican lore were characterized by call and response; the degree of response signalled approval of the topic and lyrics. A tragic fire during the Masquerade of 1963 caused an official ban of many of the typical Masquerade costumes. Dominicans began to borrow ideas from Trinidad and the Masquerade began to change rapidly to include many elements of Trinidad's Carnival (Honychurch 1975, 95). Many of the patois *chanté mas* were gradually replaced by calypsos.

Calypsos are presented for entertainment, hence their place in the pre-Lenten festivities. Calypsos rely on humor, double entendre, euphemism, eloquent wit, innuendo, pun and onomatopoeia to evoke a range of responses including laughter. The humorous approach is particularly useful for introducing serious or "delicate" subjects. The lyrics of the calypsos about Eugenia Charles lack that spark and excitement associated with calypso, but it is quite likely that stage antics, costume and props may have rendered them entertaining. Clever crafting with which "Ency" warned Mamo in "Doh Rock de Boat" of supporters who would lead her to "pain and grief" seldom flavoured the calypsos about Charles. The profusion of calypsos presented on the lady prime minister rely for their appeal on direct references to political developments. The irony, sarcasm, satire and prophecy contained in the lyrics are earnest emotional voices crying over a serious problem that continued to affect the quality of governance in the country under a leader chosen for her high credentials. The calypsonians did not seek to entertain, but to say what others dared not say. The calypsonians could not be fired from their jobs. Their calypsos could have been banned from the airwaves but this action usually heightened public curiosity and caused them to be played more frequently in private settings. The profusion and directness of these calypsos suggest that there are strong factual elements in the compositions. Their veracity was confirmed by several key informants who have known and worked closely with Charles in various capacities over two decades.

Eugenia Charles appears to have disempowered her people in many ways. The calypsos do not celebrate any sites of people's empowerment, opportunity and advancement. They do not show Charles sharing power with the people. They do not portray her government as transparent and accountable. They do not show Dominicans coming out of a crisis of governance to a situation of national self-definition, collective endeavour and attainment. Instead they show the prime minister's use of power over the citizens and the cabinet to be one of control and lack of consultation. One of the observable examples of the negative consequences of the way she used state power is seen in the decline of the labour movement.

The Social Contract

The labour movement in Dominica was one of the strongest institutions of people's power during the 1970s. Trade unions commanded mass followings; they were vocal, very influential and given to displaying their strength. The Waterfront and Allied Workers Union (WAWU) led by Louis Bennoit and Curtis Augustus, the Civil Service Association under Charles Savarin, the Dominica Trade Union led by Veronica Nicholas and the Dominica Amalgamated Workers Union under Anthony Frederick Joseph affected the development of the young nation-state from the workers' platform. The Police Welfare Association occupied that special place that did not require shows of force. Any hint that it would contemplate such action evoked speedy attention to its concerns even though the desired remedy was not always forthcoming.

It was WAWU that led the shutdown of Roseau on 16 December 1971, when it withdrew workers from the seaport. Commercial activity in the town came to a standstill as trade unions led a massive protest over the proposed Roseau Town Council Dissolution and Interim Commissioner Bill (UNECLAC 1984, 188). By noon of that day there was mounting tension in the town. The real possibility of civil unrest led to the closure of schools.[13] A large crowd of protesters confronted the police in front of the Roseau Courthouse on Victoria Street, where the House of Assembly meets. By mid-afternoon, in full view of the curious onlookers, one of the leaders of WAWU led a takeover of the courthouse and stopped debate on the bill.

This was not an issue about workers' rights, conditions at the workplace, or wages and salaries. WAWU was not confronting the government of the day over industrial relations matters. This was a matter affecting the structure of governance in the country, properly residing in the domain of the political parties and civic organizations. The bill was intended to curtail the powers of the town council and give more control of Roseau to the central government. It was cause for alarm to all citizens insofar as undermining the autonomy of one council jeopardized the integrity of the system of local government island-wide. While it was legitimate for workers to protest infringement of the powers of the local government system and to resist any impairment to its functioning, that a trade union led the protests was a testimony to its strength and influence. The Freedom Party was prominent in the town council and the bill directly sought to reduce its power. The fact that WAWU came out in defence of the Freedom Party and took the first protest action, giving the commercial sector an excuse for curtailing business that day, indicated the depth of the alliances that Eugenia Charles had with the labour movement, as well as the power of trade unions to influence national events not strictly within their purview.

The Dominica Trade Union had represented the farmers in their January 1972 protest of conditions in the banana industry. It was sympathetic to wage workers at Castle Bruce demonstrating in Roseau in July and August of the same year over land tenure, job security and their bid for worker ownership and management of the estate. It also led banana farmers in the general demonstration of 1978. The Dominica Amalgamated Workers Union often lent support to these protest actions.

The Civil Service Association (CSA) spearheaded four situations of conflict and protest against the government during the period 1973 to 1979. The first major confrontation between the CSA and government was a strike of twenty-two days' duration over the arbitrary transfer and apparent demotion of a civil servant who was a union member. The June 1976 strike of six days was in support of nurses protesting a lack of uniforms and difficult working conditions. The aim of the strike was to force the government to meet with the CSA. In September 1977, the CSA went on strike for forty-seven days to protest non-payment of wages owed to members since 1975 (UNECLAC 1984, 191–95).

On 29 May 1979 the CSA and other trade unions mounted a massive demonstration against the Bill for an Act to amend the Industrial Relations

Act, 1975, widely interpreted as an attempt to limit the ability of trade unions to initiate strike action, and the Libel and Slander (Amendment) Bill which was seen as a muzzle on the media. When events deteriorated the trade unions were major players in the formation of an extra-parliamentary solution to the state of civil unrest and helped to bring order out of the chaos. The trade unions were therefore the most prominent force in the overthrow of the ruling party (UNECLAC 1984, 204).

In sharp contrast to the muscle flexing of the 1970s, the trade unions adopted a cooperative role in the transition to a new government in 1980 and entered into a tacit social contract with the Eugenia Charles government. Trade unions became docile and acquiescent, first by choice and then by force of legislation, during the rule of the Freedom Party. During her first term of office, Eugenia Charles often took the opportunity during her speeches to thank the trade unions for their good behaviour (Dominica 1982a; 1983a, 4; 1983b, 16).

When Eugenia Charles took office she quickly paid off the civil servants' salaries that were in arrears but discontinued the automatic yearly increment. The unions cooperated. When she dismantled Statutory Boards there was no complaint (Letang 2004). Then she proceeded to preach and adhere to the gospel of wage restraint throughout her entire time in government. In 1981 she had entered into a three-year collective agreement with the CSA, which provided a limit of 10 per cent each year on salary and wage adjustments (Charles 1981, 7). She signalled that the same limits should be set in the private sector and pledged her government's vigilance to ensure the "self-discipline" of workers and their unions would not be exploited by employers (Charles 1981, 18). At the 1982 anniversary of independence she celebrated a year of "industrial peace", due to the new spirit of cooperation between workers, their unions and employers, which resulted in a slowing down in the rate of increase in the consumer price index. Despite high wage demands at the seaport, Eugenia Charles generally received the cooperation that she requested.

The prime minister negotiated a 5 per cent wage increase with the CSA in 1985 but was resentful of it and complained in the June 1986 Budget Address that it had brought "considerable pressure on the recurrent budget". In that same address she warned the CSA that persistent high wage demands do harm to the economy, and reiterated that workers and their unions have a great responsibility to create the right environment for growth and development. She also chastised one of the leading unions "whose leaders in the past have shown a responsible and mature approach to industrial relations" for a recent strike which she claimed had resulted in a lay-off of fifty workers from a new factory (Charles 1986, 12). Within a month after that address, July 1986, she had amended the Industrial Relations Act to require that unions representing workers in the three main economic industries and eight essential services[14] give forty-eight hours notice of intention to strike (Solomon 2004). This was the very Industrial Relations Act amendment that trade unions had resisted so vigorously in 1979. Seven years later Eugenia Charles used her constitutional powers with impunity. Details could not be obtained of how the unions treated this action. The workers' movement was enfeebled. Eugenia Charles's power diminished that of trade unionism during her fifteen years of rule.

At the 1992 anniversary of independence, still screeching for wage restraint, the prime minister scolded the unions, particularly the civil service union, for unrealistic wage demands (Dominica 1992b, 12). Her 1994 farewell speech did not include any thanks to the trade unions for their support.

All the trade unions in Dominica attest to a decline in the influence of the labour movement during the tenure of Charles's government. The support and cooperation that they gave Eugenia Charles when she assumed office, to stabilize the economy, polity and society, led to a lack of vigilance concerning worker protection and too much accommodation of an old "friend" (B. Nicholas 2002). Trade unions were not in the forefront of the December 1988 demonstrations (Letang 2004). In other words, the labour movement had become so weakened that workers took matters into their own hands. Elderly farmers were among several hundred demonstrators who marched to government headquarters to protest a 3 per cent sales tax and other structural adjustment austerity measures (Report of the Americas 1990, 39). This awoke the unions to the fact that they ought not to so slavishly cooperate with the government on International Monetary Fund policies, but that awareness came quite late. As individual unions sought to regain their mission and purpose, divisions and tensions began to be played out in the press and other public platforms. One trade unionist even described another, once powerful, trade union in the local newspapers as a "bulldog without teeth" (Solomon 2004).

During the second and third terms of Eugenia Charles's administration, membership in trade unions declined. Teachers withdrew from the CSA and registered the Dominica Teachers Association as a trade union in December 1990. Since Charles's departure the CSA has reinvented itself through a name change, initiated a number of non-traditional union activities aimed at benefiting members and sought additional categories of workers to represent (Letang 2004). The once powerful Civil Service Association has had to be transformed into the Public Service Union in order to redeem itself in Dominica's industrial relations environment. Other trade unions have not been as fortunate. The Dominica Trade Union is a mere historical relic whose members cannot be identified. The National Workers Union does not inspire confidence, and the stagnant Dominica Amalgamated Workers Union has been unable to replace leadership that emigrated or passed on. The Waterfront and Allied Workers Union has been able to recover some of its strength through a membership drive over the past four years. It is also contemplating combining its energies with the inert Dominica Amalgamated Workers Union, and it remains to be seen if there will be a merger, or if the weaker union will be absorbed (Rolle 2004). The trade unions are presently unable to form a common platform on any issue, constantly criticize each other in public and collectively have a diminished capacity to negotiate and to influence Dominica's industrial relations climate. In contrast to the 1970s, today the average worker has little confidence in trade unionism even while acknowledging a great need for it (Solomon 2004).

The influence and vibrancy of the labour movement has diminished throughout the Caribbean as a result of changing employment situations brought on by accelerated trade liberalization. The traditional workforce is being phased out. Downsizing, multitasking, piecework, homework and self-employment are on the increase. Stasis in the industrial relations sector is not peculiar to Dominica. However, since Eugenia Charles was such a willing disciple of economic and trade liberalization, and presided over its application in Dominica with such aplomb, some responsibility must be imputed to her for the decline of the labour movement in the island. Workers, and by extension the people of Dominica, lost the vibrancy of

one of their strongest institutions of empowerment during Charles's leadership of the country. This muting of the workers' voice is contrary to her
repeated pledge to good governance and people's participation in the
affairs of the country.

Mary, Mary, Quite Contrary

Eugenia Charles was a powerful prime minister because she used her formal and personal powers without hesitation. She succeeded in instilling
discipline, but she failed to raise the consciousness of Dominicans, organize
them and build their capacity for political participation beyond voting
every five years. Eugenia Charles knew that her methods had meant sacri-
fices on the part of many persons (Dominica 1982a, 17) but she insisted
that "firm and decisive governance" had resulted in the building of people's
confidence in themselves, in establishing a creditable image abroad, in
earning the respect of donor friends and in the provision of adequate
health, education, recreational facilities, community services and financial
institutions. She believed that her government had expanded the necessary
environment for her people to excel in whatever endeavour of life they
had chosen (Charles 1993, 14). Charles took pride in her ability to make
decisions. She admitted that many decisions were unpleasant and she
would have preferred not to have taken them, but she did not shirk from
what had to be done. She credited herself with listening to other views and
then making up her own mind: "I liked the fact that I was hard. I liked the
fact that I could take decisions" (Charles 2002f).

Before demitting office, Charles admitted that effective governance
should be attended by public education and participation. She also
acknowledged that consensual governance thrives best in a condition of
social and economic advancement. But she was adamant that consensual
governance may be ineffectual in times of national crisis and that urgent
demands for bold initiatives and effective leadership in times of national
crisis required public trust and confidence (Charles 1993, 9). Perhaps she
had seen the country as perpetually in crisis, for, if the calypsos are to be
believed, she had not delivered on the many promises of people's participation in national decision making. It could be thought, then, that while

Charles expected the people to trust her by voting her into office, she did not trust their counsel and therefore did not seek it. Certainly she had not asked their views when, quite contrary to her promise "not to play dice with the heritage of posterity" (Dominica 1983a, 3) she introduced "economic citizenship" and defended criticisms with the argument that we could not "afford to isolate ourselves, build fences around our possessions or our nationhood against foreign investment and participation" (Dominica 1992b, 10). If Charles had opened up mechanisms for citizens' participation in decision making, she might not have had to argue during her 1992 address on the fourteenth anniversary of the nation's independence that "Economic citizenship does not deprive us of any part of our country" because "the major countries of the world are joining hands in a profitable exchange of their citizens and their goods".

Conclusion

This analysis of the leadership of Eugenia Charles is taking place when power has been transferred from the first generation of post-colonial leaders to a new generation. The decision to relinquish power had been grudgingly undertaken, with old leaders fighting valiantly to define the conditions under which their departure from the political scene would be effected (Barrow-Giles and Marshall 2003, 474). Prime Minister Kenny Anthony of St Lucia has explained that the demise of the old post-colonial politics and politicians and the emergence of the new breed of leadership coincide with major transformations in the world economy, and that a new democratic ethos is needed for our time. He argues that new features of Caribbean democracy are beginning to emerge which include the conscious attempts of the new Caribbean leadership to engage civil society in the decision-making process. On one level this is reflected in a far greater tolerance towards political opponents and in more genuine attempts to include opposition groups in decision making (Barrow-Giles and Marshall 2003, 475).

These ideas were not lost on Eugenia Charles. She commented on the changing political economy of Dominica and the Caribbean in most of her speeches to the nation during her second and third terms of office. Her

notes on a draft of a party manifesto for 1990 reveal a heightened awareness of the need to implement the promises of inclusion that she had made
from the beginning of her administration. In paragraph 1, under the heading "Key Principles", Eugenia Charles wrote:

> my government will begin by taking a critical look at its own processes of deci-
> sion making, determination of development priorities, and policy formulation.
> Our goal here is to ensure that the real needs of our people, the government's
> development programs and the operational machinery or systems of our bureau-
> cracy are brought into closest harmony.

In paragraphs 3 to 5, under "Key Principles", she wrote:

> We are committed to responsible and open government. The citizens of a country
> cannot all govern. That is why they place representatives in government to do this
> work, but representatives must always function in close collaboration with those
> they represent. It is not an either or situation.
>
> We are also committed to a policy of inclusion . . . our population is too small
> for us to exclude anyone from making the contribution to our national develop-
> ment that his or her talents, gifts and resources allow.
>
> We want to build a nation with a conscience, one based on social harmony and
> caring as opposed to selfishness and conflict . . . we will attempt to place adminis-
> tration of community project in the hands of local authorities with the guidance
> of government. (DFP 1990, 1)

These were not new thoughts. It had all been said before. What was perhaps new was Mamo's admission that she might not have had the capacity
to deliver on these so-often repeated promises. She announced her inten-
sion to withdraw from elective politics soon after her 1990 victory and did
not stand for office in the general election of 1995.

The words of another of the new generation of prime ministers in the
Organization of Eastern Caribbean States have summed up what the
calypsonians spoke to in their renderings concerning the state of governance in Dominica:

> In fashioning a new structure of governance and production in the Caribbean, the
> ethic of trust between and among the people, and between them and their leaders
> in their various organisations and in government, has to be built. . . . It is the duty
> of each of us to . . . pursue . . . the most appropriate and efficacious political forms

through which to fashion a new and better governance. (Gonsalves 2003, 490)

Eugenia Charles might approve of such a vision and approach but she was unable to fulfil it. No other woman has as yet emerged as prime minister of a Caribbean state.[15] As I look forward to more women exercising political power at the highest level, one of the prime lessons to be learned from Eugenia Charles's use of prime ministerial powers was the advice articulated by "Ency" since 1986:

> Though you must maintain command
> There are times to give in to demands.

Notes

1. This spelling is of special esoteric significance to the faithful of RastafarI. The
    "I" has multiple layers of meanings; one of these is the oneness of the faithful
    with His Imperial Majesty Emperor Haille Sellassie I and, through this oneness,
    the oneness of all who are called to – RastafarI. Hence InI replaces the English
    pronoun "we". The "I" also differentiates RastafarI from "ism" and
    "Rastafarian". RastafarI and Rasta are acceptable terms. A "Dread" has the
    appearance of Rasta but rejects the covenant of "Holiness unto His Imperial
    Majesty Emperor Haille Sellassie I".

2. The United States led a military invasion in Grenada in October 1983,
    "allegedly to rescue American students . . . from a Revolutionary Military
    Council installed after the murders" of Prime Minister Maurice Bishop and a
    number of other persons (Collins 1995).

3. Eugenia Charles was unsuccessful in the general elections held on 26 October
    1970, but was nominated to the House of Assembly on the advice of the leader
    of the opposition, Anthony Moise, Dominica Freedom Party.

4. Mable Moir James was elected as representative for the Western District in the
    general elections held on 7 January 1966. She served as minister of communica-
    tions and works, 1966. Dominica was granted Associated Statehood with Great
    Britain under a constitution which became effective 1 March 1967. This
    increased the number of ministers from four to five. In the new appointments
    Mrs Mable Moir James became minister of home affairs. See Davis Pierre, 1975.

5. This seminar, held in Trinidad in November 2003, was concerned with devel-
    oping the parameters for a Sustainable Impact Assessment of the proposed
    Economic Partnership Agreement between the European Union and the
    Caribbean. The seminar was organized by the Caribbean Policy Development
    Centre in collaboration with SOLAGRAL (a consultancy firm based in
    France).

6. William Demas is a former secretary general of the Caribbean Community, and
    later was governor of the Caribbean Development Bank.

7. The labels of the reels from which their renderings were copied carried only
    stage names; therefore, the proper names of the many calypsonians cannot be
    given.

8. Dominica also has a rich tradition of *conte* (stories) and riddles told in the local
    patois.

9. The record librarian at Dominica Broadcasting Services, the national radio sta-
    tion, diligently retrieved fifteen calypsos about Eugenia Charles. The full coop-
    eration of all staff members made copying of the lyrics possible. Popular

memory lists other songs that are probably in the possession of the original
writers, many of whom have emigrated from Dominica.

10. Warrant Officer II Ashton Benjamin was strongly implicated in the attempt to
overthrow Prime Minister Eugenia Charles's government in 1981.

11. A *pui-pui* is a raft.

12. The initials "PJ" here refer to Patrick John.

13. I was at that time a member of the CSA but I do not clearly remember that the
other trade unions actually pulled their membership from their jobs. It may be
that many persons simply abandoned their posts for the day, drawn to the
excitement on the streets of Roseau.

14. These were the banana, citrus, and coconut industries; and the electricity,
health, hospital, prisons, sanitary and water, port, fire and telecommunication
services.

15. Portia Simpson Miller was elected leader of the People's National Party in
Jamaica in February 2006 and became prime minister in March 2006.

PART 4

Poverty Alleviation

and Economic

Development

7

The Economic Philosophy of Eugenia Charles and Dominica's Development, 1980–1995

EUDINE BARRITEAU

Introduction

This chapter seeks to uncover the economic philosophy of Eugenia Charles and expose how this influenced the approach to development the country experienced during her administration. The analysis attempts to unravel and analyse key economic policies formulated from 1980 to 1995 and discuss their impact on Dominican political economy. I am not overly concerned with assessing the economic viability or limitations of the Eugenia Charles administration even though these will be commented on. Instead the focus is on unravelling the whys of what was attempted and on placing these in a national and regional context. I include a discussion of the disjuncture between theorizing twentieth-century Caribbean political economy on the basis of established rules and assumptions and the pragmatic, piecemeal and unorthodox approaches executed by Charles and her administration.

Studies of women as national leaders are comparatively recent (Genovese 1993b). A comprehensive study of women as chief executive officers in seven industrialized and developing countries ignored Eugenia Charles, who was still in office when the study was published, even though she was a contemporary of most of the women whose public lives were examined (Genovese 1993b). These studies attempted, with very limited success, to identify patterns and styles of women's political leadership and locate the women as a subset of political elites (Sykes 1993).

Any approach to analysing Eugenia Charles's economic leadership cannot simply examine the political economy of Dominica and assess the policy outcomes as reactions to taming post-colonial, mercantilist capitalism gone awry. Neither can the analysis be satisfactorily concluded by resorting to a psychological approach which seeks to explain her actions in terms of personality traits or variables (Everett 1993, 104). Unlike Indira Gandhi, whose decisions were (in my opinion) unfairly portrayed by some analysts as being driven by the logic of her own political survival (Everett 1993, 104), Eugenia Charles was motivated by a deep commitment to her country's survival (Lazare 2002; Williams 2002; Douglas 2002; Yankey 2002a; Higbie 1993, 271).[1] The peculiar economic and social circumstances of Dominica were constantly at the forefront of all she did. Those adverse conditions influenced both her best decisions and the ones that proved more contentious and difficult to justify or execute. To explain why Eugenia Charles became a Caribbean political phenomenon and Dominica's longest serving prime minister, dominating her party and Dominican politics for fifteen continuous years, the analysis has to examine the political and economic context of the agrarian, small society she inherited and the character of the woman who has been described as the Caribbean's "Iron Lady" (Higbie 1993), or more affectionately, but in no less matriarchal terms, as "Mamo" (Dowe and Honychurch 1989).

Analysing the economic and political leadership of Eugenia Charles is extremely challenging. She emerged from the overlapping eras that produced many strong, often controversial political leaders and prime ministers such as Eric Williams, Forbes Burnham, Lewellyn Bradshaw, Eric Gairy, Vere Bird, Sr, Michael Manley and Errol Barrow. Like most of them she had studied abroad, and she sat the bar examinations in London like Burnham, Manley and Barrow. She came to power much later than the latter three. She assumed political leadership seven years after they had drafted the Treaty of Chaguaramas to establish the Caribbean Common Market and Community. Unlike Manley, Burnham and Barrow she seems to have held no pan-Caribbean vision. She admitted Dominica was more closely integrated into the Organization of Eastern Caribbean States (OECS):"We were not quite as close in CARICOM. OECS islands have similar income levels and culture" (Charles 2002c). This attitude was perhaps conditioned by the fact that the OECS came into being in June 1981, early in the second year of her administration (Samuel 1983, 159).[2] If she was not propelled by contemporary attempts to build functional cooperation on economic issues, there is also no compelling evidence of an appreciation of the post-Columbus Caribbean's origins in conquest, slavery and colonialism impacting on her approach to political leadership. One is hard-pressed to find evidence that she harboured a lingering nineteenth- or twentieth-century nationalist ideology that opposed European cultural disdain, North American economic and cultural penetration and political expansionism (G.K. Lewis 1983, 324).

Charles and Dominica: Leadership Style

At the political level Eugenia Charles remains a contradictory, complex leader whose actions and statements provoked strong national and regional reaction. Her political philosophy was right of centre and for many years Caribbean intellectuals and progressive thinkers found her statements and positions irritating at best, and often very galling – if not embarrassing (Higbie 1993; Dominica 1982b, 6). She was also widely admired nationally, regionally and internationally as a strong, decisive leader who was not afraid to take hard decisions and who brought respectability and integrity to Dominica nationally and in the regional and international community (Lazare 2002; Torricelli 1997; Williams 2002; Douglas 2002; Yankey 2002a; Attidore 1990). Her administration was regarded as representing a high level of integrity and respect in public life (Lazare 2002; Douglas 2002; Yankey 2002a; Williams 2002).

As an individual she was a determined, forceful, combative and God-fearing woman and was very open about her religious faith. "Every cabinet meeting began with a prayer. I prayed about major decisions. Faith is important in my life. It was in my family so it was easy to have continued it" (Charles 2002d). She was often brutally honest and confrontational in her public statements and could be relied upon to make pronouncements she strongly believed but that were highly unpopular. She cared deeply about improving the quality of life for Dominicans and made achieving improvements in the social and economic infrastructure a strategic plank of her economic and political programme. Alick Lazare reported that soon after she assumed office in 1980, Eugenia Charles

> began to look after conditions in rural areas through the provision of services and the expansion of utilities. Before the growth in the banana industry, there was an urban drift, after the growth in banana production there was a rural drift. There was an expansion of telephone, water, electricity. Within a short space of time people began to feel comfortable in their communities. (Lazare 2002)[3]

Dominicans living abroad especially appreciated the improvements in the country's infrastructure:[4]

> Some conscientious supporters of what you have done for the country to date, especially providing water, light, telephone and improved roads to the Eastern and outlying areas of Dominica, have asked me personally to write you, congratulate you, and express our appreciation on behalf of Dominicans here [St Thomas Virgin Islands]. (Attidore 1990)

As prime minister she lived frugally, abhorred ostentation and eschewed the use of public funds that could not be scrupulously justified. She was a confident woman who was comfortable with her personal power, the power of the office of prime minister and the exercise of that power.

Former financial secretary Alick Lazare thinks Charles was misunderstood as a political leader. He states that although she gave the appearance of harshness,[5] of a sense of rigidity, that she was amenable to reasonable advice: "If presented with a number of options she could bite into, she would accept it and change her mind" (Lazare 2002). Gilbert Williams, financial secretary from 1989 to 1997, also thought that her ministers misunderstood her. Having worked as cabinet secretary for some months in her third term, he concluded: "She is the kind of person, when she comes [to cabinet meetings], she puts her point of view over immediately. She put them off guard. If they had projects to present, they would lay back and let her dominate" (Williams 2002). Also, "She listened to her advisors, she would allow policy advisors to make an input. She prepared for meetings, she prepared herself, checking facts, when we were preparing budget addresses, she got it a week before so she can go through it and make changes before she presents it" (Williams 2002).

Bernard Yankey adds, "She is a very organized woman who could think analytically, conceptually, at the same time she was very detailed. She took home papers at night and went through everything very thoroughly" (Yankey 2002a).

Interestingly, almost identical statements were made of Margaret Thatcher, the woman leader with whom Eugenia Charles was compared the most:[6] "Thatcher possessed strong views, and she always completed her homework, which made her well prepared to argue her case. . . Typically, she would voice her views at the start of cabinet meetings. The response from her male ministers became predictable: They simply sat in silence" (Sykes 1993, 226).

Eugenia Charles was not driven by the desire to be popular and stated her decision making was in relation to national goals. Lazare noted that some of her decisions "displeased even people of her own class" (Lazare 2002). Her senior technocrats concur that while she had a great sensitivity to people and people's interests, when she made her case she did so in a very strong manner to the point of being almost unbending (Lazare 2002; Williams 2002; Douglas 2002). They perceived her as a leader who had the broad national interest at heart and who would not submit herself to individual favouritism (Lazare 2002; Williams 2002; Douglas 2002). Even though Charles enjoyed exercising power she had no difficulty in relinquishing leadership of the Dominica Freedom Party (DFP) and the country. When she perceived her popularity and leadership had slipped considerably, in 1993 she resigned as leader of the DFP but remained as prime minister until the end of her term. However, Gilbert Williams believed that holding onto the office and onto power as prime minister while relinquishing leadership of the party was a political blunder that hurt the party: "She felt it was time to go, she had no problems giving up. However one of the bad things she did was to hold on to the prime ministership to the end [of her third term]" (Williams 2002). In terms of understanding the anglophone Caribbean's contemporary political history, Eugenia Charles and the Dominica experience have still to be fully explored.

One of the portfolios Eugenia Charles assigned to herself and which she kept throughout her fifteen years as prime minister was that of responsibility for the ministry of finance. In anglophone Caribbean politics, the portfolio of finance or economic affairs is traditionally the responsibility of the prime minister, so Eugenia Charles set no precedent in this regard. However, she remains the only Caribbean woman in politics to have held that responsibility. An analysis of the unorthodox economic philosophy she followed and practised is essential to revealing her economic and political stewardship of Dominica. Her fifteen-year tenure as minister of finance was marked by concerted and sustained efforts to restore political and economic stability, minimize government deficits, reduce the foreign debt, improve basic social services and develop an economic infrastructure. It was also marked by controversial economic policies introduced primarily to attract foreign investment in response to shifting interests of her international patrons and declining international donor assistance.

Since the mid-1960s Caribbean governments have been determined to ensure economic and social development by pursuing deliberate and conventional economic strategies designed to attract foreign capital (Thomas 1988). Yet several of the strategies Eugenia Charles pursued to this end were frowned upon by Dominicans and Caribbean people. Guided by no easily demarcated economic philosophy, Charles was driven by the determination to bring investment to Dominica even at a political price to herself and her administration (Edwards 1992; Lazare 2002; Williams 2002; Douglas 2002; John 1992b, 1992c). Trevor Farrell categorized the approach to development pursued by Charles as "mendicant capitalism" (Farrell 1993, 20). This is a description Charles would not have denied. In her willingness to explore all avenues to raise funds for Dominica, Eugenia Charles described herself as "a very good beggar" (Charles 2002c). This supplicant approach to funding Dominica's development often involved a breathless and peripatetic chasing of donor funding wherever a possibility existed. In her 1981–82 budget address, for example, she stated the government had been unable to lay the 1981–82 estimates of revenue and expenditure in parliament in advance partly because her government had needed the time to prepare for and to attend international meetings with donors, as well as to meet with donor agencies in Dominica. They had also needed time to re-examine the draft budget in more detail before submitting the estimates (Dominica 1981d, 1).

Yet Farrell's categorization and Charles's mendicant approach on behalf of the country belie the facts about Dominica. In 1980 Dominica was a state teetering on the brink of an economic and political meltdown. It did not have the internal productive capacity required to meet its national commitments. Neither investors nor tourists were queuing to exploit Dominica's natural or human resources. To describe Dominica's development approach as "mendicant capitalism", or accept Charles's self-deprecating statement that she was "a good beggar", does not reflect the peculiarities and singular hurdles posed by the unique characteristics of the Dominican economy.

Limitations of Small Size

> I have repeatedly said to our many friends overseas that it is misleading to measure assistance to small island states like ours on a per capita basis and I have emphasized that the imperatives for growth are not the same as in already developed economies. (Charles 1984b, 9)

The problems that confront all open, dependent economies in the Caribbean are exacerbated in the case of Dominica because of its internal characteristics. It had the smallest population of all the islands in the OECS. In 1981 the population was 73,795; by 1988 it was 81,088 (Dominica 1988, 13–14). To the extent that population size indicates labour market supply as well as potential demand through internal markets for the consumption of goods and services, a small population with minimal growth can be a serious economic disadvantage. In 1983 the economically active population was 24,798 with a total of 702 employers, while in 1986 the numbers were 28,498 and 976 respectively (Dominica 1988, 15). A small labour force yields a narrow income-tax base and a linear, restricted range of economic activities. Faced with an economically active labour force of such modest size, Charles's government could not rely on a high level of internally generated savings and investment to fuel economic expansion. The scale of Dominica's government revenue and expenditure was minuscule when compared with other countries. Economic management for the Charles administration was very daunting and government's

provision of basic social goods and services remained a serious preoccupation throughout her tenure.

Dominica's terrain hindered maximum development of its natural
resources. The country is physically rugged, with virgin forests, accentuated
by a mountainous topography with the land rising steeply, seemingly
directly out of the sea. The country's beauty and natural assets predispose it
towards the development of ecotourism and not the more lucrative
tourism product of the Caribbean that combines sun, sea, sand and sex
(Kempadoo 1999). Yet the promotion of Dominica as a tourist destination
was based on the older, traditional, but irrelevant model. It was not until
the second term of her administration that economic planners abandoned
attempts to fit the Dominica tourism product into the popular Caribbean
image and packaging, and began to pursue a focus on the nature aspect of
tourism (Lazare 2002). Still, according to Lazare, the existing tourism plant
was not designed for the new marketing and promotion strategy and there
was no clear vision of what was really needed (Lazare 2002). In 1980 economic stability rested on the fortunes of the banana industry. Lazare notes,
"The marketing sector was very small, the tourism sector virtually non-
existent; [so] whatever happened in bananas determined economic stability
and the country faced volatile prices" (Lazare 2002).

Eugenia Charles meant well for the country and was determined to do
her very best for its development, as she saw it. Even her strongest critics
readily admit charges of political corruption could not be levelled against
her. But in her fifteen-year tenure there was no overriding vision of economic development that informed planning. There was not a sense of a
coherent development strategy that her government envisioned, even if the
international and national context had permitted it. In the fifteen years of
the DFP administration, there was not one five-year plan or other long-
term development plan. Eisenhower Douglas, who worked as senior economist with her from May 1988 until she demitted office, said a weakness of
her economic strategy was in not looking at the long-term challenges
(Douglas 2002). Economic policy seemed to lurch along, controlled by the
natural disasters and by the national and regional political and economic
crises that occurred. These were mediated by Charles using a combination
of her commitment to sound fiscal management and her idiosyncratic
approach to raising development financing.

Led by the larger economies in the region, the more developed countries, many Caribbean countries experimented with the "Industrialisation
by Invitation" approach to development between the 1960s and 1980s to
generate employment, transfer skills and technology and contribute to the
gross domestic product through export-oriented industrialization. Their
experience revealed that the strategy fell short of its goals, even though it
did generate some low-income employment, overwhelmingly for women
(Thomas 1988, 75–101). Dominica was unable to pursue that option successfully and remained anchored economically to its agricultural roots and
orientation. The Charles administration made several attempts to encourage manufacturing but none of these trials matured into a sustainable and
viable economic strategy. Lazare noted that Charles prioritized the expansion of small industries by trying to increase the stock of factory shells.
These were to function as incubators for small businesses. She also tried to
develop entrepreneurship particularly among young people by having
them come into cottage industries (Lazare 2002): "She converted a sports
stadium into an industrial park, attracted a few foreign industries as well as
domestic investors, but most of them disappeared during her administration, complaining of high rental fees" (Lazare 2002).

Clive Thomas demonstrates that in Dominica in 1975, 1980 and 1984,
as a percentage of the gross domestic product, manufacturing was 4.2 per
cent, 5.0 per cent and 7.3 per cent respectively. Recognized as having the
most depressed economy in the geographic Caribbean, Haiti recorded
manufacturing as a percentage of GDP at 17.1 per cent, 16.1 per cent and
19.6 per cent for roughly the same period (Thomas 1988, 89). On the
other hand, 30.8 per cent of Dominica's active population was engaged in
agriculture in 1981. Although this represented a decline from 38.1 per cent
in 1970, Dominica still had a higher percentage of its economically active
population engaged in agriculture than Antigua-Barbuda, Bahamas,
Barbados, Grenada, Jamaica, Montserrat, St Lucia, St Vincent and the
Grenadines, Trinidad and Tobago, and Suriname (Thomas 1988, 133).
Among countries of the Caribbean Community (CARICOM), only
Belize had a higher percentage of its population employed in agriculture at
35.9 per cent (Thomas 1988, 133).

Many of Charles's critics found her eager facilitation or embrace of
United States involvement in the mopping-up military exercise after the

Grenada revolution imploded as evidence that she encouraged United States economic and political intrusion and insertion in Caribbean societies, economies and political systems. In 2002 she declared: "I think we did the right thing in inviting [US military involvement in Grenada]. If they had taken over Grenada, they would have taken over Dominica next. We had no army" (Charles 2002c). She never specified who "they" were, but from other statements she made it is clear she was referring to a communist threat. It must be remembered that Eugenia Charles and Dominica shared a history of political conservatism. In the case of Dominica this is reinforced by the absence of any sustained workers' movement or trade union militancy (Riviere 1982; Midgett 1997, 49). There was an inbred suspicion among political leaders that most forms of opposition arose from communist leanings. In 1973, a two-week strike by a coalition of trade unions over the abrupt dismissal of a civil servant for criticizing government actions produced the following reaction by Chief Minister LeBlanc's administration: his government declared a state of emergency which gave security forces extraordinarily wide powers of search and arrest. It also ordered the preventative detention of three executive members of the Civil Service Association and stated in a national broadcast that "a 'Third Force' was putting into effect a communist plot to overthrow the constitutionally elected government by armed force" (Riviere 1982, 366).

Throughout the decade of the 1970s growing student militancy, influenced by the Black Power movement of the late 1960s, the "back to the land" movement by some members of the Rastafarian community and worker agitation for land ownership were all interpreted by political leaders as having connections with communist ideology. This feature was common in several Caribbean countries whose governments found it convenient to invoke "the communist threat" whenever there were strong challenges to their moral authority and political accountability.[7] By the time the Freedom Party was settling down into office in 1980 there had been two coup attempts and rumours of communist or "leftist" involvements.

Origins: Economic Philosophy of a Colonial, Landed Peasantry

For it is true to say that up until the 1950s the Windward Territories were semi-feudal economies in which merchants, the large landowners, either personal or corporate, and the middle-class civil servants ruled the inarticulate peasant and worker with an iron hand. (G.K. Lewis 1983, 150)

G.K. Lewis's conclusion that the social and economic history of the Windward Islands is in large part the history of an oppressed peasant-proprietary class fighting to maintain its precarious existence within a hostile environment is supported by Bill Riviere's analysis of class struggles in Dominica during the turbulent 1970s, even though Douglas Midgett cautions against reducing Dominica's contemporary political history to a crude and mechanical form of class analysis (G.K. Lewis 1983, 150; Riviere 1982; Midgett 1997, 59). This is the social and economic legacy Eugenia Charles inherited and in which she would practise her politics as the strong, black "mother" of the nation. It was as if she was the political mother of the country, attempting to nurse it out of its physical, economic and political disasters. Simultaneously she stood as a metaphor for Dominica, strong, rugged, unique and often harsh. Faced with a repressive, hierarchical social order with a paternalistic estate life for the majority of the labourers, as described by G.K. Lewis, Eugenia Charles inserted a new political practice – consulting with constituents:

> I think there is not enough consultation with the ordinary man in the street. People should be informed and should be kept informed. People are not aware of what is happening. We were going to meter water. They were about to put the water meters on. People in my constituency started complaining, look at all the rivers we have, why we have to pay for water? I told them why don't you go and dip your bucket in the river and take the water? If you want water in your house, you have to pay for the pipes. I went to Puerto Rico and I could tell them the cost of the pipes. They then understood, and they didn't quarrel with them anymore. My ambition was that everyone should have running water in their house. (Charles 2002d)

The metaphor of catering to the political needs of the common man, the need for continuous political consultation with John and Jane Public and a simultaneous commitment to decisive action are recurrent themes in Charles's reflection on her economic leadership. She was committed to consultation with the Dominican people and electorate: "She was not afraid to go out and talk to the community and educate them and explain to them why they have to do certain things. In that way she was a lone voice" (Lazare 2002). She was also committed to having them see her point of view. Her practice of consultation was admirable since it is often used by governments for public relations purposes only, rather than to promote understanding and to utilize the feedback generated. Many Caribbean governments do not even see the need to share their policies with their constituents. Consulting with the citizenry would not have been a common practice in Dominica; her consultations were both politically astute as well as democratic, even if only in form.

For Eugenia Charles consultation represented a form of "street level bureaucracy" (Lipsky 1980), not to be reduced simply to seeking photo opportunities and politicking with an eye to media coverage. She understood that people experienced governmental decisions in the streets, yards, communities and villages. It was an attempt by her to maintain contact with the political base beyond periodic electioneering. It seems that Charles was genuine about the processes of consultation. She wanted to hear what Dominicans thought about soon-to-be implemented policies. She stated that in daily cabinet briefings she and her colleagues would review each other's plans for the day: "I would ask what are you going to tell them? Don't go and promise them the world because we don't have it" (Charles 2002c).

She was also genuine about imparting her views about the pending policies and having Dominicans understand why the government's course of action was the correct one. Eugenia Charles seemed to believe firmly that the consent of the governed should be secured, but "governed" was the operative term, denoting where the final authority lay for the policy to be introduced:

> I used to walk around Roseau every Thursday and every Saturday. I told them what was happening and heard what they had to say. I used to hold a meeting every Thursday evening at seven for leaders within the constituencies. So people always knew what we were planning and what we were doing. I thought it was important that they were informed. I would tell them, "it is not the government that run the country, it is you that run the country". (Charles 2002c)[8]

Revealingly, in reminiscing about the introduction of metered water rates, Charles equated "consultation" with "sharing information" on the proposed changes, that is, letting constituents know that metered rates were coming and why they were necessary. But she had taken a decision for its introduction *before* she had consulted the people. While it is true there is a cost to be assigned for such services, and government has to ensure fiscal responsibility, in her reflections there was no sense that the capacity of the individual citizen to pay was considered, or that there could be feedback that would modify the proposed policy.[9] In that quotation Eugenia Charles revealed her self-image as "the benevolent, political leader knowing what is best for her people". This was a characteristic of some elitist political leaders who emerged from the colonial crucible. These were leaders who believed that, by virtue of a superior education and a secure class position, they knew what was best for their citizens.

Eugenia Charles was influenced by her experiences as a member of the colonial landed peasantry. It was a social environment where estate workers and landowners (like her parents) occupied the same social and physical landscape but from sharply divergent vantage points of privilege and power. It would have been very easy for Eugenia Charles to move around rural and urban Dominica and speak to estate labourers, urban workers, farmers, civil servants, housewives, students and children. Her rural upbringing on her father's estate in Point Michel[10] afforded an easy familiarity with workers and their lifestyles:

> "If I was talking to a labourer, I would speak to him in patois, if I was speaking to my parents I would speak English." By the time Eugenia, the youngest child was growing up, the rule had been modified so that she had to speak only English until she was 7, then she was allowed to speak creole. (Higbie 1993, 27)[11]

But Charles was very aware that her social and economic circumstances were sharply divergent from those of the men, women and children who worked and lived on her father's estate and who provided the wage labour for the Dominican economy. Her economic philosophy enabled her to simultaneously speak with Dominican citizens and speak for them.

Eugenia Charles had the best education affordable for a woman from a small British Caribbean colony in the 1940s.[12] While her upbringing was marked by a deliberate, almost studied, frugality,[13] she understood no expenses would be spared to educate her and her two brothers and a sister:

> We knew we could get any education we wanted. Whatever we wanted to study

further our father would find the means of sending us further. Our parents believed in education. Our father felt that education was vitally important. Both he and my mother only had primary school education. We always knew, we merely had to say it and we would get the education we wanted. (Charles 2002c)

Obtaining the best education in the colonial British West Indies took Eugenia Charles from Roseau to St Joseph's Convent in Grenada from 1940 to 1942. She entered the University of Toronto to study law in 1942, when Britain was caught in the ravages of the Second World War. There she met Nita Barrow and developed a lifelong friendship.[14] She went on to London after the end of the war to complete her studies in law and to be called to the bar. There she met and shared student accommodations with Lucille (Walrond) Mair and Phyliss McPherson.

As a privileged, educated young woman from the colonial Caribbean, Eugenia Charles made no sweeping analysis of the conditions affecting the region. However, by the time she arrived in Toronto the Caribbean had already experienced what the British West India Commission described as "a Hurricane of Protests" between May 1934 and February 1939. While Dominica, inoculated by the existence of a landed peasantry, experienced no labour unrest, the decade of the 1930s was a period of social, economic and political upheaval more generally in the region. The Caribbean working class were fed up with being poor and exploited. Just as they did in the nineteenth century, they displayed their dissatisfaction, became politically restless and rioted. The British Colonial Office appointed the Moyne Commission to investigate the root causes of this unrest and it visited the Caribbean between 1938 and 1939 (G.K. Lewis 1968, 66). These developments did not seem to register with her. Charles would say of her student days in London, "I did not think about Caribbean problems then and things were fine, even though things were very difficult for students then" (Charles 2002c). She had an insular outlook that went beyond being young. It was perhaps a by-product of a privileged, rural upbringing in which her father's estates, her father's economic activities and her family life were at the core of how she viewed Dominica and the Caribbean.

Time and again, in carving out an approach to the development of Dominica, Eugenia Charles would ritualistically return to the imposed frugality of her childhood, the enduring emphasis on education, and the agricultural background and rural philosophy of her father. It seems her point of reference for economic planning was her childhood upbringing. She seems to differ from other Caribbean leaders by repeatedly returning to her childhood to find guidance for approaches to development.

> As a girl I was not interested in things like that [going to the movies, new dresses], I always bought books. I got three new dresses a year, one for Christmas, one for Corpus Christie, and a cotton dress to wear in the afternoons. . . My father was in politics before me. He was a member of the Legislative assembly. We always talked politics at home. My mother never had a public life but she always had her views, she would say, "all you talking damn nonsense in this house." We had servants but my mother did a lot of the work herself. She was very good at making cakes and so on. My father had three estates, he used to leave early in the morning to go to one of them every day. (Charles 2002d)

And:

> I did not miss not being married because I was very close to my family. I could discuss anything with my father and mother. My father gave me a lot of advice, I didn't always take it, sometimes he would say what you are doing is damn nonsense. (Charles 2002d)

When Charles gained political office, her administration faced an economy that had been physically battered by two hurricanes and a society that had been politically traumatized by widespread civil unrest in response to Patrick John's schizophrenic and dangerous leadership. Asked to identify the problems the country faced when she became prime minister, Eugenia Charles said the country was poor and "there was insufficient revenue to run government's affairs, to run the country" (Charles 2002c). There were not enough Dominicans trained in specialized skills and there was an especial need for workers trained in agriculture and nursing. As a component of the gross domestic product, she stated, agriculture was not earning enough money for the country (Charles 2002c). Asked to identify what her priorities in planning were, she stated, "I prioritised roads – physical infrastructure, education, agriculture, health. I did a lot for education and I think it is because of my family background. I wanted a school in every village, sometimes children had to walk to another village, often they couldn't go to school, it was too long to walk" (Charles 2002).

Hers was an economic philosophy grounded in the rhythms of every-day life. It included respect for the local environment and culture. She firmly believed in philanthropic assistance for those less fortunate. However, that approach never yielded to a systemic concern with whether the organization of society and the means by which goods and services were produced generated the conditions that the poor knew as a way of life. Charles supported the ownership of private property, especially land: "I like people to own their land" (Charles 2002c). She believed in the state offering a basic bundle of social goods such as health, education, a physical infrastructure and functioning utilities. She also believed these established the foundation for private-sector stimulation of economic growth. She firmly believed the private sector should be the engine of economic growth; one of her regrets was not being able to stimulate the private sector to play a larger investment and entrepreneurial role in carving out an approach to the development of Dominica (Lazare 2002). Her approach to development was informed by a commitment to a free market ideology, maintaining a tight fiscal rein on government expenditure and providing a vanguard-style, crusading leadership. She was strongly convinced that she knew what was best for the poor, the peasants, rural labour and the econ-omy on the whole. The belief that private-sector investment should be the catalyst for economic growth, in a context in which the private sector in Dominica did not have the capacity or the political will to see itself in a development role, led her to search the corridors of Western, capitalist powers and institutions for this capital.

There is an implicit notion of social stasis in her view of society. Dominica still seemed to be the rural society of her childhood, a semi-feudal economy brushing against widening democratic participation. There were rich planters and poor peasants, and the latter could be eased out of conditions of abject poverty by investment to create a social and physical infrastructure. It did not include a larger vision of the reorganiza-tion of production through a modernization of the economy. There was no concern with dismantling the old, social hierarchies even though these had proven more resistant to social engineering than was previously thought.

Regional/International Political Economy: Emergency Assistance

> We survived by what can only be described as emergency assistance – grants-in-aid and ad hoc development grants and loans. This finger-in-the-dyke policy continued right on to independence in 1978 by which time the economy of the island had deteriorated to the point of disaster. (Charles 1982d, 2)

In 1980, the DFP won the election with the highest percentage of valid votes cast in all elections held between 1951 and 1990 (Emmanuel 1992, 11). Eugenia Charles received a clear mandate from the electorate to manage Dominica's political and economic affairs. Up until that point Eugenia Charles was dissatisfied with British development assistance to Dominica and was not afraid to say so: "When Dominica, as with most of the LDC's in the Caribbean, achieved partial constitutional independence in 1967, the economy was already in shambles" (Charles 1982d, 2). During one of her many trips abroad to raise development financing, one can sense Eugenia Charles's frustration at what she perceived as the reluctance of the British government, through the office of the Overseas Development Agency (ODA), to provide financial assistance to the banana industry. Instead it offered assistance in kind – fertilizer, fungicide, field boxes, export boxes (Charles 1982b, 5):

> I pointed out to the Ministers of the U.K. that all the islands required an injection of cash. That I found it impossible to understand the reluctance on the part of the O.D.A. to give such cash to Dominica and that I could not accept the excuse that they could not refinance. I pointed out that that was the language of the Commercial Banks and should not be the language of aid donors. (Charles 1982b, 5)

She was underscoring a view that in spite of internal mismanagement, the British colonial experience had not been beneficial to Dominica's economic development. She stated quite plainly that before the country attained associated statehood or partial constitutional independence in 1967 the economy was already wrecked, thus fingering the British government for most of the responsibility for Dominica's underdeveloped state (Charles 1982d, 2).

When the DFP took control of governmental affairs, the conservative political orientation of Charles and her administration met a regional and international climate inclined towards her right wing, political outlook. Ronald Reagan, Republican and arch-conservative, was elected president of the United States and introduced immediate changes in US foreign policy in the region in reaction to the following developments.

In the Caribbean three revolutions sent shock waves throughout the generally placid Caribbean community. In Grenada the People's Revolutionary Government, led by Maurice Bishop, overthrew the Eric Gairy government on 13 March 1979, and in Nicaragua and Suriname governments were also replaced by revolutionary means. Even though "[t]he US has always maintained a military presence in the Caribbean and cooperated extensively with European colonial powers in the post-war period to consolidate its geopolitical interests, it has traditionally regarded political events in the Anglophone Caribbean with benign neglect" (Barriteau 2001b, 4; on the same point, see Phillips and Young 1986).

The Caribbean left-leaning revolutions changed that. The United States responded with the Caribbean Basin Economic Recovery Act, commonly called the Caribbean Basin Initiative or CBI; and, through the United States Agency for International Development, it pressed for an expanded role for the region's private sectors and a reduction in governments' involvement in their economies (Barriteau 2001b, 4). Ironically these measures for retrenchment of the state and the services it provided were being made while many economies were beginning to experience structural adjustment programmes after failing to meet debt servicing obligations. Economically the decade of the 1980s was one of the most debilitating for Caribbean economies and all of the developments were exacerbated in an underdeveloped, mono-crop, agricultural economy such as Dominica's.

National Context: Finger-in-the-Dyke Policies

> If my government will be allowed to do nothing else that is worthwhile during its term of office, we will have introduced and maintained considerable measure of discipline in the use and accounting for public finances. (Charles 1982d, 1)

When Eugenia Charles assumed political office two conditions collided: her unorthodox approach to development, and the economic realities of Dominica and the Caribbean in the 1980s. The intersection of her philosophy with the Dominican socio-economic and cultural context produced an economic policy mix characterized by ad hoc policies seemingly out of sync with Dominica's long-term developmental needs and the economic development strategies pursued by most anglophone Caribbean countries in the 1980s. More pertinently, the economic policies pursued were not based on an overall, long-term, strategic plan for the Dominican economy, but seemed informed by the conditions facing the Charles administration on gaining office. Unfortunately what started out as a need to respond to immediate crises extended into a series of reactive, then sectoral measures over a fifteen-year period.

On becoming the minister of finance and external affairs, Charles faced an economy that had been physically battered by two hurricanes and a society traumatized by two coup attempts by disgruntled, disarmed defence force soldiers and mercenaries during her first months as prime minister. Asked to identify the problems Dominica faced when she assumed political power, she said the country was poor and there was insufficient government revenue to run the country (Charles 2002c). "Not enough Dominicans were trained and there was an especial need for workers to be trained in agriculture and nursing. Agriculture as a component of the GDP was not earning enough money. I prioritized physical infrastructure, especially roads, followed by education, agriculture and health" (Charles 2002c). Her senior economic advisers agree with her assessment. They spoke of the very extenuating circumstances confronting Eugenia Charles and her administration in 1980. The new government faced a huge public debt. In addition to the physical devastation of the economy and the climate of political instability, there were other factors challenging the new administration. The country lacked a highly skilled labour force. There was no entrepreneurial class, and the government did not have a critical mass of technocrats to assist in reconstruction or strategic planning.

To emphasize the peculiar fiscal battles her new administration had to fight, Eugenia Charles reminded Dominicans of the highly questionable agreement proposed to establish the Caribbean Southern Corporation. This was introduced (and eventually withdrawn) by the previous administration on terms very detrimental to the state and people. The agreement had established a free port authority in which no government taxes would be levied on any entity operating within the free port (Dominica 1981d, 4). According to the terms of the aborted agreement, the government would receive EC$30,000 per year in rent and 100,000 non-voting shares of the corporation. The agreement proposed to give Caribbean Southern Corporation wide-ranging powers that, according to Charles, placed it supreme in the state. The convention by which it was established "took precedence over any laws, statutes and regulations which might be in conflict with the terms of the convention" (Dominica 1981d, 4). The terms of the Caribbean Southern Convention concerned Charles greatly since it had threatened government revenue from custom duties and excise taxes which in 1981 constituted 30 per cent of government revenue. Not only did this agreement represent a serious drain on the treasury through lack of revenue but new enterprises entering the country would automatically relocate to the free port to escape government taxation (Dominica 1981d, 4).

The 1981–82 budget revealed that the Charles administration was under serious financial pressure to repair past social and physical infrastructural damage, deliver government goods and services, meet existing obligations to civil servants and undertake capital expansion (Dominica 1981d).

To attempt to control the fiscal deficit, in November 1980 the Charles government negotiated a loan with the International Monetary Fund to reduce the current account deficit and an inherited debt of EC$12 million in salary arrears (Dominica 1981d, 3). She noted that while capital grants and loans were abundant, donors shied away from aid to support consumption as opposed to investment expenditure: "With or without help domestic measures had to be taken if the country was not to collapse completely" (Dominica 1981d, 17).

In her first term she concentrated on stabilizing the economy, revitalizing the banana industry, delivering government goods and services and rebuilding the financial and political credibility of the country. Economic stability rested on bananas and Eugenia Charles prioritized this. This was before the World Trade Organization forced the removal of the preferential status for Caribbean bananas in Europe. Lazare reports that the personal attention she gave to this sector soon paid off and farmer confidence was restored and output increased: "She reformed the revenue system, eased the tax burden and spread it out more so that people began to experience the system as equitable" (Lazare 2002). She also tried to push the tourism sector but her administration felt that the absence of an international airport was a major constraint. Efforts to raise capital to finance a new airport became a preoccupation and disappointment at the end of her second term. Alick Lazare related that when Dominica switched to an ecotourism marketing strategy, the government had no clear image of what they really wanted and did not identify the market very well. While the government accepted that ecotourism did not have a mass market and required certain types of accommodation, they also recognized that the existing accommodation was substandard (Lazare 2002). Charles managed to persuade the British and French to finance the rehabilitation of the Roseau Bay Front and in fact she spoke fondly and proudly of this (Charles 2002c). The British also financed the formation of the Dominica Export Import Agency (DEXIA) in the late 1980s. The administration pushed the farmers to diversify agricultural production but this met with minimal success. While the Bay Front development enhanced cruise ship arrivals, Lazare felt they had not developed sufficient linkages with other tourism products to maximize the returns from the new facility (Lazare 2002).

Charles's first term ended with Dominica gaining international exposure from her role in the US-led invasion of Grenada. Douglas reports that her close links with the US administration took root after the Grenada invasion while her contacts within the Republican Party predisposed the Reagan administration to be favourable towards Dominica (Douglas 2002). Gilbert Williams observed that, while in the first term Charles concentrated on the reconstruction of the economy, in the second term she focused heavily on the social infrastructure, especially primary health care (Williams 2002). Charles presided over the establishment of health clinics with resident doctors in all the major villages. This was a significant innovation for Dominica and indeed for the Caribbean and was based on the World Health Organization model of preventative health care (Williams 2002). Her second term saw solid consolidation and the high point of production in the banana industry before Hurricane Hugo struck (Yankey 2002a). Bernard Yankey states Charles mastered the implementation process between 1985 and 1990.

Despite some successes, Charles "was forced to again approach the IMF" at the end of her second term in office (Williams 2002). Williams felt that the introduction of the Common External Tariff (CET) by CARICOM had had the effect of reducing revenues from custom and excises; when this was compounded by the devastation from Hurricane Hugo, which destroyed about 75 per cent of the country's banana crop (Higbie 1993, 273), the government was forced to enter into a second International Monetary Fund arrangement (Williams 2002).

Eisenhower Douglas is the only senior economic adviser to the Charles government to mention that there were some efforts to generate a long-term development plan, but he added that this was hampered by human capital constraints, and the "firefighting" of immediate issues predominated: "There was no space for taking on long term plans, we agreed to do this but in reality never got around to this" (Douglas 2002). Instead the Ministry of Finance produced eight sectoral plans with the assistance of the European Union, UN agencies and the Canadian International Development Agency (Douglas 2002). According to Douglas the intention was to integrate these sectoral plans to produce one development plan; the ministry tried to get the help of the University of the West Indies to do this but the consolidated plan was never produced. Douglas concludes that the emphasis on projects was generally beneficial but they did not examine how these projects tied together at the national level (Douglas 2002).

By the beginning of Eugenia Charles's third term political and economic problems had coalesced. A crisis occurred again in the banana industry due to a combination of economic and political factors. This was the beginning of the reduction in preferences globally and the government was challenged with finding an appropriate response (Douglas 2002). Douglas states the rate of growth in the economy in the 1990s slowed to half of the mean growth rate of the 1980s. This decline continued to the end of the 1990s. Douglas (2002) commented that as the decade of the 1990s unfolded, the level of productivity in the banana industry declined, but there was no economic substitute for the banana industry. As banana production declined, Charles placed her hopes on growth in the tourism industry: "it was beginning to take off". Tourist spending from the second to the third term more than doubled and the Roseau cruise ship terminal along with the rehabilitated Bay Front fuelled the administration's hopes (Douglas 2002).

A fiscal crisis was again looming but this one could not be attributed to poor practices of the previous or current administration. The cracks in the fiscal policy as well as the minuscule character of the Dominican economy were beginning to show. Although Charles tried to maintain foreign debt services payments, her administration was not able to pay its bills to the local private sector. It was within this context that the most controversial economic initiative of the Charles administration became attractive.

Deteriorating to the Point of Disaster: The Economic Citizenship Programme

As minister of finance, Eugenia Charles introduced the contentious Economic Investment and Citizenship Programme to generate capital to build the Layou River Hotel Project. Especially at its implementation, the project and its policies were very controversial and raised concerns nationally and regionally (Armour 1992a, 1992b; Edwards 1992; Rawlins 1992; Lazare 2002; Douglas 2002; Williams 2002; John 1992b, 1992c). This project seemed to have arrived suddenly but would have been discussed before policy papers began surfacing in 1991. As the project developed the objectives kept evolving and changing. According to the policy guidelines tabled in parliament in 1991, the Economic Investment and Citizenship Programme was aimed at investors from the Pacific Rim countries. It was introduced to enhance job creation, generate foreign exchange earnings and meet the needs of the youth population (Dominica n.d., 1). By August 1991 when the first agreement signed between the government and Grace Tung was tabled in parliament, the project was described as a business migration programme with great potential for generating investment capital. The preamble was careful to set out all the industrialized and developing countries, such as the United States, Canada, Australia, Trinidad and Tobago, and St Kitts–Nevis that had similar programmes (Dominica n.d., 1). The earlier guidelines stated the capital raised was to assist in developing local capital projects, the two main ones being financing of the local component of the international airport and the hotel and resort development project previously known as the Layou River Hotel. The latter was to be the principal beneficiary. It was described as a massive hotel complex at the Layou River Hotel site with 240 rooms and 250 villas (Armour 1992a, 1).

According to the final agreement signed between the Government of Dominica and Grace Tung the programme would work in the following manner. A potential investor and up to three dependents would gain economic citizenship after the investor applied and deposited US$35,000 in a designated escrow account.[15] The monies from the first escrow account would be paid into another escrow account in the name of Oriental Hotel (Dominica) Limited and would be used to finance the construction of the new tourism complex at the site of the old Layou River Hotel. There were several stringent regulations built into the agreement in relation to the disbursement of funds. However, the net result was that the monies raised would become the investment capital for a hotel venture owned by Grace Tung – simultaneously promoter, honorary consul and 25 per cent shareholder in the company designated to build the hotel (Armour 1993).

The programme generated a great deal of public discussion and resentment and the government was accused of selling passports. Letters were written to Charles and her cabinet, some by groups sympathetic to the government but troubled by the programme (Edwards 1992; Carlton 1992). Several of the amendments to the agreement proposed by Tung were rejected by the government on the advice of the attorney general. If her proposals had been left unchallenged, it would have put the programme beyond the regulatory reach of the government. The final agreement acknowledged and incorporated many of the suggestions made by civil society but it generated much negative publicity and confusion about exactly what was being undertaken. When the Freedom Party lost the 1995 elections, the new administration changed the terms of the agreement so that the investment income was paid to the government. To date, however, the hotel has not been built even though there was a ground-breaking ceremony on 27 April 1992.

Donor-Driven Development

Eugenia Charles responded to the early crises she faced in 1980 with a strategy that would come to define her approach to development – donor-driven financing. In the short term this strategy enabled her to stave off financial collapse of the state even though it was buttressed on two occasions by International Monetary Fund programmes. In the long run it proved disastrous. Having placed Dominica's development in the basket of donor financing, it left her administration financially vulnerable when the international climate changed and key allies were lost in the early 1990s. The very strategy that brought short- and medium-term gains by underwriting economic survival and recovery began to unravel by the beginning of her final term. I contend it contributed significantly to the Freedom Party's loss of the 1995 general elections. Much of the promised large-scale capital expansion, especially the promise of an international airport, was premised on grants-in-aid and in-kind contributions by major donors and friendly governments such as the Thatcher and Reagan administrations:

> Negotiations for the international airport began in the second term. The intention was that the Americans would assist with earth moving for the airport. The British had donated the feasibility study, the Americans would do the land clearing which would be 40% of the runway cost. The government would receive soft funding from Taiwan for surfacing the runaway and the terminal building. The momentum was lost after the Gulf War. The US administration was preoccupied, Bush lost the elections. (Douglas 2002)

When rapidly changing international events produced a shift in US policy and promised funding, Charles was forced to seek other sources of donor funding, leading her to the very controversial and ill-advised Economic Investment and Citizenship Programme. The latter had the hallmark of being hastily conceived and poorly thought through, and according to Charles's senior advisers, it was uncharacteristic of her: "Ms Charles might have been misled on that, she did not have the benefit of enough research and analysis. It was uncharacteristic of her to allow a project like that to go through – her normal style was to put together a team for analysis" (Lazare 2002).

> I saw the agreement one day, it came to my desk after it was signed. There were no checks or security to make sure the project was implemented. I was asked to open the escrow account. The Layou River Hotel existed before Ms Charles had shares in it, she was a share holder with Nassief and others. The hotel was not doing good. They used money from the Economic Investment Programme to buy the

old hotel. Ms Charles seemed to have had a conflict of interest on it. (Williams 2002)

The overriding emphasis on donor-driven development had left her administration without a development strategy when donor financing evaporated: "She was probably grasping at straws at that point" (Lazare 2002).

More than an elapsed decade separated the policies and experiences of 1992 from those of 1982. In 1982 most of the Caribbean had been supporting Eugenia Charles in what was seen as her brave, admirable attempt to return stability and respect to Dominica's politics and society. In 1992 many Caribbean people and some governments were disillusioned with her role in the Grenada invasion.

In 1982 she had been months away from dazzling conservative America and winning extensive support for her domestic policies by her support of the US invasion of Grenada: "Charles was a sixty-four-year-old passionately pro-American leader who Motley felt made British Prime Minister Margaret Thatcher seem like a kitten. Menges considered her a Caribbean Jeanne Kirkpatrick. In 1982 the United States had begun supplying funds to build a thirty-mile, $10 million road on Dominica (Woodward 1987, 290). In 1982 she had already begun an indefatigable routine of ceaseless travel in search of assistance: "I am pleased to report that the many tiring journeys I have undertaken in the past year, have brought much needed assistance to our country, and I am happy that I have been able to undertake them and to produce the results which are evident all over Dominica" (Charles 1984b, 21). By 1992 she was tired and injured, having suffered two falls, the latter on a visit to Taiwan. In 1982 she was able to successfully plan for the recovery of the banana industry; by 1992 the banana industry had suffered another battering from another hurricane, but more threateningly, Europe held foreboding of the coming loss of preferential access. In 1982 she was on the ascendancy of her political career; by 1992 she was preparing to resign as leader of the Freedom Party and to retire from active politics. In 1982 she vetted every government project and proposal with rigorous scrutiny; in 1992 she and her cabinet clearly were misled about the initial workings of the Economic Investment and Citizenship Programme.

In particular, they were unable to see, or preferred not to see, the glaring conflict of interest in the multiple and intersecting roles played by Grace Tung. Tung was simultaneously the honorary consul of the Commonwealth of Dominica in the Republic of China on Taiwan and Consul General of the Commonwealth of Dominica in Hong Kong, even as she was – not in her consular capacity but as a separate responsibility – also promoter of the Economic Investment and Citizenship Programme to the Pacific Rim countries. Additionally, she was managing director of Oriental Hotel (Dominica) Limited, the company designated to build the Layou River Hotel Project and to benefit financially from investments generated by the purchase of Dominica's citizenship, and she also was a 25 per cent shareholder of International Development and Management Limited, the construction firm that would undertake the construction of the hotel (Dominica 1991a, 1991b; Armour 1992a, 1992b, 1993, 1). Grace Tung seemed very proficient at diplomatic multitasking.

Yet Eugenia Charles, who enjoyed a reputation as a scrupulously honest politician, seemed oblivious to a possible conflict of interest in the government's seeking to resuscitate the Layou Hotel Project with funds from the Economic Citizenship and Investment Programme.

Donor development also was very costly to Charles personally. It involved numerous trips abroad which she undertook willingly and with great energy. In 1982 her travel itinerary was dizzying: she travelled to Bogotá, Colombia, for a state visit from 1 to 3 March; to Paris and London from 7 to 13 March and to Washington, DC, from 15 to 19 June. In Bogota on 2 March, she met with the minister of foreign affairs, the minister of justice, and the minister of education. On 3 March she met with the minister of agriculture, the minister of economic development, the minister of labour and social security and the director of the Bank of the Republic (Charles 1982a). On reading the report of her trip, what is discernible is the inequality between the two countries and the vulnerability of Dominica in discussing potential trade or requesting financial assistance. For example, many promises of assistance were made. On closer scrutiny Colombia wanted to export its goods and expertise. Specifically, Colombia wanted to export coffee and cement to Dominica. The meeting with the director of the Bank of the Republic was dominated by discussion on the provision of a line of credit to Dominica to purchase cement from Colombia on a bimonthly basis (Charles 1982a). In return Dominica might export grass mats to Colombia (Charles 1982a). The net proposal was that Dominica would borrow money from Colombia to buy Colombian goods, sustaining interest rate payments and employment for Colombians.

From 15 to 19 June 1982, Charles attended the fifth annual meeting of the Caribbean Group for Cooperation in Economic Development in Washington, DC, where she participated in fifteen separate meetings in two days. On 16 June she attended six meetings, the first beginning at 8:00 a.m. and the last at 6:15 p.m. On 17 June there were nine meetings bracketed between an 8:30 a.m. start and a 5:00 p.m. ending. Several years later, in 1990, when she fell and broke her leg in a hotel room while visiting Taiwan, she proceeded to work from her hospital bed.

Conclusion

Eugenia Charles deserves full credit for attempting to tackle the nuts and bolts of the country's economy. Her fifteen-year stewardship involved significant effort on her part to introduce fiscal discipline in the use of government resources. She was relatively successful in reining in runaway recurrent expenditure but this was insufficient to stimulate a sluggish, lethargic economy whose means of generating output was still characterized by the use of nineteenth-century practices. She worked hard to reduce the foreign debt, build a social and economic infrastructure and encourage the private sector to play a lead role in stimulating the local economy. Her administration also deserves recognition for trying to maintain a degree of integrity in public office. Even though towards the end of her tenure the grey areas surrounding the introduction of the Economic Investment and Citizenship Programme clouded her record, she did restore a degree of fiscal integrity to the public accounts.

Yet Eugenia Charles failed to deliver a vision for the development of Dominica. I maintain that this was an outcome of the piecemeal, programmatic manner in which she understood what needed to be done to encourage economic growth and development. As a conservative, Eugenia Charles was committed to reform, to working within the system, but the existing economic system in Dominica was too narrow to achieve much without venturing outside its imported constraints. Two additional factors made it difficult to stimulate the Dominican economy. These were the inherent constraints of size and capacity as these related to Dominica and Eugenia Charles's own economic philosophy. As a conservative committed to a modified laissez-faire economic philosophy, she believed the private sector should stimulate economic growth. However she had no training in economics and did not perceive that beyond a mercantilist, capitalist orientation, the private sector in Dominica did not have the capacity to stimulate the economy. As well-meaning as her economic planning was, it was anachronistic. It looked back to an earlier time and a simpler society. This was ironic because Dominica, more than any other eastern Caribbean country, needed to be catapulted into the twenty-first century. Dominica's economy needed radical reorganization, especially since it could not rely on a traditional tourism product and its main agricultural output was in serious decline. In the final analysis Eugenia Charles was perhaps the best person in her administration to be the minister of finance, but it was not enough. Her educational background and her economic philosophy did not predispose her to be innovative. Her articulation of what was required was a shopping list of sectoral programmes that did not add up to a long-term vision.

Notwithstanding these points, there can be no doubt that Eugenia Charles endeavoured to do the best in very difficult circumstances. All of her senior economic advisers insist she should be remembered as a woman and a prime minister who gave her best for her country. They credit her with building up a sense "of individual independence among people, and inculcating in them a spirit of independence and self-reliance" (Lazare 2002); "She brought respect back to the population" (Williams 2002), and "Dominica benefited tremendously from her administration" (Yankey 2002a). Eisenhower Douglas summed up her contribution in this way: "She sought to improve the life of the common people and believed the will of the people was very important. I believe she was our greatest prime minister" (Douglas 2002).

Notes

1. Alick Lazare was a senior economic adviser and career civil servant who worked in the Charles administration for thirteen years, first as financial secretary from 1981 to 1988 when he retired, and then as a fiscal adviser from 1988 to 1994. Gilbert Williams was financial secretary from 1989 to 1997 and also served briefly as cabinet secretary in the 1990–95 term. Eisenhower Douglas was a senior economist who worked with Eugenia Charles from 1988 to 1995. He held various positions such as head of planning and acted in various capacities. Bernard Yankey was a trusted adviser and political confidant. His official position was senior economist at the Caribbean Development Bank from 1972 to 1988, but he was appointed by the Bank to chair the reconstruction of the Dominica's economy during the first two terms of Charles's administration. He was Dominica's high commissioner to Canada from 1988 to 1992, and director of economic affairs and the OECS Secretariat in Antigua from 1993 to 1995.

2. Her more critical later comments have to be nuanced with her statements in the 1981 budget address that were supportive of CARICOM initiatives. On a closer reading, however, Charles is merely restating what the community said it would do, and her statement remains relatively guarded (Dominica 1981d, 2).

3. Lazare credits her with achieving a turnaround in the banana industry relatively early in her first term by a complete reorganization which resulted in a major rebuilding of the industry. He said she took a personal interest in this. The government restructured the banana board and allowed the board to manage. She appointed strong persons, investigated field practices, processing and marketing. She insisted on regular reports and good information systems. In a short time farmers regained confidence and rationalized production, and output grew from a low of 30,000 tonnes to a high of about 70,000 (Lazare 2002).

4. Included among her papers are several letters from Dominicans living abroad both criticizing and praising her for key developments within her tenure.

5. Especially during her first term of office and while an opposition parliamentarian, Charles did not merely give the appearance of being harsh, she revelled in her reputation for harshness. See Janet Higbie (1993) for some of the caustic statements she made and controversial positions she adopted.

6. Eugenia Charles and Margaret Thatcher were contemporaries with great similarities in background and while in office. Margaret Thatcher was elected for three consecutive terms beginning in 1979; Charles's three terms began in 1980. They both presided over all-male cabinets and both repeatedly identified their fathers as being the most decisive figures in their rise to political power. They both transformed politics in their countries and remain to date the only female prime ministers from their respective countries. Eugenia Charles has the

added distinction of being the only female prime minister in the Commonwealth Caribbean, up until March 2006 when Portia Simpson Miller became
prime minister of Jamaica. They were both leaders of conservative parties and
worked well together even though it is clear Eugenia Charles suggested at times
the British government was not doing enough for its former colony. See
Genovese 1993a.

7.   It also reflected a rabid and irrational fear of Cuba, Castro and communism in
the Caribbean fed by US cold-war propaganda. As a teenager I often heard
older people mention with fear that a particular man or woman was "red" or
communist. They made that sound as if it were equivalent to killing babies.

8.   Lennox Honychurch says the "leaders within the constituencies" to whom she
refers were all women.

9.   I am not trying to suggest here that the government introduced a flat rate that
therefore proved regressive. This is not a discussion of the actual policy that
would have been worked on by technocrats and would reflect usage and vol-
ume as a basis for pricing. Instead I am focusing on how Charles approached
her constituents with an explanation of the policy, told them there was a cost
whether they liked it or not and felt that thereby she had consulted the people.

10.   While attending secondary school in Roseau, she returned to the family home
in Point Michel by boat every Friday; she later continued her secondary education at St Joseph's Convent in Grenada.

11.   Laurence Charles, one of Eugenia's older brothers, explained their father's insistence that they speak English but underscored the ease with which they moved
in and out of the world of the workers.

12.   From 1940 to 1942, she completed her secondary education at St Joseph's
Convent in Grenada, then the most developed colony of the Windward Island
states of Dominica, Grenada, St Lucia and St Vincent. She then proceeded to the
University of Toronto to study law and, after the war had ended, to the
University of London to complete professional training as a barrister at law.

13.   "We learnt to save our money, my father learnt not to throw away our money.
We didn't live like paupers, but we didn't live like the wealthy either. We were
not made to believe we were wealthy, but money could always be found for
school" (Charles 2002c).

14.   Eugenia Charles delivered the 1995 inaugural Caribbean Women Catalyst for
Change Lecture, dedicated the following year to honouring the memory of
Dame Nita, who had died on 19 December 1995, seven weeks after the lecture.

15.   A dependent is defined as a spouse or an unmarried child under eighteen years
of age.

8

Enterprise Development and Poverty Alleviation in Dominica
The Role and Motivations of Eugenia Charles

JONATHAN LASHLEY

Introduction

The global economy during the period of Charles's rise to power in the 1970s and her tenure as prime minister of Dominica ending in the mid-1990s was characterized by a neoliberal development paradigm promoted and promulgated by the International Monetary Fund and the World Bank. This dominant paradigm emphasized an embracing of the market mechanism as the only true path to economic growth. This emphasis on economic growth has been replaced only in the last decade by a realization that development was more than economic growth, but that economic and social development were crucial.

This was the political economy of the region that framed Charles's approach to development – a political economy characterized and dominated by the oft-mentioned "Reaganomics". Reaganomics emphasized the importance of monetarism and the market: profit, weak trade unions, low inflation through macroeconomic management and the stimulation of growth through supply-side economics (Payne and Sutton 2001). The direct influence on Dominica was that this ideology was impressed by the

214

US administration upon the Bretton Woods institutions, upon which Dominica relied heavily for funding. This influence by the US government was possible because of the power the United States wielded within these major sources of funding for development initiatives. These neoliberal views were to affect Charles's approach to development in her native Dominica. However, it was not purely out of necessity that such an approach was taken by Charles, for indeed she appeared to have a belief in this mode of development due to her conservative nature.

The effect of this neoliberal approach to development was to separate the tools used to achieve economic growth directly and those used to address the problem of poverty. This dominant paradigm required governments in developing countries to provide the "enabling environment" for enterprise development – by which was meant infrastructural provision, while approaches to poverty alleviation were twofold. In the first instance, direct poverty alleviation was thought to emerge from the provision of education, health and roads, while indirect poverty alleviation was thought to trickle down from enterprise development with the creation of jobs and its associated multipliers. This was the approach Charles took to enterprise development and poverty alleviation during the majority of her term in office, as this chapter will demonstrate. However, a paradox emerges and demonstrates the separation of Charles, the prime minister of Dominica, from Charles, the community member. The paradox is seen where, as prime minister, she espoused the credentials of the neoliberal approach to development; however, in her private life she readily utilized more welfare-like approaches to supporting her community, including monetary handouts and paying school fees for the youth.

In investigating her motivations, this chapter chronicles the role of Charles in enterprise development in Dominica during her term in office as prime minister. It also considers the lack of attention paid to enterprise development as a means to assist in the alleviation of poverty among the Dominican population.

Charles's Laissez-Faire Attitude

In the late 1970s, the period of Charles's rise to power, international aid agencies were providing funding for development. On gaining office

Charles fought for and received funding from these agencies. However, despite accepting such funds and principles, Charles's administration appears to have had little impact on enterprise development or poverty alleviation during its time in power. It was not until the end of Charles's third term in office that this deficiency was recognized and greater attention paid to enterprise development as a means to alleviate poverty. Although Charles never ventured far from her original conservative orientation, there was a shift from a belief in "trickle-down" economics to one appreciative of the developmental benefits of bottom-up policy initiatives, initiatives with the small-businessperson at its base. As she stated, "We have no history or tradition of a domestic entrepreneurial class or a truly market-orientated economy. Ours is a dependent economy" (Dominica 1994b, 5). What is surprising about this statement is that Charles made it in 1994, fourteen years after Charles and the Dominica Freedom Party came to power. It amounted to a tacit admission that her administration had largely failed in its efforts to promote entrepreneurship, a fact that the evidence also shows.

During Charles's tenure as prime minister there were international funds available for enterprise development and poverty alleviation. However, these objectives were not explicitly linked. In demonstrating the importance of such funds, this external funding proved integral to the success of the National Development Foundation in Dominica (NDFD), the primary non-governmental organization (NGO) for business development in Dominica, which was founded in 1981 with direct assistance from Charles. The NDFD was established to provide support for "non-bankable" enterprises through the provision of loans and training. It is considered one of the most entrepreneurial micro-financing institutions in the Caribbean, despite recent financial difficulties (von Stauffenberg 2000). However, the effectiveness of the institution has been questioned due to excessive government intervention in recent times.

Overview of Government Initiatives, 1980–1995

The following analysis charts the evolution of enterprise development and poverty alleviation initiatives in Dominica during the period of Charles's stewardship as prime minister. During her administration there was spo-radic emphasis on the role of the entrepreneur and even less emphasis on traditional poverty alleviation measures. Over the period 1980 to 1995 there was an overriding emphasis on the development of the economy through the development of the private sector, with special attention being paid to promoting exports and attracting foreign investment. Charles appeared to firmly believe that her government's role was as a facilitator, a provider of infrastructure and guidance. This is evidenced in an extract from her budget speech of 1990, reflecting views expressed many times:

> We believe that it is government's function to provide the conditions and support systems necessary for economic and national development – to build the absorp-tive capacity of the economy for responding to growth and expansion. Once this is done, it is left to the private sector to carry on with the business of production. (Dominica 1990a, 17)

Despite this laissez-faire attitude, Charles had her own particular tilt on the ideology. As Janet Higbie recognized, Caribbean leaders of the time had two hats to wear – domestic and international (Higbie 1993). In this view, Charles was considered a "rabble-rouser" and international fund-raiser, who "begged until she got what she wanted" (Lashley and Lord 2002). In respect of this fund-raising activity, Charles believed that, despite going against free-market principles of survival of the fittest, such activity was necessary to ensure development in the Caribbean: "I believe in free enter-prise but I also believe that in the Caribbean government has to do things because you can't expect anybody else to do them . . . it's the way things are in these islands" (Higbie 1993, 261).

Although Charles believed in laissez-faire economics as an ideal, she also believed that due to the nature and level of development, governments in the Caribbean still had a large role to play in "getting things done". Overall Charles demonstrated a belief in entrepreneurship and in obtaining donor funding, and she expressed an appreciation for the specific contingent situ-ation in the Caribbean. These beliefs led to her administration being, or being considered as, "middle-right" rather than completely "right-wing" as suggested in some political circles (Higbie 1993; *Caribbean and West Indies Chronicle* 1985). For example, Michaels (1981) characterized the Dominica Freedom Party as conservative, pro-capitalist and pro-West. Michaels

(1981) viewed the Freedom Party's victory in 1980 as a "major departure from the decade of Labor [*sic*] control of Dominican politics" (Michaels 1981, 18). Michaels also noted that the role of the Freedom Party, previous to its election victory, was one characterized by concerted efforts to thwart "the socialist ideology of the party in power" (Michaels 1981, 18).

Despite these characterizations of Charles and the Freedom Party, there was an explicit belief in small-enterprise development as a means to promote economic growth. This belief is demonstrated in Charles's efforts to facilitate the establishment of the NDFD and obtain international funding for a variety of projects under the NDFD's control. As noted by Bernard Etinoff (2002), current manager of the NDFD, Charles played an integral role in the establishment of the NDFD.

However, having established that Charles supported enterprise development, an analysis of the current situation appears to show that little progress was made in terms of encouraging enterprise development as a means to promote poverty alleviation. A Country Poverty Assessment (CPA) undertaken at the end of Charles's term in office provides evidence of this. The CPA, conducted by Bonnerjea and Weir (1996), noted that there was more of an emphasis on agricultural diversification, export of manufactured goods and development of ecotourism than there was on poverty alleviation. Direct poverty alleviation strategies appeared to garner little explicit attention: that is, little attention was given to empowerment of the poor; instead, indirect approaches based on trickle-down economics were embraced. The approach to poverty alleviation was one that provided the basic needs of the population. It was thought that, once the poor had better health care, greater access to education and a better quality of living with access to water, electricity and roads, they would lift themselves out of poverty. This strategy ignored the fact that poverty was more than "simply a lack of funds, but . . . vulnerability, powerlessness, and dependency" (Bhatt and Tang 2001, 323). Bhatt and Tang (2001) go on to note that development finance institutions also need to assist the poor in overcoming these psychological problems of poverty. This may have been one of the reasons that Charles took the approach she did to poverty, where, although as prime minister and as a conservative she supported the neoliberal paradigm, she was still cognizant of the particular circumstances that existed in Dominica and the wider Caribbean. Even as she played a role in the development of the NDFD, her support for the development of the NGO movement demonstrated her commitment to the alleviation of poverty outside the neoliberal, top-down approach.

Returning to the CPA, in terms of the state of enterprise development, Bonnerjea and Weir (1996) also noted during their investigations in 1995 that there was a lack of entrepreneurial initiative among the populace of Dominica. This calls into question the effectiveness of Charles's policies and the NGO movement in Dominica specifically targeted at increasing the enterprise spirit. However, other causal issues may also be relevant, specifically, whether an historical overdependence on bananas had some role to play in retarding an entrepreneurial spirit among the peoples of Dominica.

Initially, the state of enterprise development and poverty alleviation during the period 1980 to 1995 is highlighted. This includes information on schemes adopted, the results of the CPA, and selected census data. This is followed by analysing information from a variety of sources, but primarily budgetary speeches, which highlight the direction Charles was taking towards economic development and development in general. In conclusion, the assessment provides an overview of Charles's motivation for the approaches taken to enterprise development and poverty alleviation.

Entrepreneurial Development and Poverty Alleviation in Dominica, 1980–1995

Entrepreneurial development is based on the provision of relevant training, accessible finance and technical assistance to enhance self-employment. However, a prerequisite for such an approach to succeed is the presence of an entrepreneurial culture. As Charles herself realized, no such culture existed in Dominica (Dominica 1994b). Though efforts were made to engender such a culture, these were not carried out in a very effective manner.

One of the main organizations with a mandate to develop micro and small enterprises, specifically targeting poverty alleviation, was the NDFD. Charles played a large part in the establishment of the NDFD, along with Phillip Massiph and others. The NDFD originally acted as a guarantor for small loans from two of the commercial banks on the island. Despite small contributions to the Foundation initially, due to Charles's "begging", eventually the NDFD was able to obtain substantial funding from the US Agency for International Development, and later from other major international donors. There are now several other initiatives in the country with a similar remit. Briefly, these include the following:

- *Dominican Hucksters Association (DHA)*. DHA, established in 1983, has a membership that comprises approximately 85 per cent women. The DHA provides training, loans (up to a maximum of EC$3000) and warehousing. One of the main remits of the DHA is to encourage the use of the Agricultural, Industrial and Development (AID) Bank.

- *Small Enterprise Development Unit (SEDU) of the National Development Corporation*. This is an agency of the Dominican government that provides consultancy and training services for small enterprises.

- *Small Projects Assistance (SPAT)*. SPAT was established in 1980 with a countrywide responsibility. However, by 1990 it had become more community based and it is currently operating as a catalyst for community based economic growth.

- *Dominican Save the Children*. This is an NGO to support self-reliance.

- *Christian Children's Fund*. Another NGO, this organization provides education, health care, skills and training to the youth.

Brown (1986) also notes the existence of government-run support organizations such as the Women's Bureau, local government and the Community Development Department. Brown (1986) also observes that the new "Farms to Market Limited" was timely in its provision of financing and technical assistance to the growing small-business sector. Farms to Market Limited provides refrigerated cargo-shipping facilities and farm-gate services. The mission of the company was to open up opportunities in the regional market and the huckster trade. With these developments in the support infrastructure of the small-business sector, Brown remarks that many social commentators have noted that "Dominica appears to be making every effort to devise a new path for its short and long term industrial development" (Brown 1986, 32).

Although government was keen to encourage small-enterprise growth, the orientation of commercial banks was counter to this, with an aversion to small farmers and the poor, a trend still seen across the Caribbean. Recent studies, including the poverty assessment and research by Lashley and Lord (2002), note that the poor still lack access to credit. The only institutions that provide credit to the poor are the AID Bank and the NDFD.

The AID Bank was established in 1971, while Charles had a direct role in the founding of the NDFD in 1981. The NDFD was established to provide support for "non-bankable" enterprises through the provision of loans and training with funding from the US Agency for International Development, the Canadian International Development Agency and the Overseas Development Agency. However, funding from the US Agency for International Development was lost in the early 1990s due to high default rates and what the agency considered low, unsustainable interest rates.

Despite the initiatives taken to alleviate poverty, increase enterprise development and promote self-reliance, Bonnerjea and Weir (1996) note that at the end of Charles's fifteen years in office, although there had been improvements in living conditions, poverty and vulnerability still existed to a large extent. However, there is no evidence available to judge how much the situation had improved during Charles's tenure, as this Country Poverty Assessment in 1995 was the first of its kind in Dominica and therefore provides little basis for comparison. In terms of poverty levels, Bonnerjea and Weir (1996) noted that 6 per cent of households (2 per cent of the population) were receiving assistance to counteract their poverty and that 12 per cent of households were considered as probably indigent. These observations led them to estimate that approximately 28 per cent of the population existed in poverty. The only other "estimate" that appears is that of Michaels, who notes that "[w]here ever they live, Dominicans are generally poor ... probably 35 per cent of the potential workforce, are jobless, and more are underemployed or employed part-time" (Michaels 1981, 18). Michaels also believed that the Freedom Party demonstrated a "lack of sympathy for Dominica's poor" (Michaels 1981, 19).

From their study, Bonnerjea and Weir (1996) outlined the determinants of poverty in Dominica as due to eight factors: small land plots which were too small for sustainable cultivation, landlessness, single-parent families, an underdeveloped informal sector, a weak social security system, a lack of marketing for crops other than bananas, insufficient non-agricultural employment and limited social safety nets for old age.

In addressing the first point, during her first year in office Charles implemented policy initiatives that acted as a catalyst to increase land ownership among the population. However, this initiative has subsequently led to the greater fragmentation of the land and the creation of plots that were too small for sustainable cultivation of traditional crops. In addressing the final point, Bonnerjea and Weir found that between 1986 and 1994 there was approximately a 13 per cent reduction in government services which has subsequently led to constraints on social safety nets in Dominica (Bonnerjea and Weir 1996). This can be considered as a direct consequence of the neoliberal orientation of the Charles administration and the related dictates embedded in the structural adjustment programmes of the Bretton Woods institutions. Although schemes had been implemented to deal with these issues during her time in office, there is little evidence that the schemes were successful. Where success has been seen, it has been in small isolated pockets, due mostly to the community-based Small Projects Assistance programme started in 1980.

In reviewing the main areas of concern of relevance to the current study, Bonnerjea and Weir (1996) observe the lack of non-farm employment, especially in the areas of tourism, fishing and small enterprise. In itself this acts as a sign that little was done during the Charles administration for the development of micro and small enterprises. In relation to this, the CPA also recommended that the NDFD needed to bring entrepreneurship to the poorest communities. The CPA concluded that the government's budget programmes had little direct emphasis on the poor. In relation to this it was noted that between 1989 and 1995 expenditure on agriculture and community development decreased to low levels, and was still falling. Bonnerjea and Weir (1996) attribute this as mostly due to a commitment to hiving off responsibility for poverty alleviation and community development to the NGO community. Bonnerjea and Weir (1996) also argue that another constraint in alleviating poverty among the rural poor was that NGOs in agriculture had unclear and overlapping mandates. These unclear or overlapping mandates (and the observation that cooperation among the support organizations was non-existent or sporadic) only acted to obstruct the efficient implementation of schemes aimed at poverty alleviation or enterprise development.

In looking at the apparent lack of appreciation for the specific contingent circumstances of the poor in Dominica, and demonstrating the government's preference for top-down policies, Bonnerjea and Weir (1996) note that in the area of bananas, there was greater apparent concern for the "industry" as a whole than for the needs of the smallest farmers. This was characteristic of the neoliberal economic paradigm that was dominant and influential at the time.

Despite Charles's strong belief in entrepreneurship and her overt concern for the poor, it was two years into her first term in office before measures were implemented specifically to assist small entrepreneurs (Dominica 1983b). The measures that were then implemented included the waiver of import duties on approved equipment, the provision (in the planning stage at the time) to convert the site at the Old Infirmary in the Baytown area to operate as workspace for mechanics and tradesmen who are unable to find affordable workspace and training for local handicraft entrepreneurs from all over the island so that they may return to their own communities and train others in utilizing local resources. Of these policy priorities, only the last addressed the poor entrepreneur in general, as most poor entrepreneurs were rural and unlikely to be importing production equipment. There appeared to be a lack of understanding of what characterized the poor.

The above demonstrate that there was an attempt during Charles's tenure to implement a supporting infrastructure for the development of the small business sector. However, in seeking to establish the success of such attempts, the following section compares results for the 1980 and 1990 population censuses in Dominica to demonstrate what progress was actually made.

Changes in Entrepreneurial Behaviour in Dominica, 1980–1990

Bonnerjea and Weir (1996) remarked that there was still a major need for high-risk entrepreneurial credit in Dominica after the end of Charles's admininstration as prime minister. This was borne out by the relatively static level of entrepreneurship in Dominica observed by a comparison between census data from 1980 and 1990. The following analysis is drawn from the "Population and Housing Census Report" (Dominica 1991c).

In analysing the results of the 1980 and 1990 censuses, only small increases in the number of entrepreneurs in the economy were seen:[1] in 1980, 7,677 persons had their own business or farm, 6,037 of which had no paid help; in 1990, own-account workers (no paid help) numbered only 6,238, an increase of a meagre 3.3 per cent. In terms of gender distribution, male own-account workers fell from 32.1 per cent of employed males to 29.3 per cent of employed males. Female own-account workers on the other hand increased marginally from 20.0 per cent to 20.3 per cent of employed females.

Between 1980 and 1990 there was a distinct change in the structure of the labour force. There was a decline in the share of government as an employer from 21.8 per cent to 15.3 per cent for males, and from 26.2 per cent to 22.0 per cent for females. The greatest recipient of these workers appears to have been the private sector, whose share of total employment increased from 34.1 per cent to 41.4 per cent for males, and from 44.5 per cent to 48.5 per cent for females.

It is therefore obvious that the change in own-account workers was marginal over the period 1980 to 1990. This is despite the implementation of schemes and policies to assist the development of entrepreneurship in Dominica over this period. As remarked above, this may have been due either to a lack of appreciation of the actual needs of the poor entrepreneur or perhaps to the structural adjustment policies instilled by the International Monetary Fund and World Bank, which diverted attention away from self-employment as a viable option in the search for economic growth. This and other issues are discussed in greater depth below.

Charles and Economic Development

In Charles's early years her father, J.B. Charles, ran what was known familiarly in Dominica as the "Penny Bank". It was founded in 1940 by J.B. and other Roseau businessmen under the name of the Co-operative Bank

(Higbie 1993). The formation of the bank was due to the realization that commercial banks were not serving the poor, who were only able to deposit small sums of money at any one time. The Penny Bank filled this gap and their approach mirrored a savings-led approach seen today in many micro-finance institutions worldwide.

The Penny Bank's origin was as a savings club started by P. I. Boyd. The Bank lent funds for land purchase, house construction and purchase of stock, automobiles and appliances. In this manner the Penny Bank was one of the very first formal micro-finance institutions in the world, despite the fact that micro-finance is perceived to have originated with the formation of the Grameen Bank in Bangladesh in the 1970s. Eugenia Charles's involvement with the Penny Bank began as its secretary upon her return to Dominica in 1949. Her association with the bank continued until the entity folded in the late 1970s, an event brought on by barriers implemented by the government of the time, barriers that Charles decided were too onerous to allow continued operation. As she stated in a recent interview, "The government came after us, [they] didn't want the Bank to continue so they put a lot of troubles in the way so, I say, I don't have to have that headache and I agreed and we set it down" (Charles 2002g).

In examining the development of Charles's views it is clear that she held a firm belief in the benefits of the trickle-down economics of the time. This is demonstrated by her belief that industrialization, if undertaken correctly, was a cure-all for the ills of unemployment, low standards of living, dependency, poverty and underinvestment (Dominica 1981d). What appears as a more left-wing tendency was her belief that money and time were being wasted on national defence when they could have been spent on "attempts to raise the standard of living of our own people in general and the less fortunate ones in particular" (Dominica 1981d, 4). However, if the political climate of the time is examined, including the difficulties Charles had with the defence force's loyalty to her predecessors, this can be considered simply an attack on the previous administration, especially as Charles undertook few explicit policies to address the problems she remarked on.

However, in terms of her focus on enterprise development, during her budget speech in 1981, five new strategies were proposed. Three of the five strategies, which were directed towards reconstruction and development, were business-development oriented. These three strategies included the following:

1. "Greater democratisation of the land in favour of landed entrepreneurs" (Dominica 1981d, 14). However, the issue of who were the landed entrepreneurs was not addressed.
2. "The encouragement of activities geared to agro-processing and enclave industry" (Dominica 1981d, 14).
3. "The strengthening of managerial and technological resources with particular focus on economic development" (Dominica 1981d, 14).

Other strategies proposed included the rehabilitation of infrastructure and rationalization of energy resources, mostly also geared to unlock "the potential of the directly productive sectors" (Dominica 1981d, 14). Overall, there is no explicit emphasis on policies directed specifically at the poor or small entrepreneurs.

In addressing the three strategies above, the following comments were made by Charles during her budget presentation:

1. *Land redistribution.* This would not be in the form of expropriation, but "transfers from large willing sellers to small willing buyers who demonstrate entrepreneurial commitment to develop these properties" (Dominica 1981d, 15). This was proposed to take place within the process of normal democracy.
2. *Agro-processing.* It was recognized that there was a need to change perceptions and orientations from domestic to international markets where a potential had been identified. This, however, does not appear an avenue available to the poor.
3. *Managerial and technological resources.* "Finally, the strengthening of our managerial and technological resources with a development focus is one area in which initiatives must also be taken. There is no point raising the hopes of taxpayers for cheap power if their sons and daughters are not encouraged to serve as managers and technicians in the plants which produce for the poor" (Dominica 1981d, 15–16).

In other words, participation and stakeholding were being encouraged by Charles.

As can be seen from the above, the private sector was expected to play a major role in development, and private, sector development was expected to be complementary to public sector development. This expectation is stressed several times throughout Charles's first budget address.

In addition to these policy directions, the National Development Corporation was founded to promote development in the private sector and to create employment (not entrepreneurship or self-employment), as well as to promote agro-industries and enclave industries plus others with an export orientation, both regional and extraregional. Charles also noted in her address that both local and foreign entrepreneurs were needed to promote economic development. The former were, however, (publicly) preferred.

In her budget speech in 1982, Charles further clarified her belief as to the role the state should play in development. She explicitly stated that the government considered that it should not be involved directly in industrial enterprise itself (Dominica 1982b). She believed that this should be left to the private sector, while government's role was seen to be the provider of necessary infrastructure and incentives to promote development of the private sector and, consequently, the development of Dominica.

It was not until 1983 that her administration made explicit the expected role of small entrepreneurs. In order to promote Dominica as attractive to foreign investors, Charles stated in her budget address that year that the government would need to expand industrial estates and provide assistance to small local entrepreneurs, mechanics and craftsmen (Dominica 1983b). Her intention was to remove any difficulties that were constraining private-sector development. In terms of resource allocation, Charles believed that scarce resources should not be for consumption but should be applied to export-oriented and other development enterprises. This was considered as a first priority for commercial bank resources and was thought necessary to promote technological transfer, especially skills, from foreign investors. It can therefore be seen that Charles believed that attracting foreign investment was going to be one of the main determinants of economic development, and especially the development of the human capital of the Dominican people. This was particularly important to Charles as she considered the people of Dominica as the country's most important resource, the other key resources being water and land. Charles believed that the minds of the people were the most important determinant of the development of productive power, and as such, she saw the potential to develop their minds through the promotion of foreign direct investment in Dominica. In essence, Charles saw investment in education as a part of a poverty alleviation effort.

In her 1984 budget address the private sector was again the focus for Charles. The private sector was considered to be where the "main thrust" of development would emerge (Dominica 1984). Charles sought to encourage local entrepreneurs to export, as well as encouraging investment by local and foreign companies. Related to this, Charles considered local content as important and she believed that advantage and investment should be directed towards Dominica's abundant natural resources, especially water and timber. In attempting to achieve this, concessions were offered to small businesses to encourage employment and income generation. These concessions are thought to have led to over EC$30 million in investments, mostly, however, from overseas (Dominica 1984).

During this period (1984 to 1985), the main governmental objectives included job creation, the transfer of technology and increasing export earnings. It appeared that previous policies to encourage private-sector development were working as the AID Bank's investment in industry was up from 29 per cent of total disbursement in 1980 to 60 per cent in 1983. Most of this investment was in small enterprises; consequently many who were previously employed in the public sector were now self-employed (Dominica 1984). This trend was not, however, seen in the long run as attested by the census figures discussed earlier.

In a sense Charles's attempt to develop the small business sector was merely a knock-on effect of her belief in small government: "[We] do not believe in keeping people dependent on government or in doing them favours. Our aim is to make as many Dominicans as possible economically independent and involved in some kind of gainful enterprise" (Dominica 1984, 9). Again in 1984, Charles reaffirmed her position as regards the role of government by stating that her government had no intention to engage directly in industrial enterprise; it was only seeking to promote the development of the private sector. There was the belief that this was the quickest and most effective way to increase employment, diversify and strengthen the economic base of the country (Dominica 1984).

To achieve these goals of promoting the development of the private sector, her administration developed policy goals in 1984, which were based on utilizing domestic resources, encouraging local entrepreneurship and stimulating local business development. In addition, three initiatives were noted to be assisting in achieving the objectives of private-sector development: the AID Bank's provision of more factory space, the Industrial Development Corporation's provision of industrial "nurseries" in the Bay Town area for small entrepreneurs and the construction of two small factories for small entrepreneurs with the assistance of the Government of South Korea. Charles therefore did pay specific attention to enterprise development; however, its explicit role was to assist in economic development rather than to directly alleviate poverty.

In reflecting a trend in the changing importance of micro and macro issues, in 1985 Charles returned to more macroeconomic concerns with little mention of microeconomic issues, enterprise development or poverty alleviation measures. In her 1985 budget address, Charles implicitly emphasised the dedication she paid to trickle-down economics, where the central theme of the budget was the encouragement of an export orientation for the economy (Dominica 1985a). The sole mention of small enterprise in the entire budget centred on her intention to provide credit and incentives for investment for the private sector in general, although small entrepreneurs were selected specifically to benefit from support through the Industrial Development Corporation, the AID Bank and the NDFD.

It was not until 1987 that small business issues were again on the agenda. One of the main objectives of her administration during this budget year was to encourage private-sector investment by incentives directly targeted at this sector, and by the removal of disincentives. However, in terms of the regard for the poor, there appears to be a level of ignorance as to the specific contingent circumstances surrounding the issue of poverty, where although it is recognized that rural poverty was a serious issue, and that rural entrepreneurs also suffered in this regard, Charles still stated that "[t]here is no longer a credible rationale for differentiating between businesses in different parts of the state" (Dominica 1987a, 13).

In 1989, small businesses received their greatest amount of attention during Charles's time as prime minister. The 1989 budget can be considered the most focused on small-business issues and poverty. However, as was seen in the budget two years earlier, there appears to have been a conceptual barrier to effective poverty alleviation, where the real issue of rural poverty was ignored (Dominica 1989).

One of the main measures undertaken in 1989 was that the National Development Corporation was to receive an increased subvention to upgrade staff and for promotional activities. The increase was also to be utilized to develop small business. However these actions appeared to have been motivated by the upcoming elections. Despite this, Charles's 1989 budget speech provided some interesting insights into her views on a number of issues that were specifically relevant to the issues of enterprise development and poverty alleviation. Several statements from this budget are cited below and demonstrate her views on the entrepreneur and enterprise development.

The 1989 Budget Address

Despite the concessions offered to the manufacturing sector, Charles realized that such policies were not working, as only "modest" growth in that sector was seen. For the first time, the interconnectivity of the economy was enunciated, as Charles realized that this modest growth was detrimental to the growth of the small enterprise sector due to its supply–chain link with the manufacturing sector. Charles stated that "until" the factors constraining the flow of private investment were overcome (transport, access to finance and general infrastructure), a greater focus was needed on the small enterprise sector, which possessed

> potential for import substitution, growth in exports and employment generation. This will require a new approach towards the capitalization [*sic*] of small and medium-sized enterprises, facilitating the delivery of appropriate financing, providing suitable factory space and technical assistance in management and marketing and structuring an incentive scheme that will be relevant to and appropriate for medium and small-sized businesses. (Dominica 1989, 8)

In this speech Charles announced the establishment of a small enterprise unit, a unit to coordinate enterprise development programmes and to provide technical assistance. This was grounded in an explicit belief in these enterprises' ability in "creating jobs and increasing production either for export or for import displacement" (Dominica 1989, 8). Charles went on to outline the role to be played by the financial sector: "The banking sector has a critical role to play in this strategy for development. *We intend to continue to take whatever policy measures are necessary to facilitate the development of more effective and appropriate banking policies with regard to interest rates and credit allocations"* (Dominica 1989, 9; emphasis added). This was with particular emphasis on the need to respond to the needs of small and medium-sized enterprises. In addition, it appeared that Charles was beginning to understand the importance of engendering an entrepreneurial culture among the people, especially the youth: "We believe that a well-designed scheme for providing capital, together with other forms of assistance to be provided by the small business unit, which I mentioned earlier, will be the most effective form of assistance that can be extended to young entrepreneurs" (Dominica 1989, 12).

In terms of actual actions undertaken, Charles introduced several tax adjustments in her 1989 budget speech. The tax adjustments were intended to assist "small and medium-sized enterprises to expand their equity base and improve their capacity for borrowing (Dominica 1989, 14). These actions seem to have been instigated by a belief that the business sector in general was "largely undeveloped":

> One of the problems affecting the flow of commercial bank resources into profitable and productive investment is the low capitalization [*sic*] of many small enterprises that otherwise have the capacity for growth and expansion. Some of the measures that we have proposed are directed to them in particular. The incentive for small savers to invest some of their savings in equity and for small business to convert their distributable earnings to bonus shares, should help to expand the equity base of such companies and make them more credit worthy for attracting commercial credit. (Dominica 1989, 14)

To this day, commercial credit is slow in coming forward (Lashley and Lord 2002).

Despite the recognition that businesses were floundering, especially small enterprises, the actions of the government, and Charles in particular, seem paradoxical, for within the same budget year a preferential rate of consumption tax, which was allowed as a concession to small manufacturers, was withdrawn, as most of these businesses were believed to have progressed beyond the "incubation stage". This paradox is demonstrated by the following statement: "Incentive to business, if it is used to the desired purpose, is a benefit to the worker. If, by giving concessions, we help to increase employment, to provide jobs for the unemployed, then the whole economy expands and new opportunities both for jobs and investments are created" (Dominica 1989, 18).

In returning to the views of Charles as to the role of government, they appear not to have changed after ten years in office. In 1990 she overtly stated that the function of government is to "provide the conditions and support systems necessary for economic and national development. . . Once this is done, it is left to the private sector to carry on with the business of production" (Dominica 1990, 17). It was not until 1992 that explicit mention of entrepreneurship was heard again. In speaking to the issue of deregulating trade, Charles noted that any deregulation must be cognizant of the effect on what she called the "embryonic and weak" entrepreneurial spirit in Dominica. This is despite the remark in the 1989 budget address that support for small businesses, in terms of tax incentives, was removed as they were believed to be beyond the incubation period, reaffirming the contradictory nature of the policies implemented and overt "political speak". However, Charles does make it clear which side of the fence she stands on, with a belief in the efficacy of market forces as opposed to different forms of government support for industry: "We must understand that the world does not owe us a living and that we cannot continue to seek welfare support either for the things we sell or for what we consume" (Dominica 1992a, 5).

In 1994, as elections approached, the need for the promotion of enterprise growth and the need to address the problem of poverty once again emerged. This was, however, to be Charles's last year in office. Her budget address in 1994 began by declaring that, although the NDFD's lending to small business increased by 32.6 per cent, Dominicans had "no history or tradition of a domestic entrepreneurial class or a truly market-orientated economy". Charles went on to observe that the Dominican economy "is a dependent economy. Dependent in more ways than one: dependent on a single crop; dependent on a single major market outlet. . . Above all, we must understand that we are responsible for our own advancement" (Dominica 1994b, 5).

This statement appears to be critical of the Freedom Party's lack of ability to enhance entrepreneurship during its fifteen years in office. Indeed, when asked in 2002 how successful her administration had been in enhancing the development of the small business sector, Charles replied: "I don't think we did that much . . . because you created the banks and encouraged people to borrow from the banks. So we made them responsible for themselves you know" (Charles 2002g). There appeared here a level of disappointment that her administration, despite trying, had failed to enhance enterprise development.

In terms of other measures adopted in 1994 to address the issues of enterprise development and poverty, one of the six objectives for the 1994–95 period and the medium term was to "encourage private sector development by improving the incentive regime, removing constraints to business expansion and profitability and supporting programmes for small business development" (Dominica 1994b, 6). Plans were also put in place to stimulate small business development by continued support for the NDFD. In addition to this a number of diversification strategies were introduced. One of these strategies was specifically targeted at expanding capacity in the fisheries sector and was intended to "provide supportive infrastructure and training to fishermen and fishing entrepreneurs" (Dominica 1994b, 7). This is the first real mention of a policy directed at fishery entrepreneurs by Charles, despite their being one of the main poverty groups in the island, as identified by the poverty assessment conducted in 1995 by Bonnerjea and Weir (1996).

After Charles's fourteen years in office, the 1994–95 budget address held the first concrete mention of actions to be taken against poverty with the commitment "to undertake poverty assessment study so as to access funding for the establishment of a social safety net for disadvantaged groups, especially young and unemployed persons" (Dominica 1994b, 7). This new direction may, however, have been related to the change in ethos of the major international donors, where a shift was seen that embodied an appreciation of the fact that development had both economic and social dimensions. The budget speech of 1994 also noted that prudence was needed in executing measures to increase domestic efficiency, and that consideration needed to be taken of the underdeveloped business sector and the vulnerability of low-income groups.

Two projects were implemented to improve functioning of the labour market: the Labour Force Survey and the Youth Skills Training Programme. The latter was intended to allow the youth to increase employability or allow them to become self-employed. Overall, poverty and entrepreneurship did receive special attention in this budget. In closing Charles stated:

> I appreciate the special difficulties that entrepreneurs face in our region, not least of which are the absence of supportive institutions in the areas of research and product engineering and the scarcity of appropriate capital. We have done our best to establish the right enabling environment for private sector growth and I am encouraged by reports that the domestic private sector in Dominica has expanded much further than in most of the other OECS states. (Dominica 1994b, 17)

In this respect Charles admitted defeat in her effort to promote an entrepreneurial culture. Despite being in office for fourteen years, and five years after stressing the importance of "appropriate capital" to the success of the entrepreneur (Dominica 1989), Charles realized that her administration had failed to make adequate provision for the small entrepreneur.

Conclusion

Eugenia Charles's contribution to the development of enterprise development in Dominica, and the utilization of such development to alleviate poverty in the island, was minimal on reflection. This was not, however, due to a lack of appreciation of the benefits of enterprise development. It appears that, by the end of Charles's time in office, there was a realization that the lack of success in enhancing enterprise development in Dominica was due to an inherent lack of an entrepreneurial culture among the Dominican people.

In attempting to promote enterprise development in Dominica, Eugenia Charles adopted a top-to-bottom approach. It was believed that, by creating the appropriate environment and reducing the role of government in direct support of industrial activities, enterprises would flourish. This approach was probably engendered by Eugenia Charles's fund-raising activities where "international aid donors often describe Charles's Dominica as a model for other nations" (Higbie 1993, 10). However, these donors were often conservative, right-wing organizations with a belief in neoliberal economic policies. To generate such funding Charles had to adopt an approach commensurate with such policies. This is not to say that these were not the views held by Charles, but it does indicate a lack of appreciation of the specific circumstances of the Dominican people.

Policies adopted were in a manner imposed on Dominica rather than evolved indigenously. In this sense Charles was not in a manner a puppet, but in securing aid from international donors, compromises needed to be made. Considering Charles's natural inclination to small government, and her aversion to the development of a welfare state, these compromises were perhaps not that difficult. However, towards the end of her time in office, there was a realization that policies implemented had not worked. Indeed, as early as 1985 it was noted in relation to the ineffectiveness of policies that "there have been complaints. One of the major ones is that enough of the foreign aid is not trickling down to the worse off" (*Caribbean and West Indies Chronicle* 1985, 13).

The hiving off of activities to the NGO sector was instigated to reduce the backlash from government redundancies by the promotion of support for small and micro enterprises. The NGOs themselves, however, noted that government involvement was still seen sometimes as being for political gain, rather than as a strategic plan for the alleviation of poverty through enterprise development.

Overall, the difference between the ideology of Charles in 1980 and Charles in 1995 could be said to mirror the change in ethos of the major international donors. Their neoliberal paradigm of economic development of the 1980s, which was based on top-down economic growth, was replaced by the 1990s vision of development – a vision cognizant that development was more than economic growth, that it also took the issue of social well-being into consideration. Such a vision prevented the delinking of poverty alleviation strategies from strategies aimed at enterprise development and economic growth.

Note

1.   This was estimated on the basis of the number of own-account workers, due to a lack of a more suitable variable.

PART 5

Gender, Media

and Caribbean

Society

9

Stereotyping Women's Political Leadership
Images of Eugenia Charles in the Caribbean Print Media

CARMEN HUTCHINSON MILLER

Introduction

Women's political participation is not rare within the Caribbean. Women of the Caribbean region have always been at the forefront of social, economic and political struggles. Caribbean scholars like Lucille Mathurin Mair (2000), Hilary Beckles (1989), and Nicole Phillips (2003), among others, have demonstrated that during slavery, women resisted this inhumane system using a series of strategies for their survival. During the post-emancipation and the post-independence periods, Caribbean women maintained their spirit of struggle and made evident their courage against injustices (Wilmot 1995; Sunshine 1988; Ford-Smith 1991).

Yet women's political leadership is a rarity within the Caribbean. This may seem contradictory given women's active political participation. This inconsistency should not be perplexing, if we understand and recognize the gender inequalities within Caribbean societies. How was Eugenia Charles successful in achieving political leadership within a society embedded with such inequalities? It is not my intention to try to answer this question in this chapter, since it is addressed by other contributors to this work. Instead my focus is to analyse the stereotypical images of Eugenia Charles the political leader as portrayed in the Caribbean print media during her three terms of office. In this analysis I present a brief historical context of women's inequalities within the Caribbean and attempt to explain how perceptions of assumed female capabilities, roles and even appearance affected the way Eugenia Charles was seen in her role as a female political leader. I reviewed and analysed 462 newspaper clippings gathered from five regional newspapers: *Caribbean Contact,* the *New Chronicle* from Dominica, the *Trinidad Guardian,* the *Trinidad Express* and the *Nation* from Barbados.

Historical Background to Gender Inequalities in the Caribbean

During the post-emancipation period the former members of the plantocracy were determined to hold on to the privileges they had enjoyed for centuries. They devised all sorts of strategies to keep their control. One of these strategies was the "mis-education" of the black population. The process of educating is not neutral and often was used to maintain the status quo; therefore, the type of education that the emancipated black men and women of the Caribbean were going to be exposed to was one that was going to benefit the ruling class. "Clearly education was meant to take the place of shackles and chains and its purpose was to reproduce a labouring class of black people" (Drayton 1988, 291). Drayton demonstrates in more detail the clear intention of the former slave masters as she quotes from the Stirling Report of 1834:

> A system of control now secures their conduct: Five years hence their performance of the function of a labouring class in a civilized community will depend entirely on the power over the minds of the same prudential and moral motives which govern more or less the minds of the people here [in England]. If they are not so disposed to fulfil these functions property will perish in the colonies for want of human impulsion; the whites will no longer reside there and the liberated Negroes will probably cease to be progressive, the law having already determined and enforced their civic rights. The task of bettering their contribution would be further advanced only by education. (Drayton 1984, 2)

This new vehicle of control through education was not only to keep the male slaves in their place. It also contained specific stipulations for women.

Drayton continues, "With the education system as well as the lesson books came the values of the Victorian ruling class including those which relegated women to an inferior status" (Drayton 1984, 3).

These Victorian rules were still evident in the recommendations of the West Indian Royal Report of 1945 as it relates to women's education:

> So far no specific mention has been made of the education of girls. The present low status of women in the West Indies makes it more important to secure essential equality of educational opportunity between the sexes. If there are to be happy marriages girls must be able to be companions to their husbands and therefore need every opportunity for as wide a cultural education as possible. (West India Royal Commission 1945, 130)

The provision for women's formal education was not in place in the Caribbean of the 1930s. The commission's concern to secure "essential equality of education opportunity between the sexes" was for girls to be educated to guarantee happy marriages. "The essential equality in educational opportunity for both sexes" was not an equality in terms of theirs rights and obligations but in terms of reading and writing skills with a very biased curriculum that reinforced women's subordination:

> The literary curriculum in the primary schools requires to be simplified and brought more into relation with the environment of the children. Stress should be laid on the formation of habits of clear and connected speech. The primary curriculum should in its later stages include practical and agricultural subjects for boys, and domestic training and child welfare instruction for girls. (West India Royal Commission 1945, 432)

The commission's report became more specific when it specified the type of education in secondary schools:

> The division of scholarship between boys and girls will thus be decided by the accommodation available for boys and girls respectively in the secondary schools. Plans have been completed and an Organizer engaged for a domestic training centre that will train 20 girls in a six-monthly course for domestic service. The centre will also accommodate evening classes in cookery and dressmaking. (West India Royal Commission 1945, 422)

The stereotyped roles that the commissioners envisaged for both sexes were clear. These were to be inculcated in primary schools and reinforced at the secondary level. Since women were destined to fulfil domestic roles, it should not come as a surprise that they were not perceived as potential political leaders. Female leadership therefore represented an anomaly, since what were considered the normative ideas of leadership in the region were established historically as masculine.

Anton Allahar (2001, x) states:

> the volume proposes to analyse the political successes of several Caribbean leaders going back to the early days of political decolonisation (1960s), when the climate of Caribbean politics was charged with a sense of national euphoria premised on the promise of liberation from colonial tutelage. Seizing the moment and the propitiousness of the political mood, these leaders (Michael Manley, Forbes Burham, Eric Gairy, Maurice Bishop, Eric Williams, Fidel Castro, Cheddi Jagan and Errol Barrow), to varying degrees and in their unique styles, exploited a perceived charismatic endowment, which was woven effectively into a populist politics.

This list of names reinforces the popular perception that political leadership in the region was viewed as masculine. Eugenia Charles was actively involved in politics during the same period as the male politicians mentioned, yet a study on political success and charismatic leadership excludes her, even though she is the only female to have held a top political leadership position in the region. As recently as the 1930s in the Caribbean, women were not encouraged to participate socially and politically in the shaping and decision making of Caribbean society. The West India Commission Report published in 1945 commented on the status of women in public administration at that time:

> Women can take but little part in the administration of the West Indies Colonies. When they are eligible to exercise the vote on equal terms with men or to stand with them for election to representative institutions, the prescribed qualifications are usually such that few women possess the property or income to satisfy them. . . .
>
> In Jamaica, where women are eligible for election or nomination to the Legislative Council, none has yet sat on that body. In Barbados women are not eligible to vote. Another inequality is that in three Colonies women, otherwise qualified for the vote, may not exercise it until they reach an age higher by some years than that at which a man is entitled to vote. (West India Royal Commission 1945, 217)

Caribbean women did not participate fully in the administration of the colonies, either because they did not own property and therefore were not eligible to vote, or because they did not otherwise enjoy the right to vote; even those women that were eligible for nomination – mostly white women at this time – did not come forward due to the unequal gender relations in the Caribbean. The commissioners were unable to recognize these inequalities in their reporting. Their gender bias is evident in the type of recommendations they made relating to women in education.

Barriteau "investigates the constructs and operations of relations of gender in the political economy of gender of the modernizing, twentieth century Caribbean" (Barriteau 2001b, 1). Her analysis is focused on women from the post-war, post-independence Caribbean to the beginning of the twenty-first century. In her analysis she demonstrates the unequal gender relations that continued to exist in this period. Women were perceived as belonging to the private sphere; therefore the exercise of rationality was reserved for men, who operated in the public sphere. Barriteau states:

> The private is the realm of domesticity, and for women a pivotal site to relations of domination. According to liberal political theory it comprises the world of the family, conjugal and sexual relations. The private sphere is part of civil society but it is incorporated differently. It is theorized as separate from the public world of the economy, public discourse and the state. (Barriteau 2001b, 35)

The crux of my argument in this chapter is that the Caribbean media have internalized and perpetuated this stereotype rather than challenging it or progressively attempting to present another reality.

Stereotypical Images of Women in the Caribbean and in the Media

Patriarchal ideologies have construed Caribbean woman as wives, caretakers of the home, respectable women or women of pleasure (P. Wilson 1969). In his study, Wilson directed attention to the importance of informal groupings existing in the Caribbean. He used the ideas of reputation and respectability to understand Caribbean society as it relates to the differing roles and expectations of the sexes:

> Almost every ethnographical report from the Caribbean makes mention of a "double standard" of sexual morality. Males are esteemed for their virility and are granted a freedom which they are expected to exploit. Females are, ideally, constrained in their sexual activities before and after marriage, and are expected to observe these constraints and other allied modes of behavior (such as modesty and obedience). (P. Wilson 1969, 71)

Wilson's contributions help us in understanding the stereotyped image of the Caribbean man as a free individual, in control of his destiny, not accountable to anyone for his sexual relationships. On the flip side we have the stereotypical image of the Caribbean woman as a controlled and repressed individual in her sexuality. Wilson reports a view in the Caribbean that "females are, ideally, constrained in their sexual activities before and after marriage". However, he makes it clear that there are women in the Caribbean who do not constrain themselves sexually either before or after marriage. A refusal to be constrained is also evident on the part of women in the public sphere like Eugenia Charles. As Patricia Mohammed argues in reference to the role of women in the family, "there is clearly a gap . . . between the ideology of women's role in society and that of the practice" (Mohammed 1999, 172). Another study on the perceptions of Caribbean women (Brodber 1982) explores the stereotypes of Caribbean women from emancipation to post-independence and demonstrates the tension between "the perceived idea of how a woman should behave and the real woman". This societal tension creates a paradox that makes the socializing agents (religious, educational, legal, economic and social) appear perverse in their treatment of women in the Caribbean.

In trying to force all women to behave in an "ideal way", the educational system, as I have demonstrated, plays a pivotal role in ensuring that women maintain their established societal roles. These roles are reinforced constantly and systematically, through the effective propagation of the images that emerge in the mass media. Magazines, newspapers, radio and television advertisements and general programming like soap operas and comedies help in strengthening these stereotyped images.

The media play two important roles in perpetuating women's inequalities. The media can be used to portray a racist, classist, ageist and gender-biased image of women. For example, women's magazines, especially those that advertise "beauty" products, are not representative of all classes, colours and ages of women. Most of the women represented in these magazines feed into the racial, class and gender ideologies of those who seek to cater to men's needs. These magazines use enticing and suggestive looks to sell the services women offer as wife, mothers, bitches or lovers. Women's appearances are used to make men happy and willing to enjoy the product that is offered, lured by the images of women that are used in the offering. Second, the mass media perpetuate the patriarchal system. Soap operas and comedies are designed to portray the images of women as bitches, as eternal sufferers due to the unfairness and abuse of men, as unfulfilled women who will do everything and anything to get a man to marry them or as devoted wives who stay home and run the family affairs without complaining. Some examples of these images can be seen in soap operas such as *The Bold and the Beautiful*, or comedies like *My Wife and Kids*, *Everybody Loves Raymond* and *According to Jim*, among others.

At least three specific stereotyped images of Caribbean women are portrayed in the media. In the tourist-oriented magazines, for example, there is the image of the exotic Caribbean woman who is portrayed in a way that can lure visitors to come and enjoy the beauty that the Caribbean offers. Her physical and phenotypical characteristics are stereotypical as well since she does not represent all the women of the Caribbean. This image shows a "perfect" young Caribbean woman with her relaxed hair and tanned, sexy, skinny body. The second image is of the folkloric Caribbean woman represented by the Aunt Jemima and Rachel Pringle type. These images are portrayed to feed the stereotype of the woman from the plantation with her exaggerated breasts and bottom. These images are noticeable in paintings on the walls of hotel rooms and lobbies and on the labels of some food products – such as mauby syrup and pancakes – in some supermarkets in Barbados. Third, there is the image of the gossiper, the tricky, greedy and unruly Caribbean woman. Examples of this type of representation are noticeable in some radio advertisements. All these images of these types of women are to perpetuate an unrealistic and sometimes negative image of women and to create satisfaction for that "husband" who is represented as the individual man or the "market".

Stereotyped Images of Caribbean Women in Politics

Women who participate in politics and women as political leaders are perceived in the same way as other women, by the "simple reason" of their being women. Women in the Caribbean have been and continue to be in active politics, even though their numerical representation and the type of ministries they now hold might not make many of them as visible in our minds as Eugenia Charles was in the 1980s and early 1990s.

Data from the United Nations for the period 1970 to 1990 provide an idea of women's numerical participation at the high political levels during these years.

Of the 159 United Nations member states, only six (3.8 per cent) were headed by women at the end of 1990: Iceland, Ireland, Nicaragua, Norway, Dominica and the Philippines. Also women are poorly represented in the top echelons of government. During that period only 3.5 per cent of the world's cabinet ministers were women, and women held no ministerial positions in 93 countries of the world (UN 1991, 31).

Information for 1995 shows an increase in women's political leadership: "Only 24 women have been elected heads of State or Government, since 1990. At the end of 1994 ten women were heading their governments – a number unprecedented in history" (UN 1995, 151). Despite an increase in the number of women as political leaders, these numbers should not give a sense of triumph since the gender bias toward women has changed very little ideologically. The ideology of male superiority impedes many women who do not feel confident enough to assume political leadership roles. Table 9.1 shows a recent update of women elected in the lower or single house in Caribbean states to demonstrate women's continued low representation in positions of political leadership.

The ideology of male superiority is manifested within the parties, making women's ascension to the higher ranks difficult. This is a situation that some internalize and others confront openly:

Former parliamentarian Maizie Barker-Welch has blasted the men in the Democratic Labour Party (DLP), labelling them as male chauvinists. She told people attending the party's lunch-time lecture at the DLP's George Street headquarters about the shabby treatment female party members received at the hands of

TABLE 9.1 Percentage of Women in Lower or Single House in the Caribbean

Rank	Country	Lower or Single House				Upper House or Senate			
		Latest Elections	Seats (no.)	Women (no.)	Women (%)	Elections	Seats (no.)	Women (no.)	Women (%)
7	Cuba	01 2003	609	219	36.0	–	–	–	–
15	Guyana	03 2001	65	20	30.08	–	–	–	–
24	Grenada	11 2003	15	4	26.7	11 2003	13	5	38.5
46	Bahamas	05 2002	40	8	20.0	05 2002	16	7	43.8
48	Suriname	05 2005	51	10	19.6	–	–	–	–
49	Trinidad and Tobago	10 2002	36	7	19.4	10 2002	31	10	32.3
56	Dominican Republic	05 2002	150	26	17.3	05 2002	32	2	6.3
68	Barbados	05 2003	30	4	13.3	05 2003	21	5	23.8
77	Jamaica	10 2002	60	7	11.7	10 2002	21	4	19.0
81	St Lucia	12 2001	18	2	11.1	12 2001	11	4	36.4
86	Antigua and Barbuda	03 2004	19	2	10.5	03 2004	17	3	17.6
91	Dominica	05 2005	31	3	9.7	–	–	–	–
107	Belize	03 2003	30	2	6.7	03 2003	12	3	25.0
121	Haiti	05 2000	83	3	3.6	05 2000	27	7	25.9
131	St Kitts and Nevis	10 2004	15	0	0.0	–	–	–	–

Source: Compilation from the Inter-Parliamentary Union Women in National Parliaments World Classification. Situation as of 31 August 2005. http://www.ipu.org/wmn-e/arc/classif310805.htm.

Note: When there are two houses, persons are usually appointed to the Upper House or Senate. Ranking represents classification of the countries by descending order of the percentage of women in the Lower House.

their male counterparts. She was responding to what she described as the fight by women for equal rights in a male dominated world. (*Saturday Sun* [Bridgetown] 2004, 1)

Roberta Clarke (1986, 121) demonstrated in a study done on women in political parties in three Caribbean countries that "despite the fact that female participation in the political process through voting is fairly widespread, women are still not proportionally represented in key decision-making or executive level". Clarke's study was done twenty years ago; Maizie Barker-Welch's comments about the androcentric attitude within her political party shows that this situation remains the case today.

Because of the ideology that men's superiority and strength equip them to be in public life, many women who are active political members are not encouraged to run for political leadership for fear of the attacks they might receive from the opposition and the public in general. Some of those attacks might be directed to their persona as women. To this Eugenia Charles comments: "Your partner and growing children would have beseeched you to get out of this thankless race in which nothing good could be said about you; only vile lies" (Charles 1995b, 2).

In a caricature that appeared in the *Daily Nation* (2003, 8), Prime Minister Owen Arthur of Barbados is dressed as a knight with his sword, and appears in front of Minister Mia Motley, defending her from the fear-

less, fiery dragon of public opinion. The context for this representation came from a proposal from Minister Motley in 2003 to suggest that Barbados should consider introducing legislation to decriminalize homosexuality. The Barbadian society reacted to her proposal very negatively and the prime minister came to her defence. The caption reads: "I'll defend you fair maiden. I know how to handle this heat!" Mia Mottley is an experienced politician; by now she is very aware of how hot political affairs are. However, the caption accurately portrays the attitude of the prime minister who, at a press conference, called on the public to leave Ms Mottley alone. He said she was very traumatized by the reactions of the public. The cartoon correctly captures how he handled the situation. While the media shapes public opinion it often captures and reflects particular views and opinions. In this case Prime Minister Arthur sets himself up as a knight in shining armour rescuing the poor maiden who could not handle the political heat. In the process he made her appear timid, unsure of herself and afraid of public criticism. The cartoon merely reflects his attitude.

The image of the Caribbean woman as a political leader is distorted. There are women who want to be leaders but are deterred by an ideological structure which makes it difficult for them to survive in such an environment: "The men do not have to face such onslaughts; they are reserved for women, hoping that because they are supposed to be the weaker sex they would not be able to stand the rigours for long" (Charles 1995b, 2).

Images of Eugenia Charles in the Media

Who was Eugenia Charles? Eugenia Charles was a determined woman who grew up in a family environment that nurtured her image as a woman who could achieve anything and everything she wanted. Janet Higbie's research gives a very good glimpse of her life from childhood up to her days as a political leader of the Dominican people (Higbie 1993). For a woman born in the early-twentieth-century Caribbean she was fortunate to have the support not only of her mother but also of her father to pursue her academic aspirations.

Eugenia Charles was a real challenge to a media that was accustomed to reproducing and perpetuating the image of woman as bitch or saint. What category would she fit into? She did not fit the established stereotypes: she was a single woman, she did not have children, she had an impeccable record in terms of her personal life and, besides, she seemed to be enjoying it.

My argument is that the Caribbean print media did not create a stereo-typical image of Eugenia Charles. Instead the Caribbean media used the existing stereotypical images of women who did not confirm to the norm and used them against her. Just as in the 1930s the commissioners in attempting to assess the social, economic and cultural situation of the Caribbean and striving to find the right answers fell victim to their own gender biases, in the same way the media fell victims to theirs.

The media were not capable and were not prepared to accept the uncommon image of Eugenia Charles. Examples of how individual men, and mainly men in politics, perceived her can be found in Higbie's work. It seems that when some men disagree with women, they are unable to focus on the women's point of view, but instead make women's sexuality the target of their attacks. When Eugenia Charles, among other Dominican citizens, protested the Seditious and Undesirable Publications Act that Premier LeBlanc was trying to pass in 1968, a lawyer from his government, Ronald Armour, was upset with the protesters and lashed out at them. He referred to Charles as "the eminent professional virgin" (Higbie 1993, 89). What relationship did her alleged condition as a virgin have to do with protest-ing against what she and other Dominican citizens, including many men, considered to be an injustice? "Professional virgin" here is used as a means of insulting her and implying that no man wanted her.

These types of attacks did not change when she entered the formal political arena. Armour continued to make her sexuality and age the target of his attacks. When she protested the National Dress Act in 1971 by going to parliament wearing a bathing suit, he said, "You are an old woman! Do you want me for a husband? I will make you wear minis!" (Higbie 1993, 110) and again in 1974 during a parliamentary debate he called her "a sav-age old woman" (Higbie 1993, 120). The media borrowed these fabricated images that came out of a gender-biased system and perpetuated them. Her age would be used as a political weapon against her during election times. Reporters used this as a point of entry when speaking generally about her. Of the 462 articles reviewed, reference to her age was used forty-three times (9.31 per cent).

At the beginning of Eugenia Charles's leadership, the Caribbean media did not treat her with disdain or ridicule her for being an old or single woman. Every ruling government tries to have the media on their side in order for them to promote, strengthen and advance their ideas; in addition they use the Government Information Service, the government's own medium: Eugenia Charles and her government were no different from any other government in the region in this regard. A review of the Dominican newspapers of that period helps to strengthen this point. It indicates that in the early days Charles used the media effectively and that the media were active in carrying her message. As Blumler and Gurevitch state, "The mass media offers politicians access to an audience through credible outlet, while politicians offer journalists information about a theatre of presumed relevance, significance, impact, and spectacle for audience consumption" (1995, 108). The Caribbean media offered Charles access to the Caribbean community. Initially, being the first female prime minister in the region was sufficient reason for their attention and for their coverage. But when did a shift occur and the media start to demonstrate their gender biases toward her?

Stereotyped Images of Eugenia Charles Portrayed by the Caribbean Print Media

As mentioned above, the portrayal of Eugenia Charles at the beginning of her first term in office was not distorted as a female leader, even if ideologically she was not accepted in the role she was playing; the media were not overtly rejecting her existing role as a political leader.

A shift in her portrayal occurred after her active support for the Grenada invasion in October 1983. The media not only were projecting covert gender ideologies with respect to women in the public sphere, but were also dealing with the fact that Charles was instrumental in the invasion of a Caribbean island by the United States. Many Caribbean people were against the role she played as chair of the Organization of Eastern Caribbean States (OECS).

The Perception of Strength and Weakness

Stereotypical perceptions of women as soft and submissive human beings are internalized in our social consciousness. This perception damages women both in the private and in the public spheres, causing women to be abused emotionally, physically, economically, verbally and sexually. If a woman is sure of herself and is very vocal, especially in public spaces, she is considered aggressive; if she is physically strong she is considered a "tomboy". In this male-dominated system women always find themselves in a lose-lose situation. Eugenia Charles's strong personality earned her the label of "dictator". This label did not affect her positions or personality:

> They call me a dictator but I don't think I am. The buck stops here. You cannot have everybody making decisions. Somebody must make a decision. It doesn't mean you don't listen to people. You listen and that of course makes an impression on what you decide, but in the end it is your duty to make the decisions. (*Daily Nation* 1995b, 24)

Charles demonstrated that she was not afraid to be strong and to use the power she had as a leader, even if it meant that others would be against her and the decisions she made. Because of this strong personality there are other names that were given to her, like the term "Iron Lady" (Higbie 1993).

The "Iron Lady"

The term "Iron Lady" was used to describe Eugenia Charles by the author Janet Higbie in a biography entitled *Eugenia Charles: The Caribbean's Iron Lady*. Patricia Honychurch and Jill Sheppard, reviewers of the book, reacted sharply to the label: "*Eugenia Charles: The Caribbean's Iron Lady* immediately suffers from the implied comparison with Margaret Thatcher. One wonders why the author, or perhaps the publishers, chose this unfortunate and misleading, sub-title? For Eugenia Charles is nothing if not *sui generis*" (Honychurch and Sheppard 1993, 7).

The media were unable to see her uniqueness and opted to use the term "Iron Lady" as a way to describe her. The reviewers suggested, "If any comparisons are needed then these should be with her Caribbean counterparts" (Honychurch and Sheppard 1993, 7); but the media were not able to compare her with her counterparts, who were all men, since this would have placed her in the category of "equal". That is not acceptable within a gender-biased society.

The term "Iron Lady" was utilized as a curse or as a compliment, depending on who used it. When asked in an interview if she liked to be referred to as the Iron Lady, Charles replied:

> It doesn't matter to me. I take it to mean that I have had some tough decisions to make and I have made them although I knew they were tough. If that is what it means, then it is fine. If it means that I am forthright and outspoken I am happy to be considered like that. (*Sunday Sun* 1988, 32)

Eugenia Charles accepted some of the images that portrayed her if she felt it was going to work for her, which suggests that she was not afraid to appear strong as a female political leader. Some women in decision-making positions sometimes like to appear tougher than they are, for fear of appearing weak and soft, but this doesn't seem to have been the case with Eugenia Charles. She would not have managed to serve three terms in office without being tough. As she explained in a feature interview about the nickname: "I don't think that I am an Iron Lady but I am not going to let that stop me making a decision that is necessary for the benefit of this country" (*Daily Nation* 1995b, 25).

"Blunt", "Tough-Talking", "Outspoken", "Frank"

Charles was a very vocal woman and during her time in power she was not afraid to express her views. It was impossible for this characteristic to go unnoticed by the print media and it was mentioned every time they carried a news item about her:

> To supporters, she's "Mama Eugenia." But to many people she is the "Iron Lady of the Caribbean," the tough, determined lone woman in the man's world of West Indian prime ministers, who swept to victory in yesterday's election . . . The gravel-voiced Charles is a blunt, conservative politician. (*Daily Nation* 1985a, 2)

> Mary Eugenia Charles, the Caribbean's first female prime minister and one of its most outspoken leaders, hopes to lead the Dominica Freedom Party to a second five-year term in elections today. (*Daily Nation* 1985b, 11)

Sometimes in one article these terms were used over and over:

> After 68 birthdays at the crease [*sic*] of life, the region's only female head of government is still as frank and outspoken. . . . Born May 15, 1919 in the village of Point Michel, six miles south of the capital Roseau, the tough-talking Prime Minister remembers that her parents, John-Baptiste and Josephine Charles were "strict disciplinarians." The tough-talking government boss explains "it was almost by accident", that she got into politics. (*Weekend EC News* 1988, 10)

"Unmarried" and "Childless"

Within patriarchal societies marriage provides women with social identity. Even when powerful single women like Eugenia Charles have an identity of their own and are successful in a variety of other arenas, the fact that they never married, or never wanted to be married, becomes an issue. It is as if something important and fundamental were missing from their lives. Interestingly, when men are in positions of power their marital status is never raised as an issue. The fact that Charles was unmarried was always a concern for the media: " 'I didn't meet anyone I'd like to leave home for.' So said Dominica's Prime Minister Eugenia Charles, answering a question many people would like to put to her, and explaining why she has never married" (*Sunday Sun* 1989, 34).

Eugenia Charles was suggesting with this affirmation that she was not desperate to have a husband in order to conform with the stereotypical perception that a woman is incomplete if she does not have a husband, especially when her situation was as visible as prime minister.

Yet being unmarried and childless was used as a weapon against her. Charles commented, "The fact that I was single and childless seemed to them a particularly good field for abuse of myself" (Charles 1995b, 2). Charles also recognized that being a mother and a wife would have made her task a heavier one: "I am sure that if I were not single and childless I would not have continued and persevered for twenty-five years" (Charles 1995b, 2). It is very interesting that what patriarchal ideology saw as a weakness and a target for jokes, she saw as strength and capitalized on it.

"Old Woman"

The media made Charles's age an issue, especially during the elections of 1990:

> The Prime Minister's age and a planned international airport are among the major talking points as Dominicans gear for a May 28 general election. Her opponents say that at age 71 Prime Minister Eugenia Charles should be thinking of stepping down because she is too old.... the Caribbean's "Iron Lady" says age has not impaired her ability to function effectively.... "What I want to know is—am I performing? If you are employing somebody and the person can perform do you care whether they are young or old? ... If they (opposition) could find that I am sleeping in bed all day long instead of working, they will have a right to say that. In fact, I am more active than they are." (*Trinidad Guardian* 1990, 1)

Eugenia Charles entered active politics when she was forty-nine years old and became prime minister of Dominica at age sixty-one, which proves she was very active politically before becoming a leader. Allahar (2001) notes that Errol Barrow, late prime minister of Barbados, born one year after her, joined the Barbados Labour Party at age thirty-one and became prime minister for the first time at age forty-one; he was sixty-seven years old when he died in office in 1987. Former Grenadian leader Herbert Blaize was born one year before her, and when he was in his early forties he was actively involved politically. The former prime minister of Guyana, Forbes Burnham, who was born four years after her, was head of state for twenty-one years, and was still in office when he died at age sixty-two in 1985. Information extracted from the *Daily Nation* (2002) and the *Barbados Advocate* (2002) indicates that former Dominican Republic leader Joaquin Balaguer ruled for twenty-two years and when he died at age ninety-five in 2002 he was still trying to influence political developments. These men were all her contemporaries and were of an "old age". It would be very interesting to do a comparative analysis towards discovering whether the issue of the age of these male leaders was as important to their publics as it seemed to be in the case of Eugenia Charles.

The ideology of gender inequality situates women as producers and reproducers within the private sphere during an arbitrary period of their reproductive lives. When any woman steps out of that categorization and practice, she is sanctioned. This practice is so perverse that it limits the participation and contribution of outstanding women to the development of our societies since it suggests that women cannot function as rational beings within the political sphere.

Conclusion

The portrayals of stereotyped images of Eugenia Charles were not a creation of the Caribbean media themselves. The media did not know where to situate her since they reflected and also reproduced gender stereotypes. They used the existing stereotypes ascribed to women without questioning whether they fitted her personality and political style.

At the time of Charles's emergence Caribbean society was not accustomed to seeing women in positions of power, especially a woman acting in such unconventional ways within the political sphere. Eugenia Charles was very aware of the challenges she faced as a female political leader but she was determined to lead. She was undoubtedly a remarkable woman not only in the political arena but also as an individual. She was a leader who understood the dynamics of political power, loved the exercise of power and wanted to continue having that power. The newspaper coverage did not do justice to that aspect of her public life. The media saw her strength in the political arena as something unusual for women, and portrayed her as an intruder in the public sphere. The media experienced great difficulty in seeing the woman and the politician occupying the same political space.

Appendix A
Eugenia Charles Photographed by the Media

Photograph of Dame Eugenia Charles most used by the regional media

10

The Reluctant Feminist
Eugenia Charles on Women and Gender

ALICIA MONDESIRE

> I don't think I am a feminist, really. I just felt that women had the right to do what
> they wanted to do. Men couldn't think they had the world in their pocket.
> – Mary Eugenia Charles

Introduction

In 1980, Eugenia Charles became the first woman prime minister in the Commonwealth Caribbean, and the second woman in the Western Hemisphere to be elected head of state in her own right. Before becoming prime minister of Dominica, she had distinguished herself as a lawyer, an activist who defended civil liberties and a prominent political figure during one of the most turbulent periods of Dominica's modern history. While her sex was the object of calumny and a key weapon in the arsenal of her male political opponents, she distanced herself and her politics from a women's cause or a feminist platform, asserting at times that gender inequality was not an issue for women in Dominica.

In the first of the three parts presented in this chapter, I examine the life of Eugenia Charles, focusing on gender dynamics in her family and educational environment. This sets the stage for exploring gender-related influences that would shape Charles, the political woman. I draw heavily on personal anecdotes and disclosures about her home and her family relationships. In the second part, I discuss gender and class issues in the political environment of Dominica and the Caribbean from the 1970s to the 1990s, analysing the ascent of Eugenia Charles to political leadership and exploring how her sex and her class affected her experiences as a political leader. In the third part, I focus on the institutional environment for addressing the advancement of women in Dominica and the directions followed under her leadership. There I document changes in the status of women during the fifteen-year period of the Charles leadership in the areas of education, health, employment and political participation, and compare the changes in Dominica with regional trends.

Gender Dynamics in the Family Life and Education of Eugenia Charles

In the Charles household of the early 1900s, a close and respectful relationship between and among siblings and parents prevailed. Family members were drawn to one another by a common compulsion for reasoning and argument, which nurtured the children's instinct for critique at an early age: "Whether it was a girl or boy made no difference", said Eugenia Charles (2002h).

Sibling alliances developed more around age than around gender. Although Charles identified with Jane as an older sister, it was with her brother Rennie, to whom she was closer in age, that she identified more. Rennie is portrayed in the early years as a caregiver who took care of his younger sister during an affliction with infant diarrhea (Higbie 1993, 29). Both brothers undertook domestic duties in the home, such as cleaning steps (on the outside) and helping to mix the dough their mother used for baking bread.[1] As Charles recalled:

> My mother really controlled the house; she was the person in charge. We accepted it. She had a lot of influence on us as children. Have you done your homework? She would ask. My father used to run a small dry goods store, and she was in charge of it. But she was also in charge of the house. She was the authority with my father. We had a good family life. (Charles 2002h)

Identified with the peasant class, J.B. Charles was denied privileges that left him bitter about the planter class. Ironically, more than sixty years later, his daughter would fend off working-class political opponents, who derided her class status and considered her to represent the interests of the urban, middle-class elite. As he challenged the colonial system, J.B. Charles nurtured an inquiring instinct in his children; and when he became a member of parliament, his children were directly exposed to public affairs and the policy issues of the day. Eugenia Charles remembers going to parliament and listening to the debates, and taking issue with what was said.

> [M]y father thought that you should know what was happening, so that we were always encouraged to come into the store on a Saturday, and to work with my mother in the store, and we heard what people spoke about...We were very much aware of what was happening the country. It was our business. We spoke about education, and who had access to it. We always felt we had a right to say what we thought, because it was our country, and we had a right as anybody else in the world. And I think that came from our family life. We always had our meals together. Everybody put forth their own ideas at the table. Each person was allowed to air their views. We ate together, talked together. (Charles 2002h)

She became aware of her privilege in those days: "We all had our meals together, and I found out after that all the children I went to school with did not have that opportunity" (Charles 2002h).

Her parents, who had received only primary schooling, were adamant that the children should have opportunities for education and should each pursue a career:

> They felt education was the most important thing they could give the children. My father was very interested in our education, and the children knew that whatever education they wanted they would get. We only had to show an inclination. And I think that was good for us. We always knew as children that whatever profession we wanted we would get it. Everybody was equal; it didn't matter who you were or what you were (boy or girl), what you wanted to study was the important thing. (Charles 2002h)

Her recreational interests distanced her from the female stereotype of the day, as she favoured activities that were associated more with males: playing cricket, lifting weights and rowing a boat. Despite the apparent gender neutrality in the home, she was conscious of differences in the male/female gender culture; and during her university years, she was drawn more to the males in her circle than to females. In her class at the University of Toronto, which had about the same number of men and women, she became "better friends with the men [*sic*] in the class than with the girls [*sic*], because I was accustomed to listening, to know what boys were talking about" (Charles 2002h). That she appeared in adulthood to seek out the company of males more than that of females might reflect the tendency nurtured in her early sibling relationships; and it might also suggest a latent consciousness that male companionship, for the purposes of intellectual engagement, offered more to her than female companionship.

Unquestionably, her father's political activism and his prominence in Dominican politics and business were crucial sources of inspiration to Eugenia Charles. Her mother's authority in the home and her insistence on performance standards made the children feel accountable for their parents' investments in their education. Charles says she felt obligated to her parents for affording her the opportunity to grow.

Exploring the impact of role models on women who achieved recognition in politics, Olive Senior draws attention to the enduring influence of an early immersion in a political environment and to the activism of male and female relatives. Drawing on the research findings of the Women in the Caribbean Project, she concludes that "most of these women grew up in strong family situations; that they had a sense of 'belonging' and of being 'rooted' in their societies, and were encouraged from an early age to get an education; independent thinking was also encouraged" (Senior 1991, 160).

While her father's prominence in Dominican politics would have been a compelling influence on her subsequent decision to pursue a political career, Eugenia Charles was also exposed to others who might have inspired her interest in politics. In 1956, another woman, Phyllis Shand Allfrey, had co-founded the Dominica Labour Party with E.C. Loblanc (Higbie 1993). Although Charles and Allfrey shared similar convictions about freedom of the press and other forms of civil liberties, which allied them on various issues at various historical moments, they were on opposite sides at other times. Apart from ideological differences, her colour was an issue: "She was white and I was black", said Charles, who discounted her influence as a role model.

Her consciousness of racial difference had been instilled long before. In the 1940s, when Charles confronted racism while travelling in North America, the assertion of her right as an individual to be treated equally came naturally. A passion for civil liberties was cultivated, as her intolerance of social injustice came to the fore:

> I thought nobody was better than I was. I felt that everybody was equal. I came from a little island, but it didn't mean that I didn't have a right to the things that I thought were necessary, and the things that were wrong – that I could talk about it, and say what I wanted about it. And I think that came from the home in which I lived. My father and mother always made us believe that there was nobody more equal than us to anything . . . you didn't have to keep your mouth shut because you were a child, or because you were black, or because there were others who were more senior or important than you. When they talked about Rosa Parks, I wanted to know what she had done that was so remarkable. All of us had done it, that's how I felt about it. (Charles 2002i)

At the University of Toronto, however, she was closer to the Canadians, whom she met first, than to the handful of West Indians who came after. In the university environment, race was less of an issue; it was not something she thought about while living in residence with Canadian girls.

Her first foray into politics was in 1952, when she accepted a temporary appointment as a councillor in the Legislative Council. By the time of the legislative crisis in 1968, a career in politics was virtually inevitable.

Gender and Class Issues in the Political Environment

In her writings on the interrelationship among race, class and gender, Reddock has cautioned against assigning a "hierarchy of oppressions", advocating instead an analysis which seeks to understand ways in which each type of oppression affects the others (Reddock 1993). For Eugenia Charles, it was her class and her sex that were at the root of the attacks that she faced from political opponents and from disaffected persons who had lost favour with her for one reason or the other.

As a forceful defender of justice and civil liberties, she encountered the raw hostilities and profanities of an all-male Labour Party clique that had become entrenched in power after successive political victories. Male political opponents in the Labour Party made a point of belittling her on the grounds of her sex and her class, often resorting to crude, misogynistic diatribes that challenged her legitimacy to lead and were critical of her as a single woman who had not borne children. As Peggy Antrobus argues, "Her class was a convenient excuse, a proxy for the resentment of her as a woman" (Antrobus 2002). Others saw her sex as secondary to other issues. Class issues dominated Dominica's politics at the time (Honychurch 1984), and were played out in parliament and in other aspects of public and private life. Marie Davis Pierre, the Speaker of the House in 1980, recalls the opposition Labour's taunts of "bourgeois" or "bourgeoisie" directed at her and at other members of the Dominica Freedom Party. That Charles was clearly identified with the wealthy business sector, both as a business owner and as a legal adviser, aggravated the scorn she suffered from Labour Party foes.[2] One detractor asserted that it was her business dealings, and not her sex, that was at the root of his irritation. Charles suggested that

> The worst issue for them was that they considered that I was well-off. They said that I came from a rich family. I said that if my father is rich, it's because he goes out to work at six in the morning and comes back at six in the night ... with his own cutlass in the ground. Perhaps if you had been following him you would be richer than him. I didn't have anything to be proud about; it was not my work it was his work. I ignored them, and said if you want to be as well off as he, then do a little hard work, follow him! (Charles 2002h)

Marie Davis Pierre finds the attacks were nuanced differently at various periods of her political career: "At the beginning, it was more gender. As the party gained strength, it was more her class than her sex that was at the root of the resentment directed at her by male political opponents" (Davis Pierre 2002). The scathing attacks on her by the opposition Labour Party were part of a pattern of abusive exchanges that were characteristic of party politics of the day. In her dealings with Labour in the late 1950s and early 1960s, Charles had singled out its leader, Edward LeBlanc, for derogatory attacks on his politics as well as his personal attributes (Higbie 1993). It was no wonder, then, that she appeared impervious to the virulent attacks from her political foes. It was a territory familiar to her, and one that she had herself stalked fearlessly.

One of her most dramatic gestures stemmed from her opposition to a formal dress-code in parliament which was imposed by LeBlanc in 1971. After denouncing the authoritarian (and male-biased) prescriptions of the National Dress Act, which made shirtjack suits the only legal dress in parliament, Charles astonished members and the whole country by appearing in the House in a bathing suit under her robes.

As she towered over others, both as an astute and brilliant lawyer and as a politician versed in the workings of parliamentary democracy, there were several reasons for her political opponents to resent her, especially given what by then could be identified as her "aloof" style. Her class, her sex and her age were used as weapons to belittle her. It is noteworthy that Ronald Armour, Rosie Douglas and Michael Douglas, who were all opposed to Charles, shared her class status. All three lost favour with the Labour Party at a later stage, due to clashes with the leadership and ideological conflicts. But if they were also attacked for their class, it was with a lesser intensity than that faced by Charles. Neither did her middle-class colleagues in the Dominica Freedom Party face the concerted class antagonism reserved for Charles, beyond the routine accusations that they were "bourgeois". However, the possibility of political opponents using gender as a weapon was something that male politicians were largely spared. Even within her own party ranks, her sex was the focus of an attack on her in the notable instance of the firing of a cabinet member in 1983. The sacked minister subsequently described her as "that bitch of a woman" (Higbie 1993, 219).

Gender and the Political Leadership of Eugenia Charles

In recent years there has been a considerable amount of scholarship on the gendered differences in how women and men lead and exercise power in both political and business spheres. Seminal work by Rosener (1990) identified a distinct set of attributes associated with female leadership in the corporate environment and drew attention to a complex of environmental and societal factors that affected women as leaders. More recently, others like Kawakami, White and Langer (2000), and Cowell-Meyers (2003) have elaborated on leadership styles in terms of the masculine and feminine and have broadly defined the differences in approaches. In the past, masculine leadership styles have been associated with more aggressive, hierarchical and inflexible approaches, whereas feminine styles have sought to be more horizontal, participative and responsive. However, as more and more organizations are adopting participative styles of managing, the attribution of a feminine or masculine approach has assumed less significance. Indeed, it is recognized that one or the other style need not reflect the gender of the leader, as some men might follow a style more typical of a "feminine" approach while some women might follow a style more typical of a "masculine" approach. Recent discourse on concepts of masculinity and femininity recognizes the dynamism and fluidity of both masculine and feminine behaviours (Reddock 1998; Barriteau 2000). For the purposes of this paper, I refer generally to the terminology of "masculine" and "feminine" as a convenient way of analysing how Eugenia Charles led her party and the government.

In 1974 and 1975, racially motivated attacks linked to Black Power activism and the emergence of "Dreads" in Dominica had seen the killing of several white visitors to the island. When Eugenia Charles emerged as a leader on a political stage that was set for sweeping changes, her gender seemed no more remarkable than the bizarre developments that were then gripping the country. The apocalyptic events of the period, which turned Dominica into a brutal battleground filled with thuggery and intrigue, required extraordinary resolve and leadership. The demands for aggressive leadership unleashed by these events brought to the fore an already belligerent, justice-driven personality.

In the latter years of her rule, tendencies towards militarism, hierarchy and dominance were to become emblematic of her leadership. Her tough actions in the early 1980s – promulgating the Prevention of Terrorism Act, thwarting two successive coup attempts in 1981 and disbanding the Dominica Defence Force – were outstanding examples of leadership in a difficult period, and would have been remarkable for any leader in the Caribbean during that time, male or female. Combating the violence that had seized Dominica, Charles responded to an agenda defined by male aggression and violence, the antithesis of a woman's agenda; and her response assumed the same patriarchal qualities that were inherent in the crisis.

A year after Margaret Thatcher invaded the Falkland Islands in 1982, US forces invaded Grenada, with Eugenia Charles, as chair of the Organization of Eastern Caribbean States (OECS), assuming a leadership role. In contemporary societies, Indira Gandhi was the only other female head of state who had demonstrated such a fearless, unyielding stance, when she took military action against Pakistan in the early 1970s.

Charles maintained that working in a team was something she valued highly, both during her student days at the University of Toronto and as the leader of government. In fact, her most difficult moment, she acknowledged, was relieving a cabinet minister of his duties – a process that took her almost two years. A former government official in the Dominica Freedom Party observed: "In the first term, relationships were very good. There was still a strong collegial sense in the second term, although there was some deterioration. In the third term, the party members felt they were on the outside, and members of the cabinet felt this too" (Alleyne 2002).

"She operated as a man, without much compassion", observes feminist Peggy Antrobus, likening her style to that of Thatcher, Gandhi and Jean Kirkpatrick (Antrobus 2002). A former party associate felt that the longer she stayed in power, the greater became the danger of centralization (Alleyne 2002). This became evident, he said, as she had started to become a monarchical figure, sometimes bypassing ministers and going directly to permanent secretaries (Alleyne 2002).

Although her combative style and alleged arrogance can be associated more with a masculine style of leadership, several of her male political colleagues in Dominica and in the region considered that her femininity affected the behaviour of her male colleagues, sometimes with positive results. As one of her male political allies observed:

> Miss Charles is a blend of a strong personality in her own right, and has the advantages of femininity. Being a woman, coupled with the strong personality, gave her a decided advantage. She had the ability and the capacity to lead, and people accepted her analysis and her summary of things. After a while people felt they did not want to argue with her, and she exploited that. It worked to her advantage, and to the advantage of the party. Whether you agreed or not, it was the thing to do. She was thus able to bring things to a conclusion, and reduce the tendency to squabble. (Savarin 2002b)

This once-close political associate continued:

> Eugenia Charles capitalized on being a woman in a man's world. Being the leader
> of the group, she was able to reinforce this by her dominance. If you wanted to get
> boisterous because you didn't agree, you felt constrained in shouting after a
> woman, or stamping a table, so there was a bit of frustration. But Eugenia herself
> has a significant commanding presence . . . a female commanding presence. The
> kind of jokes you would make with a group of men, you couldn't do with a
> woman present. Rather than carrying an argument to a bitter end, having stated
> your position, you would withdraw. (Savarin 2002b)

In a similar vein, John Compton, former prime minister of St Lucia, commented: "The presence of a woman in a room tends to civilize males"
(Compton 2002).

Charles's altruistic tendency to help the less privileged was known to
many, but she never boasted about it: "She was always the person representing the underdog", said Charles Maynard, a former cabinet minister
(Maynard 2002d). She would lend people money, knowing it would not be
repaid. She financially assisted children in elementary schools, and funded
thirty scholarships for university students. She also helped people with
medical needs. As a lawyer, she represented people and sought no remuner-
ation: "My father didn't have much education, but he gave us opportunities, and I feel I must return that", she said.

Another male colleague described her as "a strong mother figure" in the
party and within the government: "Caribbean people have respect for
mothers, and would not confront them." He also said,

> I think that if she had been a man, people would have stood up to her more than
> they did. Because she was a woman, people deferred to her. If you defied her on a
> matter she considered important, she would not go along, she would break it up.
> So even when you disagreed strongly, you tended to go along with her. The
> maternal thing was partly because of her age. Her integrity was unquestioned.
> People believed what she said. (Alleyne 2002)

While her allies perceived in the matriarchal image a person to be
respected, her detractors in Labour sought to turn the image of mother figure against her (Higbie 1993), coining the sarcastic sobriquet "Mamo".
Ironically this nickname worked to the promotional advantage of the
Freedom Party.

"She embodied the qualities of both the feminine and the masculine, and therefore had the advantages of both", argues sociologist Rhoda Reddock (2002). The two opposing tendencies of caring humanitarianism, associated more with the feminine; and an aggressive, commanding and manipulative approach, associated more with the masculine, made her seem unfathomable to many.

The comments of her male colleagues reflect, for the most part, the respect and admiration reserved for her as the leader of the party. By conceding her femininity, they could defend the submission required of them as subordinates, rationalized as the graciousness expected from a man towards a woman. The playing field on which they faced the dominant female leader could thus be levelled by emphasizing her femininity – by resorting to stereotypes of vulnerability traditionally associated with the feminine.

National, Regional and International Relationships

As in other countries in the English-speaking Caribbean, partisan politics in Dominica worked against a common platform for advancing women's interests (Peake 1993, 109; Reddock, 1994: 308). The first Labour Party had one woman (Mabel James); the second had none. While Eugenia Charles was prime minister, there were five women in parliament: three from the opposition, the Speaker and the prime minister. Throughout the years, the handful of women in parliament aligned themselves with their party rather than with the women's cause.[3] Charles herself felt no bond with women in opposition, asserting that it was all party, and that gender made no difference.

However, Charles spoke with pride about her relationships with prominent female figures in the Caribbean:

> I had a good relationship with Dame Nita Barrow; I knew Hilda Bynoe, I had known her before and had a very good relationship with her. I thought I had a good relationship with the women of the region. I had a good relationship with women abroad too: I became great friends with Margaret Thatcher and people like that. I encouraged her to think about what was happening in the islands, not only of England, to think about what was happening in places like Dominica . . .

because I told her we are growing up, and we are following the things you are doing, so you better do them right so you can be examples to us. (Charles 2002h)[4]

At a global level, she was preceded as a female chief of state by Sirimavo Bandaranaike in Sri Lanka (1960–65, 1970–77, 1994–present), Golda Meir of Israel (1969–74), Indira Gandhi in India (1966–77, 1980–84), Maria Pintasilgo in Portugal (1979–80) and Margaret Thatcher in England (1979–90).[5] By the end of her rule, there were in all fourteen female prime ministers or presidents in the world, with one other in the Caribbean, Maria Liberia-Peters in the Netherlands Antilles.

Charles said of other women leaders:

> I met them at meetings, but she [Thatcher] was the one I became closest to. You could tell her anything: you could tell her the things you required and why you required them, and she would listen and see in what way she could help to achieve the things you wanted for your country. I didn't hesitate to ask for the things I wanted for my country. She was easy to talk to in that respect. (Charles 2002i)

Charles supported Thatcher during the Falklands crisis. She also developed close economic, political and military ties with the United States during the Ronald Reagan administration; and those ties were solidified by the events in Grenada in 1983.

A close working relationship with other heads of state in the OECS, who were all male, developed in the wake of the Grenada crisis of 1983. The other leaders respected her for her intellect, her clarity and her confidence; and for her ability to resolve situations. Says her close ally Sir John Compton:

> She was Eugenia, and we expected something forceful from her, and forthright, and forthcoming. She not only performed as an intellectual person. You can be in a room, when you have discussions particularly in committees and in closed sessions, there is a lot of cross talk. Eugenia takes the floor and there is silence. She had accumulated the respect. It was not a woman that was there, it was a person with a strong personality. She transcended womanhood. She was an intellect, in woman's clothes. (Compton 2002)

In Compton's view, Eugenia Charles had shattered the stereotype of female/male roles and the expectations of male/female behaviours:

She was not to be "genderized." Some people confine women to a slot – being a woman. Eugenia was a person. She was more than being just a woman. Here is a woman, just behaving in this very extraordinary manner. So [it was] not only her intellectual capacity, which you would normally expect in a man. Coming from a woman, you would not expect that kind of thing. (Compton 2002)

Charles felt comfortable with the rapport that developed among the OECS leaders:

We understood each other and we said what we had to say. We were very frank with each other. We didn't hide our ideas. And if we didn't agree with something, we said it straight out. Everything was openly spoken about. All of us felt it was important to improve our education systems so that everybody would have a right to education. (Charles 2002i)

At the wider Caribbean level, there were tensions in the 1970s during the time of the Grenada Declaration, as smaller territories perceived an imperialist threat led by the Guyanese leader Forbes Burnham.[6] As John Compton recalls: "The things that Eugenia could tell Forbes, nobody else could tell him. She would cut off Forbes, put him down. It was a clash of ideology; it was a clash of intellect; it was a clash of the sexes, all combined in Eugenia's parrying thrusts with Burnham" (Compton 2002).

It is said that abroad, she benefited from being the lone woman to whom courtesies were extended: a chair given, a conversation started. "Courtesies that may not have been offered to male colleagues, such as paying her passage, arranging a good hotel", says Charles Savarin. He added, "Other leaders were drawn to her, because she came from a little island in the Caribbean. The other guys were lost among the rest. So you would want to form a committee, say with John James, and the Prime Minister of Dominica" (Savarin 2002b).

Throughout the 1980s, and up to 1995 when she demitted office, she was a much sought-after speaker for national, regional and international events focusing on women. Her international affiliations include membership in the International Foundation for Election Systems and the Harvard-based Council of Women World Leaders. She was president of the International Federation of Women Lawyers while she was prime minister in 1992.

Women and Gender in Dominica: The Institutional Environment

The period during which Eugenia Charles ruled Dominica was an unusually favourable one for advocating women's issues, due to United Nations leadership of global efforts to advance the status of women that began in earnest with the Mexico Conference of 1975. Governments all over the world were inspired to take actions to correct gender-based imbalances in various spheres of public and private life, creating new units called women's desks or bureaus, and in some cases a ministry for women's affairs. Much of the support for the operations of these units was procured from external donor sources and it often proved inadequate to sustain their operations at a level that could be considered effective. Moreover, the dynamism of donor priorities meant that funding was never assured over a long-term period, and this rendered the units vulnerable to sudden shifts in their resource base. The government of Eugenia Charles was no different from others in the Caribbean, in having a marginal allocation of financial and human resources for implementing global conventions that promoted the status of women. However, in 1982, her government created a Women's Bureau, replacing the Women's Desk that had been set up by the previous government.[7]

During the fifteen-year period that Eugenia Charles was in office, significant groundwork was laid for policy, legislative and institutional measures that were intended to promote women's advancement and gender equality. In 1989, the government ratified a National Policy on Women, and the following year it signed the Convention for the Elimination of All Forms of Discrimination Against Women (CEDAW). However, legislative reforms lagged behind the legal prescriptions for advancing women's status. No report on the CEDAW was ever prepared. According to a former official of the Women's Bureau, "The government's position was that existing legislation covered most of the requirements" (Alleyne 2002). He went on to explain that other international conventions besides the CEDAW had been sidelined by government's lack of resources to achieve their full implementation, and that government was guided by the OECS legal department in deciding which conventions would be given priority (Alleyne 2002).

Charles's view was that Dominica had already gone past the CEDAW:

> The UN declarations were not the most important things in life. For instance, when I appointed the Speaker, the opposition foresaw what I was getting at. Because I thought it was important for us to be ahead of other countries in that respect; we would have already established our ideas. As a lawyer in my office, I had worked on some of the issues, such as domestic violence, disposal of assets in marital and common law relationships. (Charles 2002i)

The eleven policy goals in the national policy included provisions for women in employment, in the family, and in politics and government. By 1993, however, plans to realize the policy were still to be articulated (Dominica National Council on Women, National Consultation, September 1993). Up to 1993, the model legislation of the Caribbean Community (CARICOM) was not considered for incorporation into the Dominican law, although amendments were made to the Sexual Offences Act and to the Child Maintenance Act. In the mid-1990s, after the operations of the Women's Bureau had been suspended for several months with the position of director unfilled, Eugenia Charles moved the Bureau from the Ministry of Community Development to the Economic Development Unit, where it was directly under her supervision (Blaize 2002). The move was generally seen as having a positive effect on the status of the Bureau, and was made during what turned out to be the prime minister's last term in office. It also coincided with what was then one of the most difficult periods of Dominica's economic history.

The economic order framed by a structural adjustment programme which began in 1981 created a policy climate in which real income declined, the cost of certain government services increased and employment levels fell. By 1989, unemployment levels for women were double those for men, and more women were in low-income situations compared to men (cited in UNICEF, Bureau Five-Year Action Plan, 1989, 14). Budget cuts in health had caused deterioration in services and, in some cases, new or higher costs. In 1990, recurrent expenditure on health dropped to 12.9 per cent from 13.7 per cent in 1986. An estimated 40 per cent of the nursing professionals were lost to the system, as Dominican nurses sought more lucrative jobs abroad (Dominica n.d., 16).

Employment

In line with most CARICOM countries, Dominica recorded for 1980 to 1992 sharp increases in the number of women employed in primary, secondary and tertiary industries. However, employment trends in Dominica reported in the 1990–91 census showed a gender gap that placed Dominica in the upper ranking of CARICOM countries (Mondesire and Dunn 1997). Whereas 67.8 per cent of males had secured employment, only 35.3 per cent of females had managed to do so, leaving a gender differential of 32.5, the highest in the Windward Islands. Labour force participation rates showed a similar trend, with Dominica recording the highest gender differential among the Windward Islands and Barbados. As employers, Dominican women experienced one of the more severe gender gaps among CARICOM countries, second only to the Bahamas.[8]

Commenting on the Freedom Party's strategy of job creation, Josephine Dublin (2002) draws attention to differences in how job creation was perceived by government, and by some in the women's movement in Dominica: "What she saw as jobs for women, we saw as 'feminization of poverty' ", she says of the sweatshops that were encouraged under Charles's government.

Education

In 1991, female enrolment in secondary schools in Dominica was among the highest in CARICOM, with 68 per cent for females compared to 32 per cent for males (Mondesire and Dunn 1997). During the same period, Dominica had one of the highest gender differentials in male/female primary enrolment, favouring males; and one of the highest gender differentials in secondary enrolment, favouring females (Mondesire and Dunn 1997). At the tertiary level, however, the gender differential was among the lowest in CARICOM, with 6.2 per cent of males compared to 6.8 per cent of females (Mondesire and Dunn 1997). Results of the Common Entrance Examinations from 1980 to 1991 show a higher percentage of girls than boys passing the Common Entrance; but the figures also show a performance decline for males and females, with the decline for females twice the magnitude as for males (Mondesire and Dunn 1997).

In adult education programmes, women's enrolment more than doubled that of men – 1,351 compared to 541, according to the "Report on the Status of Women in Dominica, 1976–1985" (Dominica 1985c). Adult education was of particular interest to the government of Charles, and was seen as a means of increasing the income earning opportunities for women.

Participation in Politics and Government

Up to the end of 1978, there were no female permanent secretaries in the civil service, although the government of the day had declared a concern for elevating the status of women in Dominica. Moderate advances by women in the political arena were recorded under the leadership of Eugenia Charles, with slightly more women participating in parliament and in national government in 1992 compared to 1980, although the numbers in local government had declined between 1980 and 1992. During the tenure of Charles, four Dominican women held leadership positions: in addition to the prime minister herself, these were Mayor Cynthia Butler and Speakers of the House Marie Davis Pierre and Neva Edwards. While the data on elected and appointed women may be discouraging, there were more women participating in politics in the 1980s than at any other point in Dominica's history. It is worth noting that several women came in as senators. How much of that was a result of the role model Charles offered, and how much came from the awakening of women through the UN Decade, remains to be studied.

Eugenia Charles as a Role Model

Undoubtedly, the presence of a woman as prime minister boosted the confidence levels of Dominicans in general and of women in particular. How this translated into gains can only be assessed in relation to whether this confidence inspired other actions leading to women's independence. Anecdotal accounts suggest that this did in fact occur:

> I gained confidence through my exposure to Miss Charles. I saw how she dealt with a US ambassador, as the only woman among several men in a meeting, six of them. The ambassador was one big man. . . . When I have a point, I talk about it. I can fit into a discussion; not fearful that someone will hate me for what I say. She encouraged me to take courses to further myself professionally. (Zamore 2002)

By working at the personal or individual level rather than at the policy level, Eugenia Charles opened doors for some women in Dominica to enter the workforce and in a few cases to assume management and leadership roles within the public service and in the private sector. It was a conscious strategy she followed, as explained in her own words:

> I personally believe in the personal touch: that you had to be talking to people directly, you couldn't just stand from a platform and issue an edict about what had to be done . . . so women had a role in encouraging their fellow women to state their position. I realized women had to go out to work, so one of the first things I did was arrange to have a day centre where children could be dropped off in the morning and picked up in the afternoon. (Charles 2002h)

Yet there were policy directives that were aimed at women, notably, one concerning the participation of women in the police force. Before the Dominica Freedom Party assumed power, women were coming in fairly significant numbers into the police force (Alleyne 2002). According to one member of the party, she issued an internal policy directive to the commissioner of police that stopped the recruitment of women and required that women not be promoted above the level of sergeant. Her rationale was that the senior policemen were using the policewomen as their playthings, and she did not want to give them that opportunity.

Although these instances of actively seeking the interests of women were indicative of her concern, she distanced herself from a women's cause or a feminist platform. She supported the Beijing process, but frequently asserted that gender inequality was not an issue for Dominican women. While insisting that she was not an advocate for women, she promoted equal rights in her statements and her actions.

She discounted perceptions that she singled out women:

> I think they thought I was preferential to women. I wasn't. The thing is the first speaker I chose was a woman. But she was a very good speaker and did a very good job. And the second speaker was also a woman, Neva Edwards she was very good.
>
> I did not particularly advocate for women's issues. I spoke out, never kept back. I made utterances. I didn't think I had to pretend about that and not say where I stood on those things. I did anything that I thought was necessary for the benefit of the country. And I always felt that women were important in this respect,

because women have always done so much of running the things of the country. If you look at the families here: a farmer has his little piece of land, but he can't work it unless his wife is there working side by side with him and they are producing something that is useful for the family. So I spoke out about those things, but not advocating policy, just saying that . . . and I did it in my work too – that a woman had as much right as a man. (Charles 2002h)

In March 1975, the year in which the Decade on Women began, women in Dominica rallied behind Charles after a local newspaper launched a singularly demeaning attack on her, characterizing her as "the Danger Lady". Objecting to the debasement that had become the hallmark of Labour's assaults on Eugenia Charles and the efforts to belittle women in general, the newly formed Dominica Women's Action Committee took to the streets in a protest action (Higbie 1993, 133). The event served to introduce a feminist analysis on a public issue, and further served to establish a women's agenda in the politics of the country early in the UN Decade on Women.

Marilyn Zamore, her former personal secretary, saw Charles as wanting to put women on the agenda by giving women opportunities such as training so they could assume management positions, and by setting up the government housing loans board for the benefit of civil servants who could then access loans at lower interest rates. "This was done with women in mind", said Zamore: "She encouraged women to take positions in the civil service where they could be upwardly mobile, and identified positions that women could fill. She also encouraged women to enter politics" (Zamore 2002).

A number of initiatives that were ostensibly gender-neutral actually redounded to the benefit of women, notably the adult education schemes launched in the 1980s and the housing loans programme. Deliberate efforts to enable women to pursue work and their careers saw her active support for the Social Centre day care.

Consciously and unconsciously, she became a role model for Dominican women and for women all over the world. "We used her as a role model in activities of Dominica National Council of Women [DNCW]", says Neva Edwards, former president of the DNCW:

She never took sides for women particularly, because she wanted to be fair and deal with men and children as well. However, she supported women's programs through the DNCW and through the Social League. Sometimes it was financial support in the form of a subvention from government. She made it easy for women to opt for prominent positions, as permanent secretaries, magistrates, judges and bank managers. (Edwards 2002b)

According to Gertrude Roberts, women's organizations flourished under her leadership.

Noting that she was a pragmatist who was given more to practical than to strategic gender issues, Peggy Antrobus identifies as a weakness in her leadership a failure to challenge oppressive structures of class: "She was not a transformational leader" (Antrobus 2002).

Conclusion

In her analysis of women's attitudes to participation in party politics, Olive Senior has described several factors that deter women from entering politics. The main deterrent, according to Senior, is socialization: many women identify power with the masculine; and view politics as anti-feminine, dangerous and dirty (Senior 1991). Other deterrents to women's participation in politics are family life obligations, lack of economic resources, lack of male support even within their own parties and lack of female support. With the exception of the issue of male support, which became a concern only during the latter years of her rule, none of these considerations applied to Eugenia Charles.

Eugenia Charles was a unique personality who assumed leadership through an unusual confluence of political events and natural disasters. She possessed the conviction, the grit, the verve, the professional credibility, the contacts and the money to launch a successful bid for power in a Dominica that was in a state of social, political, economic, physical and indeed spiritual decline. Her social status and her gender were both enabling and disabling factors. How attentive she was to women's needs and to gender equality issues was determined more by the exigencies of the situation that confronted her on her ascent to the office of prime minister, than by her passion or otherwise for these issues. While her development priorities as prime minister – education and infrastructure – were aimed at improving the lot of all Dominicans, there were particular initiatives that redounded to the benefit of women as a distinct group. Dominican women benefited from initiatives that were not specifically targeted, including the Education Trust Fund and access to housing loans.

Gains for women under her leadership might be expressed more in terms of improvements in women's morale and confidence, and less in material terms. In particular, setbacks in employment and education for the female population during her rule indicate that the policies pursued fell short of improving the situation for the vast majority of women. While her concern to open doors for the advancement of individual women saw increases in women's participation in government and politics, and in some private-sector firms, the majority of women were not afforded such opportunities for growth. Most observers agree that women's advancement would have been further ahead had a guiding policy framework been formulated earlier. As it happened, by the time the Five-Year Action Plan and National Policy on Women were developed, the government of Eugenia Charles was on its way out. Indeed, the government's policy commitments to the International Monetary Fund and the World Bank were inconsistent with the aspirations of the National Policy on Women.

In the words of her colleague Sir John Compton:

> She made Dominica proud on the regional and international stage. As soon as you speak about Dominica, she comes to mind. People still ask about the woman prime minister. When anybody heard about Dominica they asked about Eugenia Charles. She raised the whole profile of Dominica. She blazed a trail for Caribbean women. When people look at her, they would then say she was a woman. (Compton 2002)

Being a woman added to the mystique of Eugenia Charles, but her grandeur transcended her gender. She remained an enigma to many, embodying the activist, the shrewd politician and the compassionate humanitarian. By any standard, she was an extraordinary individual.

Acknowledgements

The research for this chapter was conducted between May and December 2002. It involved fieldwork and interviews in Dominica, Barbados, St Lucia, Port of Spain and Toronto. The author gratefully acknowledges the contribution of the following people who took part in interviews during the research phase: Dame Eugenia Charles, Sir John Compton, Neva Edwards, Marie Davis Pierre, Charles Savarin, Brian Alleyne, Lucia Blaize, Gertrude Roberts, Myrtle Solomon, Rhoda Reddock, Joycelin Massiah, Peggy Antrobus, Pamela Liburd, Charles Maynard, Kerry Harris, Yvette Barzey, Josephine Dublin, Marilyn Zamore, Josephine Jean Baptiste, Mrs Robinson and Cuthbert Seignoret. The kind assistance and cooperation of Professor Eudine Barriteau and the staff of the Centre for Gender and Development Studies, Cave Hill, is greatly appreciated. The author extends special thanks to Dame Eugenia Charles and her staff, who were warmly accommodating and helpful during the visit to Dominica.

Notes

1.   Whether these chores can be identified as male or female in early twentieth-century Dominica is debatable. In those days, baking, as an occupational trade, was associated with males and females (personal communication, Cuthbert Seignoret); although gender differences may have arisen in the ownership of the enterprise, with the tendency being towards male ownership. What is significant about the example is the notion of a male child assisting with household chores, which would usually devolve to the female children. In more recent discourse, Barriteau (2000) has challenged the gender-based characterization of chores, emphasizing that chores necessary for household maintenance should be categorized as neither male nor female.

2.   Honychurch describes the resentment of the leader of the Dominica Labour Party in terms of "his deep-rooted dislike of the traditional establishment, particularly the powerful Roseau-based group of farmers, merchants and professionals usually identified by the DLP as 'the mulatto gros-bourg' " (Honychurch 1984, 180).

3.   For example, when the leader of the United Workers' Party, Edison James, wanted to appoint Ossie Symes as Speaker of the House to replace Neva Edwards, who was also from his constituency, Marigot, the nomination was seconded by Vernice Bellony, an MP for the ruling United Workers' Party. Edwards and Bellony had both been associated with the Dominica National Council on Women. According to a Freedom Party affiliate, women in the Labour Party

disgraced themselves by siding with people who attacked Eugenia Charles because she was a woman.

4.   Both Eugenia Charles and Nita Barrow attended the University of Toronto in the 1940s. Nita Barrow was enrolled at the School of Nursing in 1941. Charles started her studies two years before Barrow arrived on campus.

5.   This information was obtained mainly from records of the Council of Women World Leaders at the John F. Kennedy School of Government, Harvard University.

6.   Several of the leaders, John Compton, Forbes Burnham and Eugenia Charles, had met as students in London in the 1940s.

7.   On the attainment of independence in 1978, a Ministry of Health, Industrial Relations and Women's Affairs was established, replacing the Ministry of Home Affairs, Health and Welfare.

8.   Compared to the average regional gender differential of 3.1, Dominica had a differential of 4.3 and the Bahamas 4.9.

References

I. Primary Sources

A. Manuscripts in the Dame Mary Eugenia Charles Collection held on deposit in the Main Library, University of the West Indies, Cave Hill, Barbados

Armour, Jenner B.M. 1992a. "Economic Citizenship Programme". Cabinet Paper no. 176/92.

———. 1992b. "Statement by the Minister of Legal Affairs on the Economic Citizenship Programme Laid in the House of Parliament, Roseau, Dominica".

———. 1993. Letter to the Cabinet Secretary, Office of the Prime Minister, enclosing three copies of the final agreement between Ms Grace Tung and the Government of the Commonwealth of Dominica (Roseau: Office of the Attorney General and Minister of Legal Affairs). 2 July.

Attidore, Anthony. 1990. Letter to Honourable Mary Eugenia Charles, "Appreciation for your development of Dominica". 4 June.

Boghoert, Arnold. 1964. Letter to M. Eugenia Charles. 8 November.

Caribbean Community Secretariat. 1987. "Review of Programmes of the Community as Administered by the Secretariat". Eighth Meeting of the Conference of Heads of Government of the Caribbean Community, Castries, St Lucia, 30 June–3 July 1987. 29 June.

Carlton, Ralph. 1992. Letter to the Chairman of the Dominican Freedom Party. 29 October.

Charles, Mary Eugenia. 1974. House of Assembly Opposition File.

———. 1977. House of Assembly Opposition file.

———. 1982a. "Statement by the Honourable Prime Minister Re:Visit to Bogota, Colombia from 1–3 March".

———. 1982b. "Statement by the Honourable Prime Minister Re:Visit to Paris and London, March 7–13".

———. 1982c. Report on a mission to Washington, DC, 15th–19th June.

———. 1982d. Statement by the Honourable Mary Eugenia Charles, Prime Minister of the Commonwealth of Dominica, at the meeting of the Caribbean Group for Cooperation in Economic Development, Washington, DC, 16 June.

———. 1983a. "Interview with Prime Minister and Press Secretary on Human Rights". Typescript.

———. 1983b. "Presentation Address at Norman Manley Law School Graduation Ceremony". 15 October.

———. 1984a. "Address by the Hon Eugenia Charles Prime Minister of the Commonwealth of Dominica and Chairman of the Organisation of Eastern Caribbean States 31st May 1984".

———. 1984b. "Address by the Honourable Mary Eugenia Charles on the Occasion of the 6th Anniversary of Independence" [Draft]. Roseau. 3 November.

———. 1984c. "Address to the Waterfront and Allied Workers Union at the Opening of a Seminar on Organising Work of Trade Unions and the Role of Trade Unions in Society. 9 October".

———. 1987. "Address by the Prime Minister of the Commonwealth of Dominica to the Conference of the World Affairs Council of Philadelphia and Philadelphia Bar Association on the Occasion of the Bicentennial of the US Constitution. Philadelphia. 19 June".

———. 1993. Letter to Lennox Honychurch. 3 December.

———. 1995a. "Inaugural Lecture: Caribbean Women – Catalysts for Change". University of the West Indies, Cave Hill, Barbados.

———. 1995b. Interview, "The Experiences of the First Female Prime Minister of the Commonwealth Caribbean", *Cave Hill News* (UWI, Barbardos) 1, no. 6 (December) 2.

———. N.d. "Statement".

Doctrove, M.C. 1980. "Report on Visit to Barbados by Honourable H.G. Dyer, Minister for Communications, Works and Tourism and Mr M.C. Doctrove, Permanent Secretary, October 23–24, Roseau".

Dominica Freedom Party (DFP). 1980. "Election Manifesto". Roseau.

———. 1990. "Election Manifesto 1990". Handwritten draft by Eugenia Charles.

Dyer, Henry G., and M.C. Doctrove. 1981. "Report on a Visit to New York by the Minister for Communications, Works and Tourism and Mr M.C. Doctrove, Permanent Secretary, Roseau".

Edwards, Neva. 1992. Letter to the Honourable Prime Minister, "Views on the Economic Citizenship Programme from the Dominica National Council of Women". 16 October.

Honychurch, Lennox. 1993. Letter to M. Eugenia Charles. 8 November.

John, Patrick. 1992a. Letter to Acting Prime Minister, "Covert actions by persons in the Tiwanese [*sic*] Consulate in Dominica". 26 October.

———. 1992b. Letter to the Honourable Prime Minister, "Views of the National Workers Union on the Economic Citizenship Programme".

———. 1992c. "Statement by National Workers Union on Economic Citizenship Programme". Roseau, Dominica.

Manoncourt, Erma. 1995. Letter to M. Eugenia Charles, "Thank you for participating in the Survey on How Decision Makers see Communication for Development". 31 March.

Rawlins, F.A. 1992. Letter to the Honourable Charles Maynard, acting Prime Minister, "Radio statement over the alleged incompatible behaviour of persons in the Tiwanese [*sic*] Consulate in Dominica". 30 October.

Torricelli, Robert. 1997. Letter to Honourable Dame Eugenia Charles. March.

West Indies (Associated States) Council of Ministers Secretariat. "Conclusions of the Special Meeting of the Council of Ministers Basseterre, St Kitts–Nevis 18 June 1981: Annex IV: Address by Hon. Eugenia Charles, Prime Minister of Dominica", and "Annex V: Address by Hon. Maurice Bishop, Prime Minister of Grenada".

Yankey, Bernard. 1990. Letter to Honourable Prime Minister Dame M. Eugenia Charles, "Information on Canada's Business Immigration Program". 5 July. Facsimile copy.

B. Interviews in the Dame Mary Eugenia Charles Collection held on deposit at the Main Library, University of the West Indies, Cave Hill, Barbados

Aaron, Pat. 2002. Interview by Keturah Cecilia Babb. Notes. 18 May. Roseau, Dominica.

Agar, Daphne. 2002. Interview by Joan Cuffie. Audiotape. June. Roseau, Dominica.

Allen, Angelo. 2002. Interview by Keturah Cecilia Babb. Notes. 10 December. Roseau, Dominica.

Alleyne, Brian. 2002. Interview by Alicia Mondesire. July 8. Roseau, Dominica.

Antrobus, Peggy. 2002. Interview by Alicia Mondesire. May 29. Toronto, Canada.

Baptiste, Jean. 2002. Interview by Keturah Cecilia Babb. Notes. 15 May. Roseau, Dominica.

Blaize James, Lucia. 2002. Interview by Keturah Cecilia Babb. Notes. 16 May. Roseau, Dominica.

Bruney, David. 2002. Interview by Eudine Barriteau. Note. 20 March. Roseau, Dominica.

Bruno, Alexander. 2002. Interview by Keturah Cecilia Babb. Notes. 10 December. Roseau, Dominica.

Charles, Mary Eugenia. 1986. Interview by Sue MacGregor. Transcript of broadcast on *It's Your World*, BBC Radio 4. 18 May. London.

———. 2002a. Interview by Alan Cobley. Tape recording. 9 July. Roseau, Dominica.

———. 2002b. Interview by Cynthia Barrow-Giles. Notes. 15 March. Roseau, Dominica.

———. 2002c. Interview by Eudine Barriteau. Notes. 20 March. Roseau, Dominica.

———. 2002d. Interview by Eudine Barriteau. Notes. 21 March. Roseau, Dominica.

———. 2002e. Interview by Joan Cuffie. Audiotape. June. Roseau, Dominica.

———. 2002f. Interview by Keturah Cecilia Babb. Notes. 17 May. Roseau, Dominica.

———. 2002g. Interview by Tracy Robinson. Tape recording. 21 August. Roseau, Dominica.

———. 2002h. Interview by Alicia Mondesire. 2 July. Roseau, Dominica.

———. 2002i. Interview by Alicia Mondesire. 4 July. Roseau, Dominica.

Compton, John. 2002. Interview by Alicia Mondesire. 11 July. Castries, St Lucia.

Davis Pierre, Marie. 2002. Interview by Alicia Mondesire. 2 July. Roseau, Dominica.

Douglas, Eisenhower. 2002. Interview by Eudine Barriteau. Tape recording and notes. 19 October. Roseau, Dominica.

Dublin, Josephine. 2002. Interview by Keturah Cecilia Babb. Notes. 17 May. Roseau, Dominica.

Edwards, Neva. 2002a. Interview by Joan Cuffie. Audiotape. June. Roseau, Dominica.

———. 2002b. Interview by Keturah Cecilia Babb. Notes. 5 July. Roseau, Dominica.

Etinoff, Bernard. 2002. Interview conducted by Jonathan Lashley. NDFD offices, Roseau. March.

Green, Ronald. 2003. Interview by Keturah Cecilia Babb. 10 December. Roseau, Dominica.

Honychurch, Lennox. 2002a. Interview by Eudine Barriteau. Notes. 21 March. Roseau, Dominica.

Honychurch, Lennox. 2002b. Interview by Joan Cuffie. Audiotape. June. Roseau, Dominica.

Jno Charles, Vanoulst. 2002. Interview by Keturah Cecilia Babb. Notes. 17 May. Roseau, Dominica.

Lazare, Alick. 2002. Interview by Eudine Barriteau. Tape recording and transcript. 16 October. Roseau, Dominica.

Letang, Thomas. 2004. Interview by Keturah Cecilia Babb. 10 December. Roseau, Dominica.

Lewis, Eucivila. 2003. Interview by Keturah Cecilia Babb. July. Roseau, Dominica.

Liverpool, Nicholas. 2002. Interview by Tracy Robinson. Tape recording. 19 August. Roseau, Dominica.

Maynard, Charles. 2002a. Interview by Cynthia Barrow-Giles. Notes. 17 March. Roseau, Dominica.

———. 2002b. Interview by Joan Cuffie. Audiotape. June. Roseau, Dominica.

———. 2002c. Interview by Keturah Cecilia Babb. Notes. 18 May. Roseau, Dominica.

———. 2002d. Interview by Alicia Mondesire. 5 July. Roseau, Dominica.

Nicholas, Bernard. 2002. Interview by Keturah Cecilia Babb. Notes. 15 May. Roseau, Dominica.

Nicholas, Peterson. 2002. Interview by Keturah Cecilia Babb. Notes. 15 May, Roseau, Dominica.

Piper, Mona. 2002. Interview by Keturah Cecilia Babb. Notes. 15 May. Roseau, Dominica.

Reddock, Rhoda. 2002. Interview by Alicia Mondesire. 14 July. Port of Spain, Trinidad.

Rolle, Donald. 2004. Interview by Keturah Cecilia Babb. August. Roseau, Dominica.

Savarin, Charles. 2002a. Interview by Cynthia Barrow-Giles. Notes. 16 March. Roseau, Dominica.

———. 2002b. Interview by Alicia Mondesire. 5 July. Roseau, Dominica.

Solomon, Catherine. 2004. Interview by Keturah Cecilia Babb. August. Roseau, Dominica.

Sorhaindo, Rupert. 2002. Interview by Keturah Cecilia Babb. 16 May. Roseau, Dominica.

Williams, Gilbert. 2002. Interview by Eudine Barriteau. Tape recording and transcript. 17 October. Roseau, Dominica.

Yankey, Bernard. 2002a. Interview by Eudine Barriteau. Tape recording and transcript. 18 October. Roseau, Dominica.

———. 2002b. Interview by Keturah Cecilia Babb. 18 May. Roseau, Dominica.

Zamore, Marilyn. 2002. Interview by Alice Mondesire. Roseau, Dominica. July.

C. Calypsos

1. Calypsos referring to Charles and her administration as recorded on reels at the Dominica Calypso Monarch Competitions and held in the Record Library of the Dominica Broadcasting Services

Aaron, Pat [Musician]. 1984. "Mama". Reel no. 084.

———. 1986. "It's Traditional". Reel no. 067.

Brown Sugar. 1981. "Cry to the Nation". Reel no. 027.

Checker. 1981. "Soca for My Prime Minister". Reel no. 027.

Cyrille, Morris [Ency]. 1982. "Banana Association Song". Reel no. 045.

———. 1986. "Doh Rock de Boat". Reel no. 075.

DBS. 1994. "Tell Eugenia". Reel no. 228.

Dyno. 1982. "De Coup". Reel no. 045.

Element. 1981a. "Eugie the Highest". Reel no. 034.

———. 1981b. "Lady of the Year". Reel no. 028 (Junior Monarch Competition).

General Natty. 1995. "I'll Ask Her". Reel no. (none).

Haxey. 1984. "Visions". Reel no. 052.

Loblack, Levi. 1984. "Mother Mary". Reel no. 084.

Rabbit. 1986. "My Grandmother's Prayer". Reel no. 067.

Spider. 1982. "Coming Soon". Reel no. 038.

———. 1988. "Bob Hope". Reel no. 116.

Tronada. 1983. "Freedom Fighters". Reel no. 049.

Winston, Artherley [Venturer]. 1986. "Woman Take Over". Reel no. 067.

Zeye. 1981. "Hold Dem Down Ms Eugie". Reel no. 028 (Junior Monarch Competition).

———. 1982. "Save the Nation". Reel no. 038.

———. 1984. "We Wont Fall by the Gun". Reel no. 052. (Same calypso as "Save the Nation", performed to refer to the political events in Grenada, October 1983.)

Ziko. 1981. "Hold Dem Down Ms Eugie". Reel no. 034.

2. Calypsos about Eugenia Charles and her administration found documented in other sources

Mendes, Albert ("De Man Himself"). 1990. "Iron Lady". Quoted in Higbie 1993.

Mighty Chalkdust (Hollis Liverpool). 1987. *Sea Water and Sand*. US: Straker Records Ltd.

"Rabbit". 1988. "Three Percent Calypso". Quoted in "Dominica: Privatize and Pauperize" in *Report of the Americas: The Caribbean* 23, no. 5. (February 1990): 33–40.

D. Publications of the Government of Dominica to November 1978, continued as Commonwealth of Dominica from December 1978

Dominica. 1968. Hansard of the Meeting of the House of Assembly, 5 July.

———. 1971a. Hansard of the Meeting of the House of Assembly, 12 February.

———. 1971b. Hansard of the Meeting of the House of Assembly, 8 July.

———. 1973a. Hansard of the Meeting of the House of Assembly, 18 April.

————. 1973b. Hansard of the Meeting of the House of Assembly, 12 July.

————. 1974a. Hansard of the Meeting of the House of Assembly, 19 November.

————. 1974b. Hansard of the Meeting of the House of Assembly, 6 December.

————. 1975. "Report on the Problem of Dreadism in Dominica: A Committee under the Chairmanship of Rev. A. Didier appointed by the Government of Dominica". Roseau: Ministry for Home Affairs, Social Security and Youth.

————. 1976. Hansard of the Meeting of the House of Assembly, 13 April.

————. 1977a. Hansard of the Meeting of the House of Assembly, 26 May.

————. 1977b. Hansard of the Meeting of the House of Assembly, 8 August.

————. 1977c. Hansard of the Meeting of the House of Assembly, 14 November.

————. 1977d. "Report of the Constitutional Conference London, May".

————. 1978a. Hansard of the Meeting of the House of Assembly, 23 February.

————. 1978b. Hansard of the Meeting of the House of Assembly, 13 April.

————. 1978c. Hansard of the Meeting of the House of Assembly, 29 May.

————. 1978d. Hansard of the Meeting of the House of Assembly, 3 November.

————. 1981a. "Address by the Honourable Prime Minister on the Occasion of the 3rd Independence Anniversary Celebrations". Roseau.

————. 1981b. Hansard of the Meeting of the House of Assembly, 5 March.

————. 1981c. Hansard of the Meeting of the House of Assembly, 10 June.

————. 1981d. "1981–82 Budget Address by the Honourable Prime Minister and Minister for Finance and External Affairs". Roseau.

————. 1982a. "Address by the Honourable Prime Minister on the Occasion of the 4th Anniversary of Independence". 3 November. Roseau.

————. 1982b. "1982–83 Budget Address by the Honourable Prime Minister and Minister for Finance and External Affairs". 14 June. Roseau.

————. 1983a. "Address by the Honourable Prime Minister on the Occasion of the 5th Anniversary of Independence". 3 November. Roseau.

————. 1983b. "1983–84 Budget Address by the Honourable Prime Minister and Minister for Finance and External Affairs". 11 July. Roseau.

————. 1984. "Whatever progress we make must come from our own efforts: 1984–85 Budget Address by the Honourable Prime Minister and Minister for Finance and External Affairs". 18 June. Roseau.

————. 1985a. "1985–86 Budget Address by the Honourable Prime Minister and Minister for Finance and External Affairs". Roseau.

————. 1985b. Report on the House of Assembly General Elections.

————. 1985c. "Report on the Status of Women in Dominica, 1976–1985".

————. 1986. "1986–87 Budget Address by the Honourable Prime Minister and Minister for Finance and External Affairs". 16 June. Roseau.

————. 1987a. "1987–88 Budget Address by the Honourable Prime Minister and Minister for Finance and External Affairs". Roseau.

———. 1987b. "Report on the Activities of the Women's Bureau, 1986–1987". Ministry of Community Development, Housing and Social Affairs.

———. 1988a. "1988–89 Budget Address by the Honourable Prime Minister and Minister for Finance and External Affairs". 11 July. Roseau.

———. 1988b. *Statistical Digest: Ten Years of Growth 1978–1988*. Roseau, Dominica: Central Statistical Office, Ministry of Finance.

———. 1988c. "Structural Adjustment Facility, Policy Framework Paper". 14 July. Roseau.

———. 1989. "1989–90 Budget Address by the Honourable Prime Minister and Minister for Finance and External Affairs". Roseau.

———. 1990a. "1990–91 Budget Address by the Honourable Prime Minister and Minister for Finance and External Affairs". Roseau.

———. 1990b. Report on the House of Assembly General Elections.

———. 1991a. "Agreement between the Government of the Commonwealth of Dominica and Grace Tung Honorary Consul of the Commonwealth of Dominica in the Republic of China, Taipei, Taiwan, Republic of China [Schedule C of Cabinet Paper 176\92], 23 August. Roseau".

———. 1991b. "Economic Citizenship Investment Programme. [Schedule B of Cabinet Paper 176\92] debated and passed in the House of Parliament, 27 May. Roseau".

———. 1991c. "Population and Housing Census Report". Roseau.

———. 1992a. "1992–93 Budget Address by the Honourable Prime Minister and Minister for Finance and External Affairs". Roseau.

———. 1992b. "Join Hands to Build Our Nation". Address by the Honourable Prime Minister to the Nation on the Occasion of the 14th Anniversary of Independence. November.

———. 1993a. "1993–94 Budget Address by the Honourable Prime Minister and Minister for Finance and External Affairs". Roseau.

———. 1993b. "Strengthening the Bonds of Unity: Address Given by Dame Eugenia M. Charles, Prime Minister on the Occasion of the 15th Anniversary of Independence". 3 November. Roseau.

———. 1994a. "Dominica Medium Term Economic Strategy, 1994–1996", final draft. April.

———. 1994b. "1994–95 Budget Address by the Honourable Prime Minister and Minister for Finance and External Affairs". Roseau.

———. Dominica. 1994c. "November 3 Address to the Nation on the Occasion of the Sixteenth Anniversary of Independence". Roseau.

———. 1995. "Five-Year Action Plan for the Women's Bureau, 1995–2000". June.

———. N.d. "Economic Citizenship Investment Program. Policy Guidelines, Roseau".

E. Legal references

1. Court cases cited

Active v Scobie & Davis (1969) 13 West Indian Reports 189 (High Court, Dominica).

Attorney General and the Minister of Home Affairs v Antigua Times [1975] 3 All England Reports 81 (Privy Council, Antigua and Barbuda).

Bahamas Methodist Church v Symonette [2000] Law Reports of the Commonwealth 196 (Privy Council, The Bahamas).

Beckles v Dellamore (1965) 9 West Indian Reports 299 (Court of Appeal, Trinidad and Tobago).

Charles v Phillips and Sealy (1967) 10 West Indian Reports 423 (Court of Appeal, WIAS).

Chief of Police v Powell, Chief of Police v Thomas (1968) 12 West Indian Reports 403 (High Court, West Indies Associated States).

Collymore and another v Attorney General (1969) 15 West Indian Reports 229 (Privy Council, Trinidad and Tobago).

Francis v Chief of Police (1973) West Indian Reports 550 (Privy Council, St Christopher-Nevis-Anguilla).

Joseph v The State of Dominica (1988) 36 West Indian Reports 216.

Kelshall v Pitt, Munroe and Bernard, ex parte Kelshall (1971) 19 West Indian Reports 136 (High Court, Trinidad and Tobago).

Lestrade v Roseau Town Council and Another (1970) 15 West Indian Reports 18 (Court of Appeal, West Indies Associated States).

Maximea and others v Attorney General (1974) 21 West Indian Reports 548 (Court of Appeal, Dominica).

Maximea and others v Attorney General (unreported) 17 July 1973, High Court, Dominica (No. 144 of 1973) Faculty of Law Library, University of the West Indies, Cave Hill.

Pratt & Morgan v Attorney General [1994] 2 Appeal Cases 1 (Privy Council, Jamaica).

Robinson et al. v Sealey (1974) 1 Cases on Commonwealth Caribbean Bills of Rights 94 (High Court, Trinidad and Tobago).

Weekes v Montano and May (1970) 16 West Indian Reports 425 (High Court, Trinidad and Tobago).

2. Legislation

Antigua and Barbuda

Newspapers Registration (Amendment) Act No. 8 of 1971.
Newspaper Surety Ordinance (Amendment) Act No. 9 of 1971.

Dominica

Constitution of Dominica 1967.

Constitution of Dominica 1967, Schedule 2 to the Dominica Constitution Order 1967, Statutory Instrument No. 226.

Industrial Relations (Amendment) Act (No. 2) No. 13 of 1979.

Libel and Slander (Amendment) Act (No. 2) No. 11 of 1979.

Seditious and Undesirable Publications Act No. 16 of 1968, *1990 Revised Edition of the Laws of Dominica* Vol. 3, Chap. 10:03.

Seditious and Undesirable Publications, *1961 Revised Laws of Dominica*, Chap. 254.

St Kitts–Nevis

Press and Publications Board Act No. 27 of 1971.

Public Meetings and Processions Ordinance, 1961 *Revised Laws of St Christopher Nevis and Anguilla*, Vol. 5, Chap. 302.

St Christopher Nevis and Anguilla Constitution, Schedule 2 to the St Christopher Nevis and Anguilla Order 1967, Statutory Instrument No. 228.

Trinidad and Tobago

Sedition (Amendment) Ordinance No. 36 of 1971.

Sedition Ordinance, *1950 Revised Laws of Trinidad and Tobago*, Chap. 4: 6.

United States of America

Sedition Act 1798, 1 Stat. 596. 1848. The Public Statutes at Large of the United States of America, from the Organization of the Government in 1789, to March 3, 1845. Boston: Little, Brown. Vol. I, p. 596.

F. Newspaper and periodical articles

Barbados Advocate (Bridgetown). 1996. "Men Say Law Courts Favour Women". February 17: 7.

————. 2002. "Dominicans Say Adieu to Balaguer . . . But Event Marred by Long Delay and Scuffle". 19 July: 17.

————. 2005. "Workplace Not Always Suited to Women". 28 March: 5.

Caribbean and West Indies Chronicle (London). 1981. 97, no. 1560 (February–March): 6.

————. 1985. "Eugenia Prepares for Battle". 100, no. 1585 (April–May): 12–13.

CARICOM Perspectives. 1984. "Excerpts of Interview with Prime Minister Eugenia Charles". No. 23 (January–February): 5–6.

Chronicle (Roseau). 1967. M. Eugenia Charles. "Freedom from Criticism". 22 May.

Daily Nation (Bridgetown). 1985a. "Charles Stays at Controls". 2 July: 2.

————. 1985b. "Mary Eugenia Charles". 1 July: 11.

———. 1995a. "Owen Arthur: The Way Forward Is Economic Development". 30 August: 18A–19A.

———. 1995b. "Will of Iron, Heart of Gold". 26 May: 24–25.

———. 1998. "Iron Lady Still Going Strong". 13 April: 21.

———. 2002. "Former Dominican Leader Dies at 95". 15 July: 12.

———. 2003. Cartoon captioned "I'll defend you, fair maiden. I know how to handle this heat!" 17 November: 8.

Economist. 2005. "Obituary: Eugenia Charles". 26 September.

New Chronicle (Roseau). 1993a. Commonwealth of Dominica 85, no. 2 (8–29 March).

———. 1993b. Commonwealth of Dominica 85, no. 3 (9–16 July).

Report of the Americas. 1990. "Dominica: Privatize and Pauperize". *Report of the Americas: The Caribbean* 23, no. 5 (February): 33–40.

Saturday Sun (Bridgetown). 2004. "DLP SLAP: Barker-Welch Blasts Male Chauvinists in Party". 17 April: 1.

Sunday Sun (Bridgetown). 1988. "How Dominica Is Faring . . ." 3 April: 32.

———. 1989. "Dominica Remains Love of Her Life". 31 December: 34.

———. 1997. "Liz Pours It Out at Oistins". 8 June: 10A.

———. 1998. "Caribbean Boys in Crisis". 10 September: 14A.

Trinidad Express (Port of Spain). 1990. "What's Age Got to Do with It?" 3 May: 21.

Trinidad Guardian (Port of Spain). 1982. " 'Fowl' Names Don't Bother Me: Says PM Eugenia Charles". 21 March: 1.

———. 1990. "Age No Drawback Says Dominica's 'Iron Lady'. Eugenia, 71, Going for a Third Term". 17 May: 1.

———. 2000. "Men Belittled in Dominica – Minister". 18 March: 7.

Weekend EC News. 1988. "Iron Lady of the Region". 31 March: 10.

G. Other primary sources

Charles, Mary Eugenia. 1981. "Address by the Honourable Prime Minister on the Occasion of 3rd Independence Anniversary Celebrations, 1981". Pamphlet held in the Main Library, University of the West Indies, Cave Hill, Barbados.

———. 1983c. Letter to the Ambassador of the United States to the Eastern Caribbean. 23 October. Appendix E in Dominique 1984: 107.

———. 1985. "Caribbean Challenge". Address presented to the Opening of the National Symposium on Women and Development. Bureau of Women's Affairs, Kingston, Jamaica. Copy held in the Main Library, University of the West Indies, Mona, Jamaica.

Dominica National Council of Women. 1993. "Report on the Proceedings of a National Consultation held as part of the Preparatory Process for the fourth World Conference on Women, 1995". September.

Dominica National Council of Women. N.d. "Report on the Status of Women in the Commonwealth of Dominica".

Gilmore, William C. 1984. Appendix 2: "Treaty Establishing the Organisation of Eastern Caribbean States (Extracts) of 18 June 1981". In *The Grenada Intervention: Analysis and Documentation*, 76–87.

———. 1984. Appendix 4: "Memorandum of Understanding (Between Antigua and Barbuda, Barbados, Dominica, St Lucia and St Vincent and the Grenadines) Relating to Security and Military Co-Operation (Extracts) of 29 October, 1982". In *The Grenada Intervention: Analysis and Documentation*, 88–92.

———. 1984. Appendix 11: "Address to the Barbadian People by Prime Minister Adams (Extracts) of 26th October 1983". In *The Grenada Intervention: Analysis and Documentation*, 102–5.

Scoon, Paul. 1983. Letter to President Ronald Reagan. 24 October. Appendix F in Dominique 1984: 108.

II. Secondary Sources

Alexis, Francis. 1983. *Changing Caribbean Constitutions*. Bridgetown: Carib Research and Publications.

Allahar, Anton, ed. 2001. *Caribbean Charisma: Reflections on Leadership, Legitimacy and Populist Politics*. Kingston, Jamaica: Ian Randle.

Allsopp, Richard, ed. 1996. *Dictionary of Caribbean English Usage*. New York: Oxford University Press.

Anderson, Nancy Fix. 1993. "Benazir Bhutto and Dynastic Politics: Her Father's Daughter, Her People's Sister". In Genovese 1993b, 41–69.

Andre, Irving W., and Gabriel J. Christian. 1992. *In Search of Eden: Dominica, The Travails of a Caribbean Mini-State*. Upper Marlboro, Md; Brampton, Ontario; and Roseau: Pond Casse Press.

Anthony, Kenny D. 2003. "New Horizons in Caribbean Democracy". In Barrow-Giles and Marshall, 473–81.

Baker, Patrick L. 1994. *Centring the Periphery: Chaos, Order and the Ethnohistory of Dominica*. Kingston: The Press, University of the West Indies.

Barbados Holiday Guide. 2004. Bridgetown, Barbados: Cot Brochure Display.

Baron, Robert A., and Donn Byrne. 2002. *Social Psychology*. 10th ed. New York: Allyn and Bacon.

Barriteau, Eudine. 1982. "The Caribbean Basin Initiative and the Commonwealth Caribbean". *Bulletin of Eastern Caribbean Affairs* 7, no. 6 (January–February): 11–20.

———. 1998a. "Engendering Local Government in the Commonwealth Caribbean". Working Paper No. 1 (April), Centre for Gender and Development Studies, University of the West Indies, Cave Hill, Barbados.

———. 1998b. "Theorizing Gender Systems and the Project of Modernity in the Twentieth-Century Caribbean". *Feminist Review* no. 59 (Summer): 186–209.

———. 2000. "Examining the Issues of Men, Male Marginalization and Masculinity in the Caribbean: Policy Implications". Working Paper No. 4 (September), Centre for Gender and Development Studies, University of the West Indies, Cave Hill, Barbados.

———. 2001a. "Before WID, Beyond GAD: Caribbean Women Creating Change". In Barriteau and Cobley 2001, 3–16.

———. 2001b. *The Political Economy of Gender in the Twentieth Century Caribbean*. London and New York: Palgrave International.

———, ed. 2003a. *Confronting Power, Theorizing Gender: Interdisciplinary Perspectives in the Caribbean*. Kingston: University of the West Indies Press.

———. 2003b. *Constructing a Conceptual Framework for Developing Women's Transformational Leadership in the Caribbean*. Monograph, Centre for Gender and Development Studies, University of the West Indies, Cave Hill, Barbados.

———. 2003c. "Constructing a Conceptual Framework for Developing Women's Transformational Leadership in the Caribbean". *Social and Economic Studies* 52, no. 4: 5–48.

Barriteau, Eudine, and Alan Cobley, eds. 2001. *Stronger, Surer, Bolder: Ruth Nita Barrow, Social Change and International Development*. Cave Hill, Barbados, and Kingston: Centre for Gender and Development Studies and the University of the West Indies Press.

Barrow-Giles, Cynthia. 2002. *Introduction to Caribbean Politics*. Kingston: Ian Randle.

Barrow-Giles, Cynthia, and Don Marshall. 2003. *Living at the Borderlines: Issues in Caribbean Sovereignty and Development*. Kingston: Ian Randle.

Beck, Robert J. 1993. *The Grenada Invasion: Politics, Law, and Foreign Policy Decision-making*. Boulder, Colorado: Westview Press.

Beckles, Hilary. 1989. *Natural Rebels: A Social History of Enslaved Black Women in Barbados*. London: Zed Books; New Brunswick, NJ: Rutgers University Press.

Beiner, Ronald. 1995a. "Introduction: Why Citizenship Constitutes a Theoretical Problem in the Last Decade of the Twentieth Century". In Beiner 1995b, 1–28.

———. ed. 1995b. *Theorizing Citizenship*. Albany: State University of New York Press.

Benn, Denis. 1987. *Ideology and Development: The Growth and Development of Political Ideas in the Caribbean 1774–1983*. Kingston: Institute of Social and Economic Research, University of the West Indies.

Bhatt, N., and S. Tang. 2001. "Delivering Microfinance in Developing Countries: Controversies and Policy Perspectives". *Policy Studies Journal* 29: 319–33.

Bickel, Alexander M. 1962. *The Least Dangerous Branch: The Supreme Court at the Bar of Politics.* New Haven: Yale University Press.

Blackman, Francis W. 1995. *Dame Nita: Caribbean Woman, World Citizen.* Kingston: Ian Randle.

Bledsoe, Timothy, and Mary Herring. 1990. "Victims of Circumstances: Women in Pursuit of Political Office". *American Political Science Review* 84, no. 1 (March): 213–23.

Blumler, G. Jay, and Michael Gurevitch. 1995. "Politicians and the Press: An Essay on Role Relationships". In *Approaches to Media: A Reader*, ed. Oliver Boyd-Barret and Chris Newbold, 108–16. London: Arnold.

Bolland, O. Nigel. 2001. *The Politics of Labour in the British Caribbean: The Social Origins of Authoritarianism and Democracy in the Labour Movement.* Kingston: Ian Randle.

Bonnerjea, L., and A. Weir. 1996. *Commonwealth of Dominica. Poverty Assessment. Report Prepared for the Government of Dominica.* Roseau: Government of Dominica.

Brill, Alida, ed. 1995. *A Rising Public Voice: Women in Politics Worldwide.* New York: Feminist Press at City University of New York.

Brodber, Erna. 1982. *Perceptions of Caribbean Women: Towards a Documentation of Stereotypes.* With an introduction by Merle Hodge. Cave Hill, Barbados: Institute of Social and Economic Research (Eastern Caribbean), University of the West Indies.

Brown, B. 1986. "Facilitating Development in Dominica: An Alternative Approach". *Bulletin of Eastern Caribbean Affairs* 12, no. 5: 30–33.

Charles, Mary Eugenia. 1982. "Address Delivered by the Honourable M.E. Charles, Prime Minister of Dominica at the Graduation Ceremony, January 27th 1982, University of the West Indies, Cave Hill". *Bulletin of Eastern Caribbean Affairs* 8, no. 1: 1–4.

———. 1992. "The Challenge of Health and Social Development in Dominica". *Caribbean Affairs* 5, no. 3: 78–83.

Clarke, Roberta. 1986. "Women's Organization, Women's Interest". *Social and Economic Studies* 35, no. 3 (September): 107–55.

Col, Jeanne-Marie. 1993. "Managing Softly in Turbulent Times: Corazon C. Aquino, President of the Philippines". In Genovese 1993b, 13–40.

Collins, Merle. 1995. "Epigraph: Signs". In *Caribbean Quarterly* 41, no. 2 (June): vii.

Commonwealth Foundation. 2002. *The Citizens and Governance Programme: Issues for Debate.* Vol. 1. London: Commonwealth Foundation.

Conger, J.A. 1991. "Inspiring Others: The Language of Leadership". *Academy of Management Executives* 5 (no. 1): 31–45.

Cowell-Meyers, Kimberly. 2003. *Women Legislators in Northern Ireland: Gender and Politics in the New Legislative Assembly.* Occasional Paper No. 3. Belfast: Centre for Advancement of Women in Politics, School of Politics, Queen's University.

Craig, Paul. 1990. *Public Law and Democracy in the United Kingdom and the United States of America*. Oxford: Clarendon Press.

Craig, Susan, ed. 1982. *The Contemporary Caribbean: A Sociological Reader*. Port of Spain, Trinidad: Susan Craig.

Davis Pierre, Marie. 1975. *House of Assembly Dominica Procedure and Working Methods*. Roseau, Dominica: Davis Pierre.

Demas, William G. 1975. *Change and Renewal in the Caribbean: A Collection of Papers*. Challenges in the New Caribbean, no. 2, ed. David I. Mitchell. Bridgetown, Barbados: CCC Publishing House.

Denning, Lord. 1973. "The Right to Dissent". *Commonwealth Judicial Journal* 1: 10–12.

Dominique, Francois, ed. 1984. *Grenada: Intervention? Invasion? Rescue Mission?* TS pamphlet. Copy held in the Main Library, University of the West Indies, Cave Hill, Barbados.

Dowe, Marion, and Lennox Honychurch. 1989. *Mamo! A Personal Portrait*. Roseau: Tropical Printers.

Drayton, Kathleen. 1984. "The Development of Higher Education for Women in the Commonwealth Caribbean with Special Reference to Barbados". MA thesis, Smith College, Northampton, Mass.

———. 1988. "Ideology and Culture in the Caribbean: Transmissions through Language Policy in the Education System". In *Gender in Caribbean Development*, ed. Patricia Mohammed and Catherine Shepherd, 290–99. Kingston: Canoe Press.

Duncan, Neville, and K. O'Brien. 1983. *Women and Politics in Barbados 1948–1981*. Cave Hill, Barbados: Institute of Social and Economic Research, University of the West Indies.

Emmanuel, Patrick. 1992. *Elections and Party Systems in the Commonwealth Caribbean 1944–1991*. St Michael: Caribbean Development Research Services.

Everett, Jana. 1993. "Indira Gandhi and the Exercise of Power". In Genovese 1993b, 103–34.

Farrell, Trevor. 1993. "Some Notes towards a Strategy for Economic Transformation". In Lalta and Freckleton, 343–52.

Ford-Smith, Honor. 1991. "Women and the Garvey Movement in Jamaica". In *Garvey: His Work and Impact*, ed. Rupert Lewis and Patrick Bryan, 73–83. Trenton, NJ: Africa World Press.

Genovese, Michael A. 1993a. "Margaret Thatcher and the Politics of Conviction Leadership". In Genovese 1993b, 177–210.

———, ed. 1993b. *Women as National Leaders*. Newbury Park: Sage Publications.

Gilbert, D., and J.J. Connolly, eds. 1991. *Personality, Social Skills, and Psychopathology: An Individual Differences Approach*. New York: Plenum Press.

Gilmore, William C. 1984. *The Grenada Intervention. Analysis and Documentation*.

London and New York: Mansell Publishing.

Gonsalves, Ralph E. 1994. *History and the Future: A Caribbean Perspective*. Kingstown, St Vincent: Quik-Print.

———. 2003. "Governance in the Caribbean in the Age of Globalisation". In Barrow-Giles and Marshall, 482–90.

Guy, Levis. 1995. "Dame Eugenia Charles: Dominica". In Brill, 136–40.

Hall, Kenneth O., ed. 2000. *Integrate of Perish: Perspectives of Leaders of the Integration Movement 1963–1999*. Mona, Jamaica: University of the West Indies, Office of the Principal.

Hartman, Mary S., ed. 1999. *Talking Leadership: Conversations with Powerful Women*. New Brunswick, NJ: Rutgers University Press.

Heinl, Robert D., Nancy Gordon Heinl and Michael Heinl. 1996. *Written in Blood: The Story of the Haitian People, 1492–1995*. Lanham, Md.: University Press of America.

Henry-Wilson, Maxine. 1989. "The Status of the Jamaican Woman, 1962 to the Present". In *Jamaica in Independence: Essays on the Early Years*, ed. Rex Nettleford, 229–53. Kingston, Jamaica, and London: Heinemann Caribbean and James Currey.

Higbie, Janet. 1993. *Eugenia Charles: The Caribbean's Iron Lady*. London: Macmillan Press.

Hogan, R., and J. Hogan. 1991. "Personality and Status". In Gilbert and Connolly, 137–54.

Honychurch, Lennox. 1975. *The Dominica Story: A History of the Island*. Roseau: Lennox Honychurch.

———. 1984. *The Dominica Story: A History of the Island*. Roseau: Dominica Institute.

———. 1995. *The Dominica Story: A History of the Island*. Rev. ed. London: Macmillan Press.

Honychurch, Patricia, and Jill Sheppard. 1993. "Eugenia: Iron Lady of the Caribbean". *Daily Nation*, Bridgetown, Barbados.

Hoyte, Harold. 2003. "Political Essence: Fiery Mother, or Unmarried – Which Woman Would You Choose?" *Daily Nation, Campaign Express,* 5 May: 9.

Inter-Parliamentary Union. 1997. "Men and Women in Politics: Democracy Still in the Making: A Comparative World Study". Geneva: Inter-Parliamentary Union.

———. 2005. "Women in Parliaments: World Classification". http://www.ipu.org/wmn-e/classif.htm. April 1.

Jones, Kathleen B. 1988. "Towards the Revision of Politics". *The Political Interests of Gender: Developing Theory and Research with a Feminist Face*, ed. Kathleen B. Jones and Anna G. Jonasdottir, 11–32. London: Sage Publications.

Judge, T.A, and J.E. Bono. 2000. "Five-Factor Model of Personality and

Transformational Leadership". *Journal of Applied Psychology* 85: 751–765.

Kawakami, Christine, Judith B. White and Ellen J. Langer. 2000. "Mindful and Masculine: Freeing Women Leaders from the Constraints of Gender Roles". *Journal of Social Issues* 56, no. 1 (Spring).

Kempadoo, Kamala. 1999. *Sun, Sex and Gold: Tourism and Sex Work in the Caribbean.* Langham, Md: Rowman and Littlefield.

Kenrick, Douglas, T., Steven L. Neuberg and Robert B. Cialdini. 1999. *Social Psychology: Unravelling the Mystery.* Boston: Allyn and Bacon.

Kirkpatrick, S.A., and E.A. Locke. 1991. "Leadership: Do Traits Matter?" *Academy of Management Executives* 5, no. 2: 48–60.

Kitzinger, Celia. 1991. "Feminism, Psychology and the Paradox of Power". *Feminism and Psychology* 1, no. 1: 111–29.

Knight, Franklin, and Colin A. Palmer, eds. 1989. *The Modern Caribbean.* Chapel Hill and London: University of North Carolina Press.

Lalta, Stanley, and Marie Freckleton, eds. 1993. *Caribbean Economic Development: The First Generation.* Kingston: Ian Randle.

Lashley, J., and K. Lord. 2002. "Microfinance in the Caribbean: Experiences and Best Practice". Report prepared for IADP Network for Poverty Reduction. Washington, DC: Inter-American Development Bank.

Lent, John. nd. *Press Freedom in the Commonwealth Caribbean.* Pamphlet, Faculty of Law Library, University of the West Indies, Cave Hill, Barbados.

Lewis, Gordon K. 1968. *The Growth of the Modern West Indies.* New York: Monthly Review Press.

———. 1983. *Main Currents in Caribbean Intellectual Thought: The Historical Evolution of Caribbean Society in Its Ideological Aspects, 1492–1900.* Baltimore: Johns Hopkins University Press.

Lewis, Linden, ed. 2003. *The Culture of Gender and Sexuality in the Caribbean.* Gainesville: University Press of Florida.

Lijphart, Arend. 1984. *Democracies: Patterns of Majoritarian and Consensus Government in Twenty-One Countries.* New Haven and London: Yale University Press.

———, ed. 1992. *Parliamentary Government versus Presidential Government.* Oxford and New York: Oxford University Press.

Lipsky, Michael. 1980. *Street Level Bureaucracy: Dilemmas of the Individual in Public Services.* New York: Russell Sage Foundation.

Liverpool, Nicholas. N.d. [1980?]. "A Study in Peaceful Extra-Constitutional Change on the Caribbean Island of Dominica: An Application of the Legal Doctrine of Necessity". Unpublished, Faculty of Law Library, University of the West Indies, Cave Hill.

Macmillan, W.M. 1936. *Warning from the West Indies: A Tract for Africa and the Empire.* London: Faber and Faber.

Maingot, Anthony P. 1989. "Caribbean International Relations". In Knight and Palmer, 259–92

———. 1994. *The United States and the Caribbean*. Basingstoke and London: Warwick University Caribbean Studies, Macmillan Press.

Manley, Michael. 1974. *The Politics of Change: A Jamaican Testament*. London: Andre Deutsch.

Mathurin Mair, Lucille. 2000. "The Rebel Woman in the British West Indies during Slavery". In *Caribbean Slavery in the Atlantic World: A Reader*, ed. Verene Shepherd and Hilary McD. Beckles, 984–1,000. Kingston: Ian Randle.

McAfee, Kathy. 1991. *Storm Signals*. London: Zed Books.

McClelland, David. 1985. *Human Motivation*. Glenview, Ill.: Scott Foresman.

McIntosh, Simeon. 2002. *Caribbean Constitutional Reform: Rethinking the West Indian Polity*. Kingston: Caribbean Law Publishing.

Meeks, Brian. 1993. *Caribbean Revolutions and Revolutionary Theory: An Assessment of Cuba, Nicaragua and Grenada*. Basingstoke and London: Warwick University Caribbean Studies, Macmillan Press.

Meeks, Brian, and Folke Lindahl, eds. 2001. *New Caribbean Thought: A Reader*. Kingston: University of the West Indies Press.

Michaels, R.A. 1981. "Changing the Guard in Dominica: Elections and a Hostage Crisis". *Caribbean Review* 10, no. 2 (Spring): 18–19, 49.

Michelman, Frank. 1988. "Law's Republic". *Yale Law Journal* 97: 1,493–537.

Midgett, Douglas. 1997. "Fact and Interpretation in Dominican Political History". *Journal of Eastern Caribbean Studies* 22, no. 3 (September): 48–63.

Mitchell, Lionel A. 1995. "Microstates Marketing and Development: An Investigation of Dominica". Paper submitted to the Seventh Bi-Annual World Marketing Congress, Academy of Marketing Science and Monash University, Melbourne Australia, 6–10 July.

Moglen, H. 1983. "Power and Empowerment". *Women's Studies International Forum* 6, no. 2: 131–34.

Mohammed, Patricia. 1999. "The Caribbean Family Revisited". In *Gender in Caribbean Development,* ed. Patricia Mohammed and Catherine Shepherd, 164–75. Second edition. Kingston: Canoe Press.

———. 2003. "Blueprint for Gender in Creole Trinidad: Exploring Gender Mythology through Calypsos of the 1920s and 1930s". In Linden Lewis, 129–68.

———. 2005. "Academic Call and Response: Calypso and the Caribbean Literary Imagination. Reflections on the Conference on Calypso and the Caribbean Literary Imagination". Sponsored by Caribbean Literary Studies, University of Miami, Coral Gables, and the Historical Museum of Southern Florida, 17–19 March. Mimeo. Centre for Gender and Development Studies, University of the West Indies, St Augustine.

Mondesire, Alicia, and Leith Dunn. 1995. *Towards Equity in Development: A Report on the Status of Women in Sixteen Commonwealth Caribbean Countries*. Georgetown: Caribbean Community Secretariat.

———. 1997. *An Analysis of Census Data in CARICOM Countries from a Gender Perspective: 1990–1991 Population and Housing Census of the Commonwealth Caribbean*. Georgetown: Caribbean Community Secretariat.

Mulla-Feroze, Aashiana H., and Venkat R. Krishnan. 2000. "Consideration, Initiating Structure, and Transformational Leadership: the Role of Gender". In *Proceedings* of the 37th Annual Meeting of the Eastern Academy of Management, Danvers, Mass., May.

Müllerleile, Christoph. 1996. *CARICOM Integration: Progress and Hurdles. A European View*. Kingston: Kingston Publishers.

Neft, Naomi, and Ann D. Levine. 1997. *Where Women Stand: An International Report on the Status of Women in 140 Countries 1997–1998*. New York: Random House.

Nettleford, Rex. 1988. "The Dame Nita Affair: Of Commonsense and Cousinhood". *Money Index*, March: 19–20.

Paravisini-Gebert, Lizabeth. 1996. *Phyllis Shand Allfrey: A Caribbean Life*. New Brunswick, NJ: Rutgers University Press.

Pateman, Carole, and Mary Lyndon Shanley. 1991. "Introduction". In *Feminist Interpretations and Political Theory*, ed. Carole Pateman and Mary Lyndon Shanley, 1–10. University Park, Penn.: Pennsylvania State University Press.

Payne, Anthony, and Paul Sutton, eds. 1993. *Modern Caribbean Politics*. Baltimore and London: Johns Hopkins University Press.

———. 2001. *Charting Caribbean Development*. London: Macmillan.

Peake, Linda. 1993. "The Development and Role of Women's Political Organizations in Guyana". In *Women and Change in the Caribbean*, ed. Janet Momsen, 109–31. Kingston: Ian Randle.

Phillips, Anne. 1993. *Democracy and Difference*. University Park, Penn.: Pennsylvania State University Press.

Phillips, Dion, and A.H. Young, eds. 1986. *Militarization in the Non-Hispanic Caribbean*. Boulder: Lynne Rienner.

Phillips, Nicole. 2003. "Producers, Reproducers and Rebels: Grenadian Slave Women 1783–1838". Working Paper No. 10, Centre for Gender and Development Studies, University of the West Indies, Cave Hill, Barbados.

Pitkin, Hanna. 1981. "Justice: On Relating Private and Public". *Political Theory* 9: 327–52.

Pohlmann, Lisa. 1995. "Ambivalence about Leadership in Women's Organisations: A Look at Bangladesh". *IDS Bulletin* 26, no. 2 (July).

Pope, James. 1990. "Republican Moments: The Role of Direct Popular Power in the American Constitutional Order". *University of Pennsylvania Law Review* 139: 287.

Reddock, Rhoda. 1993. "Primacy of Gender in Race and Class". In *Race, Class and Gender in the Future of the Caribbean*, ed. J Edward Greene, 44–73. Kingston: Institute of Social and Economic Research, University of the West Indies.

———. 1994. *Women, Labour and Politics in Trinidad and Tobago: A History*. Kingston: Ian Randle.

———. 1998. "Women's Organizations and Movements in the Commonwealth Caribbean: The Response to Global Crisis in the 1980s". *Feminist Review* 59, no. 1 (June): 57–73.

Riviere, Bill. 1982. "Contemporary Class Struggles and the Revolutionary Potential of Social Classes in Dominica". In S. Craig 1982, 365–84.

Riviere, Bill. 1993. "The LeBlanc Era: Electoral Politics in Dominica, 1951–1975". In *Bulletin of Eastern Caribbean Affairs* 18, no. 2 (June): 30–35.

Roberts, Peter A. 1988. *West Indians and Their Language*. Cambridge: Cambridge University Press.

Robinson, Tracy. 1994. "Periods of Emergency in the Commonwealth Caribbean: Judicial Review and the Constitutions". Bachelor of Civil Law thesis, University of Oxford.

Robinson, Tracy. 2003. "Beyond the Bill of Rights: Sexing the Citizen". In Barriteau 2003a, 231–61.

Rosener, Judy B. 1990. "Ways Women Lead". *Harvard Business Review* (November–December): 119–25.

Ryan, Selwyn. 1999. *Winner Takes All: The Westminster Experience in the Caribbean*. St Augustine, Trinidad: Institute of Social and Economic Research, University of the West Indies.

Saint-Germain, Michelle A. 1993. "Women in Power in Nicaragua: Myth and Reality". In Genovese 1993b, 70–102.

Samuel, Wendell. A. 1983. "Caribbean Economic Integration". In Lalta and Freckleton, 159–73.

Sartori, Giovanni. 1997. *Comparative Constitutional Engineering: An Inquiry into the Structures, Incentives and Outcomes*. Second edition. London: Macmillan Press.

Schulz, Donald E., and Douglas H. Graham, eds. 1994. *Revolution and Counter-revolution in Central America and the Caribbean*. Boulder and London: Westview Press.

Serbin, Andres. 1990. *Caribbean Geopolitics: Towards Security through Peace?* Boulder: Lynne Rienner.

Senior, Olive. 1991. *Working Miracles: Women's Lives in the English-Speaking Caribbean*. London: James Currey.

Simonton, D.K. 1994. *Greatness: Who Makes History and Why*. New York: Guilford.

Smith, Lindel. 1979a. "Patrick John, Dominica and a Sign of the Times: A Comment". *Bulletin of Eastern Caribbean Affairs* 5, no. 2 (May–June): 23–28.

Smith, Lindel. 1979b. "The Political Situation in Dominica". *Bulletin of Eastern Caribbean Affairs* 5, no. 3 (July–August): 20–31.

Statham, Anne. 1987. "The Gender Model Revisited: Differences in the Management Styles of Men and Women". *Sex Roles* 16 (April): 409–29.

Stern, Geoffrey. 1995. "In Discussion with Eugenia Charles". *Economic and Political Sciences, LSE Magazine* 7, no. 1 (Summer): 16.

Sunshine, Catherine A. 1988. *The Caribbean: Survival, Struggle and Sovereignty.* Washington, DC: Epica.

Sykes, Patricia Lee. 1993. "Women as National Leaders: Patterns and Prospects". In Genovese 1993b, 219–29.

Taylor, Douglas. 1972. "Tales and Legends of the Dominica Carib". In *Aspects of Dominican History,* Government of Dominica, 44–55.

Thomas, Clive Y. 1988. *The Poor and the Powerless: Economic Policy and Change in the Caribbean.* New York: Monthly Review Press.

Thorndike, Tony. 1993. "Revolution, Democracy, and Regional Integration in the Eastern Caribbean". In Payne and Sutton, chap. 6.

Tribe, Lawrence. 2000. *American Constitutional Law.* 3rd ed. New York: Foundation Press.

United Nations (UN). 1991. *The World's Women: Trends and Statistics* 1970–1990. New York: UN.

———. 1995. *The World's Women: Trends and Statistics* 1995. New York: UN.

United Nations Economic Commission for Latin America and the Caribbean (UNECLAC). 1984. *Social Structural Changes in Dominica.* Restricted AHG/SEM/SSC/84/1 Sub-Regional Headquarters for the Caribbean.

Vassell, Linette. 2003. "Women, Power and Decision-Making in CARICOM Countries: Moving Forward from a Post-Beijing Assessment". In *Gender Equality in the Caribbean: Reality or Illusion*, ed. Gemma Tang Nain and Barbara Bailey, 1–38. Kingston: Ian Randle.

Von Stauffenberg, D. 2000. *Microfinance in the English Speaking Caribbean.* Bridgetown, Barbados: Caribbean Development Bank.

Waldron, Jeremy. 1999. *Law and Disagreement.* Oxford: Oxford University Press.

West India Royal Commission. 1945. *West India Royal Commission Report.* London: His Majesty's Stationery Office.

White, Dorcas. 1977. *The Press and the Law in the Caribbean.* Bridgetown, Barbados: Cedar Press.

Wilmot, Swithin. 1995. "Females of Abandoned Character? Women and Protest in Jamaica, 1838–65". In *Engendering History: Caribbean Women in Historical Perspective*, ed. Verene Shepherd, Bridget Brereton and Barbara Bailey, 279–95. Kingston: Ian Randle; London: James Currey.

Wilson, Peter J. 1969. "Reputation and Respectability: A Suggestion for Caribbean Ethnology". *Man,* n.s., 4, no. 1: 37–53.

Wilson, Woodrow. 1992. "Committee or Cabinet Government". In Lijphart 1992, 72–74.

Wint, Carl. 1989. "Where Have All the Men Gone?" *Daily Gleaner* (Kingston). 15 August: A6.

Woodward, Bob. 1987. *Veil: The Secret Wars of the CIA 1981–1987*. New York: Simon and Schuster.

Young, Iris Marion. 1995. "Polity and Group Difference: A Critique of the Ideal of Universal Citizenship". In Beiner 1995b, 175–208.

Contributors

EUDINE BARRITEAU is Professor of Gender and Public Policy, and Head of the Centre for Gender and Development Studies, University of the West Indies, Cave Hill, Barbados. She is the author of *The Political Economy of Gender in the Twentieth Century Caribbean*. Her edited collection *Confronting Power, Theorizing Gender: Interdiscipinary Perspectives in the Caribbean* won the inaugural Best Selling Textbook award from the University of the West Indies Press in 2004. She has published several articles on feminist theorizing and is currently coordinating three research projects that collectively examine Caribbean political economy and social change from the perspective of gender. She is the inaugural Dame Nita Barrow Women in Development Fellow, Ontario Institute for Studies in Education, University of Toronto (1997).

ALAN COBLEY is Professor of South African and Comparative History, University of the West Indies, Cave Hill, Barbados. A graduate of the Universities of Manchester and York, he completed his doctorate in South African history at the School of Oriental and African Studies, London. He has worked at the University of the West Indies since 1987, and has served as head of the Department of History and dean of the Faculty of Humanities and Education. He has published widely on aspects of South African and Caribbean history.

KETURAH CECILIA BABB is a RastafarI woman. A national of the Common-wealth of Dominica and of Barbados, she is a worker skilled in project design, management and evaluation. She has a background in history and an interest in economics. Her research and teaching aim to democratize the ownership of information and empower the grass-roots communities of which she is a part. She is devoted to gender justice and this has led to involvement in a range of projects at national, regional and international levels. Keturah has been an NGO activist for the past twenty years. She is currently deputy coordinator of the Caribbean Policy Development Centre based in Barbados.

CYNTHIA BARROW-GILES is St Lucian born. She received her undergraduate and postgraduate degrees from the University of the West Indies, Cave Hill and Mona campuses. She joined the academic staff of the University of the West Indies, Cave Hill, in August 1989 in the Department of Government, Sociology and Social Work, where she teaches comparative government and politics. She is currently head of the Department of Government, Sociology and Social Work. She is the author of *Introduction to Caribbean Politics* and co-editor (with Don D. Marshall) of *Living at the Borderlines: Issues in Caribbean Sovereignty and Development.* She is a member of the edi-torial committee of the *Journal of Eastern Caribbean Studies,* University of the West Indies, Cave Hill.

JOAN CUFFIE is an educational psychologist and currently a lecturer in behavioural sciences in the University of the West Indies HIV/AIDS Response Programme (UWIHARP), Cave Hill, Barbados. She is a mem-ber of the American Psychological Association. Her current research inter-ests are in the area of the psychological impact of gender issues on educational achievement and participation, students' learning styles, coedu-cation and gender, sexuality and HIV/AIDS. She has published in a num-ber of journals and edited texts.

CARMEN HUTCHINSON MILLER is a research assistant and co-editor of the working paper series at the Centre for Gender and Development Studies, University of the West Indies, Cave Hill, Barbados. She is also a postgradu-ate student in the Faculty of Humanities and Education pursuing a PhD in the Department of History. Hutchinson Miller is an Afro–Costa Rican and a third-generation descendant of Jamaicans who, as part of the Caribbean diaspora, migrated in the late nineteenth century to Port Limon, Costa Rica, for the construction of the railroad. She has published "In Memory of Ancestors: Contributions of Afro-Jamaican Female Migrants in Port Limon, Costa Rica 1872–1890" in the Centre for Gender and Development Studies working paper series.

JONATHAN LASHLEY is a fellow at the Sir Arthur Lewis Institute of Social and Economic Studies, University of the West Indies, Cave Hill, Barbados. He works on several projects for international agencies and Caribbean governments, as well as doing independent research in the areas of poverty alleviation, microenterprise development, entrepreneurship and industrial organization and policy. His publications include "Making a Strategic Commitment to Microfinance in the Eastern Caribbean" *Journal of Microfinance* 6 no. 1 (2004); "Evaluacíon del empresariado juvenil en le Caribe (An Evaluation of Youth Entrepreneurship in the Caribbean)", *Inter-American Developing Bank*; and "Securing Opportunities for Secure Livelihoods", in *The OECS Human Development Report* (2002).

ALICIA MONDESIRE is an international development consultant and gender analyst. A national of Dominica, she has written and spoken extensively on gender equality issues in the Caribbean and globally, and on social and political affairs in the Caribbean. She was lead author of the widely cited publication *Towards Equity in Development: Report on the Status of Women in Sixteen Commonwealth Caribbean Countries*; and co-author of the first-ever gender analysis of census data in the Caribbean. As CUSO's Eastern Caribbean director in the 1980s, she interacted directly with the government of Dame Eugenia Charles.

TRACY ROBINSON is a lecturer in the Faculty of Law, University of the West Indies, Cave Hill, Barbados. She teaches Gender and the Law, Family Law, Constitutional Law and Caribbean Commonwealth Human Rights Law and is the editor of the *Caribbean Law Bulletin*. Her present research interests include gender, citizenship and constitutionalism, family law, and culture and violence against women.